Twin Sisters

Order this book online at www.trafford.com
or email orders@trafford.com

Most Trafford titles are also available at major online book retailers.

Printed in Victoria, BC, Canada.

ISBN: 978-1-4269-0172-0 (sc)
ISBN: 978-1-4269-0173-7 (hc)
ISBN: 978-1-4269-0174-4 (eb)

*Our mission is to efficiently provide the world's finest, most comprehensive book publishing
service, enabling every author to experience success. To find out how to publish your book, your
way, and have it available worldwide, visit us online at www.trafford.com*

Trafford rev. 1/12/10

Trafford
PUBLISHING®   www.trafford.com

North America & international
toll-free: 1 888 232 4444 (USA & Canada)
phone: 250 383 6864 ♦ fax: 812 355 4082

ACKNOWLEDGMENTS

I want to thank my husband, who spent many months editing, and translating.

My close friend Ms. JingShi, in Chicago who had great patience reading, advising, and rereading.

Dr. Weihong Liu in New York who has given me tremendous support and encouragement.

Forward

THIS SUBJECT MATTER IN Twin Sisters still highly controversial for a novel in China.

This book reveals an army cadre seducing a girl that comes from deep in the author's memories from her childhood. She was author's neighbour who gave up her virginity in an attempt to gain her mother's freedom, a beautiful girl with a slightly pale face, often in tears at home; this is the prototype of YingLi.

YongHong is a typical representative of the Red Guards who denounced the capitalist roaders, and traitors, who often were family members or neighbours; creating many grievances, and injustices.

This book differs from most accounts of the Cultural Revolution that label the "Red Guards" as a "sin" or criminals; this book explains firsthand the motivations, influences, mentality, and personal growth of the fanatical Red Guards.

Twin Sisters, reveals the characters of many different people in great depth; Lian was a woman who's good intentions were betrayed by the party, lost the love of her life, and lived with life-long regret, and suffering. Zhang was disabled in a battle on the Russian frontier due to the incompetence of his captain and later died at the hands of his wife. Crippled Sun was a veteran of the Korean war that had cost him a leg, became a hero, and the work group leader in his village; who went on to recruit and abduct women as incentives for the village men to produce more. LinLin was a college professor who lost his position because of his wife; he went on to become a refuse collector, and was subsequently accused of being an anti-revolutionary and condemned.

The innocence of juveniles, justice, and the goodness of people are portrayed in depth; as are the rivalry and confrontations of opposing factions of the Red Guards, as well as life in the countryside versus the city.

It is acknowledged by historians that history has usually been written about leaders, and the victorious; that history has been written by or for the winners. *Twin Sisters* is a departure from the traditional; depicting the real lives of common people impartially in historical context.

Because the subject matter *Twin Sisters* is still considered "too sensitive" for Chinese publishers it has not been published in book form in China yet. I hope that this book will give English readers the same surprises, insights, and delights as the Chinese who have read it. *Twin Sisters* has received great acclaim on the web in China, and among Chinese living in North America.

The relationships of the main characters.

Ying Li: youngest twin sisters.

YongHong: elder twin sister.

LuDongChun: the twin sister's mother.

LinLin: YingLi's first husband.

NianLin: YingLi's second husband.

ZhangYong: YongHong's husband.

WenJun: YongHong's lover.

Lian: LinLin's first wife.

DaShan: YingLi &LinLin's son.

DaHai: YingLi & NianLin's son.

Guoqing: YongHong & WenJun's daughter.

LiuJiahuai: a low level cadre in the army.

Qi-Sanhai: a high level cadre in the army

Crippled Sun: The mountain village's production team captain.

Chapter 1

THIS BOOK TELLS THE love stories of twin sisters during the Cultural Revolution. YongHong the elder sister joined the cultural revolution and became an excellent Red Guard who rose to become the provincial women's leader, she unwillingly married a disabled soldier who she did not love, and became involved in an extramarital affair with an army officer. The younger twin sister YingLi, was naturally kind, gentle, and shunned politics but her husband became involved in a case by accident, and in an instant became an anti-revolutionary, resulting in great suffering in her love life.

The story begins in the summer of 1966, with their mother LuDongChun.

The family lived in a small city in Northern China named Long Shan City, the English translation is "Dragon Mountain City."

Such a small city, but on this day there would be a great action known as the ten thousand peoples meeting that had just begun.

The woman mayor LuDongChun was on the stage on her knees; body curved; short hair dishevelled; face pale; arms tied behind her back, and a large square paper board hanging from her neck labelled: "Traitor and Capitalist-Roader." A microphone with a stand was close beside her so the crowd could hear her. Because the microphone was so close to her face her breathing in it radiated into the plaza, and was carried by the wind to the sky.

Since the fire of the Cultural Revolution had gripped Long Shan City, she had been removed from her position, and was being denounced by the crowd supporting the revolution.

The city plaza was very large, and almost all major mass gatherings were held here.

Today many factory workers, many levels of officers, and students with a sense of mission had been gathered and squeezed into the plaza by a group of Red Guards. The people standing in the sun became a hot wave.

With LuDongChun on the stage was a young man, acting as a master of ceremony, he used a portable microphone to speak loudly to LuDongChun: "Confess your traitor's crime honestly." The young man was wearing a Red Guard army style uniform grass green in colour, without the army's badge. His forceful voice resounded through the microphone and flooded the plaza.

LuDongChun with a hoarse voice replied: "Chairman Mao's teachings say: 'There is no right to accuse without making an investigation.' I am not a traitor." She was wearing a men's style bluish grey Chinese tunic suit. She had been raised as a gentleman but had changed to a lady many years ago had got married and had twin daughters: YongHong and YingLi, who were now eighteen years old. But she still preferred to wear men's clothes, and spoke and walked like a man.

It was clear that her words dissatisfied the crowd; a great disturbance was beginning to stir in front of the stage.

The young man spoke loudly into the microphone: "The Japanese surrounded your village, and all the people of the village were killed, only you survived; do you dare to say that you did not turn traitor?"

LuDongChun corrected him. "Chairman Mao teaches: 'There is no right to accuse without making an investigation'; it was not all the people of the village that were killed, only the men of the village were killed."

"Yes, you were acting and dressed as a man at that time, why did the Japanese not kill you?"

LuDongChun was silent.

The young man stretched his neck out toward the crowd and shouted. "This traitor Capitalist Roader hopes she does not have to answer. What do you say?"

"Answer, answer..." The people shouted, they were agitated, getting madder, and began screaming now.

"Let her confess her traitorous crimes!" Pandemonium erupted suddenly in front of the stage with impassioned countless fists were raised to the sky.

"Does the one that explains need to give more details?"

"Yes!" "Yes!" "Yes!"... Uproar arose in waves one after another.

Then, he turned to face LuDongChun speaking loudly and sternly. "This is the demand of the revolutionary masses."

"How detailed?" LuDongChun asked, and then began to cough. Her face turned red and then dark brown. Her body was shaking; the board hanging from her neck started to swing from her chest. This kind of meeting had been held a few times already. The most interesting part of the story to many people was her rape by a Japanese army officer. This was an inhumane act but at that time, humane acts were considered harmful to the revolutionary ideology, people had to learn how to deal firmly with all questions.

The people's mood was not softened when LuDongChun coughed, but strengthened even more. Another person took the lead and read aloud, with everyone following. "Chairman Mao teaches us to say: 'The revolution, is not to invite people to go to dinner, not for embroidery, not to write an essay. Revolution is a class overthrowing the action of the violence of another class.' "

The front of the stage immediately took the appearance of an ocean of the pious. The ones that would be affirmed said that any kind of religion in the world would be inferior to Chinese. This bragged about atheism, nationality, and being proud of the proletariat; they were accepting another kind of baptism voluntarily. When they felt hungry and thirsty, Chairman Mao's quotations were food and water, when they were lost, Chairman Mao's quotation was a compass. They quickly assumed that LuDongChun was coughing to avoid answering.

Suddenly a middle-aged man jumped on the stage, ranting and snatched the microphone and waved it high, "Don't resist and act shamelessly." He was rousing the people to anger.

"Don't resist and act shamelessly." was chanted universally.

Eventually LuDongChun continued speaking: "At the time that the Japanese devils entered the village, they suspected that the village was hiding anti-Japanese allied forces. They separated all the men in the village, and a devil's officer ordered us to take off our clothes. When they saw that I was a woman, they left me, and killed the men."

The young Red Guard tried to regain control of the meeting, but he was unsuccessful.

The middle-age man asked loudly: "So at that time, you were in the anti-Japanese allied forces?"

"Yes."

"Then why did not they kill you?"

"They wanted..." She paused a moment, and then continued saying: "... to rape me."

"How did they rape you?" the middle-aged man like a pervert wanted explicit details; a loud gasp rose from the front of the stage.

At the time the youngest daughter of LuDongChun, YingLi was standing outside of the plaza. She was about 5.8 feet tall, but was very thin, and somewhat fragile. Her facial features were partially hidden beneath a huge straw hat because she was crying, and afraid of being seen. At her side was a big yellow dog, the beloved family pet. The yellow dog wasn't paying attention and didn't realise that YingLi was sad, it was excited at being in such a big crowd, and ran about smelling the strangers, barking friendly greetings, and then running back and around her with out stopping, licking her hand, and her sandals.

The meeting was being broadcast through speakers around the square and carried on the wind through out much of Long Shan City.

YingLi hated her older sister very much now since she had been the first one to put up posters denouncing their mother.

She had brought the dog wishing it would bite her sister, and some of the other people too, but she was too timid to confront anyone herself.

YingLi knew her sister would be there today, because she had become the commander of a Red Guard faction.

YingLi was right, her older sister YongHong was standing in the crowd; she was wearing a Red Guard uniform that de-emphasized her breasts with a tight fitting green tunic that complimented her face like a peach with green leaves, her hair was cut short in the new popular style, called "revolution hair" that created an overall masculine appearance.

YongHong was a Red Guard group leader and also the first person to accuse LuDongChun of being a "traitor". She was young and very immature when she accused her own mother of being a traitor. At that time, the names of "Traitor", "Antievolutionary", or Capitalist Roader" were almost always attached to a powerful person; she thought since her mother was the mayor of the city she should have that name too. When she had first tried to join the red guards they had refused her so she used her first revolutionary action denouncing her mother to win their approval; she was quickly accepted based on her action and rose quickly in her group. Now faced with her mother's plight, she had mixed feelings that exacerbated her sense of unease. Several times she wanted to jump on the stage and turn the crowd back in the direction of criticizing and denunciation. Now her thoughts about LuDongChun were not of mother and daughter, they were of the Revolution and the class struggle, using revolutionary purpose as the criterion. She would not come out boldly to protect her mother, but for the benefit of the revolution she would be brave, stand out and resist. She felt the struggle had deviated far from the intended direction of the revolution.

At this very moment she needed to show her great love for the CPC and Chainman Mao; there was only one way to be loyal: listen to the CPC and Chainman Mao's words, and carry out the Cultural Revolution.

She heard the middle-aged man yell: "Then explain."

"You want me to continue from where?" LuDongChun asked seeming to have forgotten what he said.

The middle-aged man was stupefied; he followed her and asked the crowd. "Where did she stop?" His voice passed through the microphone and his gaze wandered up and down over the square, range upon range of duck's necks stopped moving. Then he said: "The rape process."

"The getting raped process." LuDongChun corrected him again.

A middle-aged man lifted his foot to kick LuDongChun, and taking the microphone he faced the front of the stage yelling. "We want her to be honest and to explain her own question to the revolutionary masses, right?"

"Yes, yes..." Many voices from the front of the stage shouted.

The middle-aged man was extremely excited; he raised his arm and shouted.

"Overthrow LuDongChun!"

People were following: "Overthrow LuDongChun!"

"Long live the Cultural Revolution of the proletariat!"

"Long live the Cultural Revolution of the proletariat!"

Just as this chant ended, a person in front of the stage called out to the young man: "Commander Liu, telephone!"

The crowd chanted: "Commander Liu, telephone!"

After a moment, the masses realised the mistake: wow! What is this? It was not chant material! Wow! Realising their mistake they started laughing. The whole square broke out laughing uproariously their voices soared into the sky.

"Quiet! Serious!" The young man was greatly embarrassed by the mistake. Before going down to answer the call, he whispered to the middle-aged man, and then said loudly: "Comrades, continue the meeting."

LuDongChun closed her mouth tightly, sweat covered her face making it look glossy, but her waist board was straight and upright all the time. Even after she was pushed down, she quickly rose up again.

"What do the Japanese's things look like?" middle-aged man used the word "things" to allude to a man's penis. In China the noun of sexual organs, is usually replaced by a pronoun.

The middle-aged man seemed only interested in sex , he was asking repeatedly, and everyone knew he was referring to a Japanese penis. He seemed to have already peeled off LuDongChun's clothes in his mind, seen her naked body, and he is imagining this naked body being ravaged by the Japanese. He was drooling at the mouth and wanted to know: how the sex organ of Japanese was different than Chinese.

Some schoolgirls bowed their heads in embarrassment, and most of the boys' faces began to turn different shades of red. The people sweated and gaped under the burning sun, waiting for them to get to the familiar procreation function the unfortunate woman was required to describe.

LuDongChun answered: "The same as you."

She should have said: "The same as yours." The meaning was changed completely, no one knew if LuDongChun had intended to insult them or not, but immediately she had caused a disaster. To liken the revolutionary masses to a penis was being too arrogant for sure.

The middle-aged man was so mad he kicked her lower back, pushed her down on the stage, took off his belt, and lashed her. His actions excited the crowd; they became restless for a moment, someone yelled. "Hit her, hit..." More people began waving their fists and jumping on the stage. Someone seized LuDongChun by the hair someone was pulling on her arm, hitting and kicking. At that time the big yellow dog jumped on the stage, growling and biting people... the meeting became a people versus the dog battle.

Chapter 2

YongHong recognized the yellow dog as her family's dog at once. The confusion caused by the dog, moved her to decide to take the stage. She had good reasons; she would stop this disturbance between the people and the dog, and lead the meeting into the proper direction of the Cultural Revolution.

Her understanding of the revolution was not like what she had witnessed. Therefore she watched first and then appeared on the stage, taking over the microphone, she spoke with confidence about Mao Zedong revolutionary theory.

She had been extraordinarily calm watching the development of the state of affairs and quietly scheming. If she said it was her mother who was the subject of the masses' struggle, it would not be so good for her, as proclaiming the party line and verifying the purpose of the meeting in revolutionary eyes. It took nearly an hour, with shouting and fierce debate, but she convinced the people with reasoning, to cite the authorities, and persuaded the masses; and she finally brought the situation under control.

Afterwards, YongHong's behaviour was highly praised by the revolutionary committee in the city. Her name had already been spread from the high school throughout Long Shan city. Such a woman, who dared to speak out, print big posters, and strike at injustice, should be the women's model. The directorship of the Women's Federation of the garrison post of the Long Shan city would be hers.

Chapter 3

Aᴄ FEW MONTHS LATER YingLi had finally found a way to get her mother set free.

Since her mother had been arrested, 153 days had past, and every single waking moment she had felt uneasy about her mama. On the day her mother had been accused in the plaza the big yellow dog's bravery had made her feel ashamed of herself. In the past months, she was ran around everywhere, looking for a way to save her mother.

She heard from her classmate Qing, that her mama had been in trouble too, but she had her used her body to free her mama.

Qing was half Russian and half Chinese; and her sex life had started early.

YingLi was a young girl just eighteen years old and had not had any sexual experience; sex in her mind was another name for love, without love, it was something to be abhorred. But to free her mother, she was willing to do anything.

Long Shan city had just been buried in a heavy snow that fallen for seven days, such a snowfall had not occurred in a hundred years.

That evening, YingLi was struggling through the heavy snow to meet with a young man, who was the army cadre in charge of her mama's case. The dimly lit street lamps, looked like they were not fully awake yet. The wide road under a heavy blanket of snow, stretched into the distance like a silver snake following a rolling wheel. With wrenching movements, from foot to foot she struggled through the snow that seemed to be trying to take her feet captive. The sound of loud noises came from the far horizon, and the glare of a red light was rising in the sky. YingLi plodded on, staring at the rising red glow, and began to feel very apprehensive.

The red glow was coming from a battle between two factions of Red Guards. She was sure her older sister would be there.

YingLi was having great difficulty moving her feet through the deep snow, but finally she arrived at the gate of Qing's house. She knocked repeatedly on the door, and eventually the fat girl appeared.

"Hi, Qing!" YingLi said.

"Why are you here?" Qing asked.

"I feel nervous, will you come with me?" YingLi asked hesitantly.

"It is not I that do not want to go with you, it...it...I mean that you must understand the situation." Saying this Qing saw YingLi had tears on her face, flowing quietly. She understood for YingLi to give her body to a man to ravage, felt like going to a death.

By this time, the red light from the fire began to intrude into Qing's vision.

"Oh, my god! Our school is on fire! They have been talking about it for months, now it is coming true. It is on fire! How will we return to study?" Qing said with wonder.

"I will go now." YingLi said, heading in the direction of the light from the fire.

"Wait." Qing called running to catch up. "Wow, is your elder sister at risk? Is she in there with many class mates?"

Chapter 4

YINGLI HAD GUESSED THE source of the red light of the fire was the school. YongHong was leading more than thirty Revolutionary young Red Guards in a final defence of their high school building.

Following revolutionary developments the Red Guard groups had become factions who fought for improvements that only one faction could win.

Looking back many of those acts were naive and ridiculous, but at the time they faithfully executed on their understanding and beliefs.

The corridor and doors on the first floor of the school had been blocked with desks and chairs. This was just an ordinary building; it had no history like that of the Louvre in Paris or the Palace Museum in Beijing but now it was the symbol of a great victory that two feuding Revolutionary groups wanted to win. They may not really understand the real purpose of this revolution but they would be loyal and faithful to what they believed. Dense smoke and tongues of fire filled the corridor. A student who wanted to escape death opened a window, but YongHong rushed forward and caught the coward by her belt, pulling her back upbraiding her in a stern voice: "Don't try to escape".

Outside the building, the opposition laid siege to the defenders with fire becoming increasingly fierce. The opposition was cheering and jumping with joy, their shouts rose to the sky loud enough to make the planet and the moon tremble.

YongHong believed she would die.

She had been a little nervous in the beginning, but she switched quickly. She thought she would become a hero, proud of her thoughts she conquered fear.

Chapter 5

THE CITY HALL OFFICE contained many bungalows in a big complex, with a wall around it, and only two entrances, one back and one front. Door men had worked 24/7, and required that all who entered must register first; but since the Cultural Revolution began, all the old rules had changed, now, people could go in freely. Here, at night, only the representative of the army LiuJiahuai stayed in the office, because he was a low rank army officer, and had no family in Long Shan city.

LiuJiahuai was the special cases department's second in command. The head Qi-Sanhai, was the army leader in command taking over mayor LuDongChun's position; he did not serve as mayor he only handled big case judgements. Routine matters were the only things that second leader LiuJiahuai could make decisions on. His position was not high enough to decide matters concerning people's life or death. The handful of people held here, like LuDongChun, were like screws that had just been unloaded from the big machine of society. Whether the screw was good, or bad, was the only question that required his judgement.

He had promised YingLi to help get her mama out, just like a fisherman using little bait to lure the fish to the hook. He knew LuDongChun's case was very complicated. LuDongChun the former head of the city government, had not been accused of any wrongdoing as the head of the government during her seventeen years in the position; but she was accused of having been born in a landlord's family, and having been a "traitor". For the case of checking out, it was all based on the testimony of witnesses. Finding people to prove the family origin of LuDongChun would be easy; but it was very difficult to prove that a Japanese officer had raped her before the liberation of China. They could search the whole of China but they could not go to Japan to check.

LuDongChun's case was like a hot sweet potato that could burn one's hand. However, using sex to make a deal with YingLi, he thought was safe.

He knew face was as important to a Chinese woman as her life. When YingLi arrived at LiuJiahuai's room, her body felt numb; she didn't have any feeling for him, she lay on a simple wooden bed, and received his kissing.

Later she thought that his hot tongue licking her nose and mouth, must be like a black bear from the mountains tasting its' prey. His tongue brought a foul taste of liquor and felt stiff in her mouth, like a dentists' tongue depressor, and it caused her stomach to convulse violently. She was nauseous and bile from her mouth went to his tongue, and stuck like glue. He was very unhappy, he moved his face from side to side trying to get rid of the taste rubbing his tongue on the bed.

Her soul went out in the dark and squatted in a corner crying. Her body went numb, she felt like a duck roasting in an oven. She imagined her classmate Qing was encouraging her: "Yes, that is the right way, if you want to help your mother do it that way."

"YingLi," The man was calling her name softly but her mind was in another world. She was remembering that her mother's hand and foot had looked terrible, as if a wild dog had just bitten her, her leg was swollen too. "Mother, I want to rescue you and take you home." Mother had said. "Don't worry; I'll get out some day."

"YingLi." He said again, his voice was becoming rough and impatient "Are you dumb?"

"What did you say...what?" From under his weight, her voice sounded so weak, he almost couldn't hear her.

The man was drunk, the blood in his body surged like a runaway wild horse. "Can you tell me...?" His tongue was on her face, she felt cold saliva running down her neck. "Why were you crying?" When she didn't reply he said. "If you don't want to continue, you can leave now."

YingLi did not move.

She did not really understand what she was expected to do. In the darkness she felt her panties being taken off.

"You can't." She said. Her panties stopped moving.

YingLi turned her face to the side, to escape his tongue, saying: "I...now, I...already..." YingLi made great efforts to open the dictionary in her life, but could not find suitable words to describe anything; she thought she had already done that.

YingLi's breasts were being assaulted by big rough hands trying to be gentle. YingLi felt her skin getting hot, and sore. In her dreams, she had always been scared of a ghost that had appeared since her mama left. The ghost peeled her skin and flesh at this moment, opened her breastbone, and took out her heart ...she wanted to cry, but could not utter a sound.

YingLi felt like a dead fish, she did not have any resistance left.

Also she did not know that the man's penis was still as soft as jelly, and that he was trying to get himself aroused.

"Do you like me?" he asked trying to get worked up. He was nipping YingLi's ears with his teeth, his beard scratched her and made her itchy, and she tried to avoid him. "Speak." he ordered. "I...I want you to say you like me."

"You like me." YingLi repeated. She just wanted to be finished like a homework assignment and leave as soon as possible. She never thought about the meaning of the words or that they could be used to stimulate sexual arousal, later she understood, but she did not want to say she liked him. No, it was just an ugly deal; it was an exchange, this page of her life would cause her pain forever.

"Say, you like me!" He said loudly and pointing to her head said, "It is you, you who like me. Yes, I like you, but I want you to say, you, like, me!"

YingLi replied:: "I can't say that."

Stalemated for a while, LiuJiahuai started to compromise. "Can you sing for me?"

YingLi knew she could not refuse him again so she sang: "The east is red, the sun rises, and there emerged a Mao Zedong in China, he works for the happiness of the people, he is the people's ..."

This was the national song, and all Chinese could sing it very well, but hearing this song his penis went limp. "Stop...singing!" he said.

"Not that. Sing a love song."

"That is illegal, you know that."

At that time all love songs had been replaced by revolutionary songs, people who dared to sing about love would be in trouble. Of course, LiuJiahuai knew that very well, therefore he said: "Don't be afraid, I'll support you." He started singing a traditional obscene ditty, "18 and touching."

He began breathing very rapidly. YingLi felt him thrust deeply within her, and her nerves cried out.

Chapter 6

WHILE YINGLI WAS USING her body to try to help her mother, YongHong was standing on the windowsill looking down wards, into a scene of a sea of fire. Someone ignored her order and jumped down.

"Jumping out is forbidden". She shouted.

YongHong's given name was YingHua: Ying was her middle name; Hua was her first name. The practice of naming Chinese children is much different than Western culture; the middle name came from the family tree. Accordingly the middle name tells who hah seniority in the family, and can identify people who are from the same family. YongHong and YingLi both had the same last name Wang, but the last name usually was an important person or relationship that was not related by blood. Therefore she was named YingHua at birth but when the Cultural Revolution began she had changed it, and since had become the leader of the students in her school. Since Long Shan city caught the fire of the Cultural Revolution YongHong had already surprised the party several times: first she denounced her own mother as a traitor; second at the ten thousand people's meeting she talked very well and had the ability to control the masses...and she was famous in all Long Shan City now. People who mentioned "YongHong's" name, would blurt out: "She is beautiful and a very smart girl! She denounced her mother, she is perfect revolutionary material."

In order to show her revolutionary loyalty, she had even changed her name; YongHong, means forever red.

She became Commander-in-chief of the red guards' headquarters in Long Shan city.

Now facing this critical moment of life and death, YongHong really wanted to jump, but the feeling of impending death is not as appealing or as beautiful as it appeared in books and films. In the thorax there are no heroes falling, just the opposite, she believed she would die, and her heart was full of unexpected regrets; she was still young, and had just started on the path of the revolution, she suspected that her mother was a traitor but that was just from revolutionary logic. She believed she was right and felt it was too bad she did not have the opportunity to wait and prove it. Her thoughts wandered between becoming a martyr or perhaps turning into dog's dung. She closed her beautiful eyes, and posed like a "phoenix", ready for nirvana in the sea of fire.

Chapter 7

YONGHONG WAS ENGULFED IN a sea of fire, with her brave and noble-minded companions who must surely die. A soldier rescued YongHong, but two of her companions died in the school building. She escaped from death with severe burns and was in the hospital for several weeks.

When the gauze was finally taken off YongHong ran back to her own group's headquarters without stopping. She faced the portrait of a companion who had died in the fire and full of hate swore revenge for all those who had died; the group responsible must repay with the same price they had paid.

The next day, YongHong went to a chicken farm in the city's suburbs, and leaving a pile of RMB that she regarded as payment for the chickens. She pulled a kitchen knife from her waist sash and began killing chickens. YongHong was building her courage, she had been afraid of the sight of blood, from childhood; and fainted when she saw others bleed. This weakness had not been important in the past, but the situation was different now; she wants to lead her companions into battle against the other group, and to die bravely. Being afraid of the sight of blood would never do. She was carrying the chickens by their wings, as she wanted to lift her enemies by their arms, and she twisted the chicken's necks, as if they were her enemies' necks. Then she placed the knife against the neck and pushed...once...twice...blood spurted from the neck and splattered on the ground; she could not distinguish between humans and chickens necks now. When she killed the first chicken, her hands shivered and her legs trembled; everything went pitch-dark the moment she saw the blood. She stood there shaking and trembling and nearly fell down; then she killed a second, third, and fourth chicken without feeling anything. This hatred and lack of empathy was born from her tragic experience; she recoiled from several drops of pitch-black blood that had a strong smell with the odour of fish. In order to overcome these natural instincts, she dropped more RMB again, and caught another chicken; she held the chicken in her hands for a long time feeling the chicken trembling. The chicken was desperately squawking and struggling, none of these things aroused her pity. YongHong stared into the eyes of the chicken ruthlessly as it struggled against its' enemy, the blade of the knife she noted with satisfaction that the enemies (chickens) she had killed, had finally quit running about and fallen one after another in pools of blood.

Chapter 8

I T WAS A PITY YongHong had no chance to go into combat against
the other group because she was promoted to the position of
Director of the Women's Federation of Long Shan city. The job was
like a modern family court of arbitration; an ancient proverb said,
"Even an upright official finds it hard to settle a family quarrel,
especially issues of family, contradictions between couples mostly
involving sex." YongHong was without sexual knowledge or sexual
experience so this job gave her big headaches.

The morning of the third day after she took up her official post,
she had a case of a female worker from a clothing factory in the
city who had been hit by her husband causing a bloody nose and
swollen face.

YongHong asked, "What happened?"

Three people started speaking at the same time all thinking
that she was asking them to speak first. YongHong said: "Speak one
at a time."

The leader of clothing factory gave the female worker a push
saying, "You talk first."

The female worker wiped away her tears, and opened her mouth
to speak, but the words did not come; she cried loudly, wailing
uncontrollably in front of everybody.

YongHong turned to interrogate the husband: "You please speak first, why did you hit her?"

The man said: "I did not intend to hit her."

YongHong severe in countenance and voice asked: "You did not intend to; the fact is you did hit her, why?"

The man bowed his head and pouted saying: "She does not sleep with me in the evening."

YongHong was puzzled and asked: "Then where does she sleep?"

YongHong's question made people laugh, including the woman who had been crying. She knew explicit sex was taboo, but had never heard about talking about one's sex life as simply sleeping together, or handling personal affairs.

The clothing factory leader explained smiling: "He means that she does not handle affairs with him."

YongHong asked again: "What was not done?"

Three people laughed. The female worker who got a thrashing raised her face, and shyly told YongHong: "The matter of relations, between men and women."

YongHong was even more confused: "You have three children don't you?"

The female worker's smile changed to a gloomy expression and she said: "He is not a reasonable man. he wants to have sex every day, I need to work to support three children, and I do not have enough energy; in the evening; I am so tired that my eyelids need rods to prop them open. When do I have time to be in a leisurely mood with him? He said I had unfaithful intentions, and hit me. "

YongHong finally understanding, turned to face the man and said: "You have done wrong." She felt her face burning as she talked and wanted to finish this case as soon as possible.

YongHong threw a shabby oil pen, and piece paper to the husband and said: "Write a warranty."

After writing several lines, the husband stopped and asked: "Can I ask a question?"

"Yes, speak." YongHong said.

"She and... I." He said pointing to his wife: "I and she..."

"Don't hesitate, get to the point."

"Can we handle affairs together?"

"You are a couple, certainly."

"If, if she doesn't want to, what can I do?"

YongHong wrinkled her brows and asked the female worker: "Do you want to handle affairs with him?"

The female worker was very shy; she smiled, bowed her head, and muttered: "Yes."

"Done, does she need to give a guarantee too?" He asked.

YongHong asked the man: "What will she have to guarantee?"

"Guarantee that she will handle affairs with me."

"Do you want to guarantee?" YongHong trying to keep her patience asked the female worker.

The female worker became delighted unexpectedly: "I don't need to guarantee."

The husband said: "You must guarantee."

"What kind of guarantee do you want her to make?" The clothing factory leader asked the man.

"Guarantee...how many times a week with me."

The female worker looked at YongHong, and waited for her to speak.

YongHong wrinkled her brows tightly; she had an impatient expression on her face, she was thinking: what kind revolutionary work is this? Then she faced the factory leader shaking her hand and said: "This problem you can take back to the factory and solve your selves, OK?"

Chapter 9

YINGLI AFTER HER NIGHT with LiuJiahuai had really believed that her mother's problem was solved. Optimism, and confidence showed in YingLi's' walking posture: in the past, she had walked with her head lowered, the feet of a wall do not walk on the surface; there are paths that do not follow the main road.

Today, she entered the gate of the government compound with her head held high.

YongHong saw her sister entering from the front door and followed her silently, until she was in front of the office of LiuJiahuai. YongHong stretched out her hands and covered YingLi's eyes from behind.

"Take your dog's paw off me! I know who you are." YingLi said loudly as she pulled the fingers away from her eyes.

YongHong dropped her hands and craned her neck asking: "Hello! Who is the dog?"

"Of course, it is you!" YingLi said: "Even a dog would be better than you! A dog knows how to protect, you even betray your own mother; you are not as good as a dog."

Standing next to each other it was easy to see that YingLi was a little bit taller than her older sister, but her face and slim body shape was almost the same. Their complexions were bright, like ripe peaches, large round eyes, aquiline nose, lips moderate thickness, with their oval shaped faces and sharp chins, really looked like two movie stars. In high school they had been the two school beauties, causing many boys to have romantic fantasies.

YongHong interrupted her younger sister and said: "I tell you. If I had not been there that day, our mother would have suffered much worse. If you do not believe me, ask people who were there."

I tell you seriously, it was a very wise move for me to write the big-character poster for our mother, so that I could get ahead of the others; if I did not write that big-character poster, others would have; it is the way of the times. The situation in the whole country is the same; you have not seen, but there are many veteran cadres, with children like you, who want to protect their parents. Does what you protect live? You cannot protect anyone. You look at me with your bosom filled with hatred; it is meaningless... don't look for an excuse there."

YingLi interrupted YongHong saying angrily: "shut up; I don't want to hear you make excuses, I don't believe you! Get out of here, and leave me alone!"

YongHong looked her younger sister up and down from head to toe, and determined to regard her with kindly tolerance and asked: "Who did you come here to see?" she had mistakenly thought her sister had come here to see her. The attitude of her younger sister did not surprise YongHong; she knew she was still angry with her because of their mother's situation. Since YongHong's revolutionary zeal had caused their mother such problems, the sisters had taken different paths, and drifted far apart.

"Who I came to see is none of your business." YingLi replied, she did not intend to tell her purpose to her sister, but suddenly she changed her mind and said: "I came to find people who can help me get my mother out of here."

"Oh, did you come to see him?" YongHong asked pointing to LiuJiahuai's office: "Younger sister, please listen to me; go back home, no one can help you right now."

"You are a big liar, he can help me." YingLi said not believing her.

"What did he say?" YongHong asked examining her younger sister closely with the eyes of an inquisitor.

"He said..." YingLi wanted to use this against her conscienceless elder sister. "You forsook family loyalty for position and power, and betrayed your own mother for the revolution. He is a representative of the army, his position is higher than yours, and he is a revolutionary too! But he wants to help mom." YingLi answered with a sneer.

"Did he say that he would help you? Did he invite you to go to his office to talk etc. in the evening?" YongHong asked

Seeing that her older sister had become very nervous, YingLi began to think that her words had put a thorn in the heart of her sister; then she began to wonder why she had asked about an evening meeting in his office? Maybe her sister knew something about him? YingLi felt an ominous premonition.

"No." Was all she replied.

It was a typical mid day in spring, the sun hung in an ashen sky, it was not hot; but YingLi's forehead was sweating excessively. She thought it was probably the clothes that she was wearing; following the fashion of the day, she was wearing a female grass green army uniform that her elder sister given her. It had three small open-neck collars inside a traditional Chinese cotton-padded jacket. The cotton-padded jacket really did not fit her and it made it difficult for her to breath. The Sun on her head felt like countless acupuncture needles causing pain in her eyes; she narrowed her eyelids trying to hide her feelings.

YongHong looked very closely for a moment examining her young sister's face that was sweating abnormally, and said, "I tell you, you had better not contact him in the future."

"Who I contact is none of your business."

YongHong spoke in a low voice as her eyes glanced about saying: "He is very horny, and wants to have sex with any woman except his mother. Do you understand? You need be careful."

YongHong did not know that her warning was already too late.

YingLi thought about her sister's words; she felt compelled to believe her but didn't want to either. Her elder sister had such bad image of LiuJiahuai; she remembered clearly that when LiuJiahuai had first come to the city they had dated a few times. Afterward YongHong broke off with him for no apparent reason. YingLi glared at her elder sister and felt in her heart, even if he was a lecher, even if he has had her cheaply, as long as he does rescue her mother, she will not regret it. Her filial piety was not a new thing. Throughout several thousand years of history in China, filial piety had been the primary moral basis for conducting oneself; ones parents must be respected, and cared for. If she did what her elder sister told her, how would she be able to help her mother? She was also afraid that if her elder sister found out what she had done through continuing this conversation she would be the one to suffer.

"Mother's chilblains are re-occurring." YingLi said in a softer voice; when her sister did not say anything, she asked: "Why don't you ask the government to help mother?"

"My young sister, do you think the government is controlled by me, that I let who I want to enter, and who I want to leave?" YongHong lowered her voice and continued, saying: "As long as the central authorities do not have a policy there is nothing we can do". YingLi just became even more agitated and asked her self: "Why does there need to be a central policy?" She felt confused, and couldn't decide between her older sister and LiuJiahuai, who was right who was lying, she needed to go home where it was quiet and do some deep thinking about it.

YingLi lowered her head and said: "I do not believe that there is no one who can help my mother." She was determined to go home, did not say "goodbye" to her older sister. YingLi started walking toward the city hall with her head hanging low; as she passed through the gate of the government compound she heard her elder sister's voice following her: "Wait, wait"

She slowed down.

Chapter 10

YONGHONG CAUGHT UP AND said. "I heard that ZhangYong has been demobilized from the army."

ZhangYong was YingLi's ex-boyfriend; after her mother LuDongChun lost her position, they had broken up.

"So he demobilized what does that have to do with me?" YingLi asked and continued walking, resuming her pace; wanting to get away as soon as possible and end any talk on this subject, but the persistence of her elder sister following her made her stop.

"I know you broke up with him, but I thought you would like to know, he is disabled."

"Disabled?" YingLi repeated, she turned, staring at her elder sister's mouth, seeming not to believe what she had heard, at the same time, her eyes revealed a desire to know more.

"Yes, he lost a leg." her elder sister said slowly; as if she was squeezing toothpaste out of a tube, watching her sister closely trying to read her reaction.

YingLi did not dare to believe, even though he didn't have a relationship with her any longer she was also unwilling to believe her sister..

"Is that really true?"

"Do you think my news is false? Go and see how that good for nothing one of yours looks, and ask yourself if he was worth trying to commit suicide for. It is a good that you have the chance to see for your self and resolve your heart ache." YongHong saw the face of her younger sister getting dark; and she made a big show of her power unconsciously.

Several months before when the relationship ended YingLi had taken a lot of sleeping pills, and tried to end her life, because of ZhangYong. Fortunately YongHong with her Red Guards had raided the home to loot it, found her, and had her admitted to hospital.

"I know you are too soft-hearted, while others only shed a tear, you cannot forget any thing. Did you hear what I said? Don't forget: you wanted to end your life because of him and he still did not come around to the right way of thinking."

"In the past our relationship already died." YingLi said.

YongHong left.

And YingLi stood there like a statue. The image of ZhangXianmin entered her thoughts again; his forehead was sweating: "Tell my son, with your own mouth, that your relationship is finished, I am asking you to set my son free."

YingLi wrote several letters, breaking off relations with Zhang Yong; but in her heart she had believed that she was secure in Zhang Yong's love. Zhang Yong, like the protagonist in a novel, when he read her 'Dear John' letter would write back immediately; or return to her side to declare his undying love to her. He would criticize her for being hasty and absurd... but she had waited in vain for his reply.

Zhang Yong had been in the northern border area when armed conflict took place along the Sino-Soviet border; and he had been awarded a Merit Citation, Third Class. The hero had returned to his native city with great honour, bestowed by the people. A public appearance and speech was arranged so that Zhang Yong could relate his heroic deeds to the people. It was said, that the scene that day, was unprecedented in the history of the Long Shan city. The largest meeting room in the whole city could only hold a thousand people, but the city welcomed hundreds of thousands from the masses. The main meeting place was in the meeting room, the great outdoors served as a branch hall. ZhangYong's speech did not live up to the people's expectations; however the atmosphere was still warm and unusual. The speech was interrupted repeatedly; with the sound of slogans and applause coming like commas and periods in an essay.

YingLi did not go to listen to the speech and did not go out in the evening either, she waited until the next morning. Feeling crazy in her heart, she abandoned all restraint and went to Zhang Yong's house without a second thought to meet with him face to face, to clear up and solve the misunderstandings that had taken place.

Zhang Yong's mother stopped her at the gate.

Chapter 11

YongHong worked in government but these affairs did not differentiate between big and small and looked like a grandmother's job. She was annoyed beyond endurance, and really wanted to tell her leaders that she did not want to do this work. However, it is the party member's sacred duty to become a good party member and obey the party; her life belonged to the party.

A few days later, an old married couple came in who looked to be over 60 year's of age, with black and white hair and wrinkled faces. The old woman was very angry and said to YongHong: "I want to divorce him."

"We have different revolutionary views and belong to different groups." The old man added.

At the time, a gust of wind of change was blowing from the national leadership. The political view was a popular subject and had become the focus of discussion.

The resulting increase in family problems: husbands and wives fighting or getting divorced, sons or daughters were becoming enemies of their parents...YongHong's sense of the political potential of the issue caused her to become really excited.

She was about to set an example, to prove that the Cultural Revolution was firmly planted in people's hearts, and now a perfect example stood before her. She told the couple: "Ok, I will support your request."

From the moment that YongHong made her decision, she knew how she would exploit the case. It had been several months since her involvement in LuDongChun's criticizing and denouncing conference; the revolutionary storm had taught her much about becoming a chess player and choosing the right piece.

She knew that breaking up this marriage would not accord with Chinese moral standards; but as a first in the new times in political standards this was a challenge.

The interests brought forward in this challenge were double; the old woman would rise to national political circles, and her own personal reputation would soar for her keen sensitive political perception. Out of loyalty to the party, she was a chess player who would personally break up this revolutionary family of 30 years. The old woman who should have lived an easy life in old age and ended up with dementia would become a piece, on the chessboard; a sad ending.

But as a national player on the board; she been used as a chess piece too when she had accepted a marriage without love, and then experienced a tragedy of love.

Chapter 12

INSIDE ZHANGYONG'S HOME, A hoarse voice was croaking: "Wine...wine...wine..." bellowing hoarsely from the bedroom intermittently.

His father ZhangXianmin and his wife were standing outside the bedroom door, appearing anxious and helpless.

Zhang's wife was being gentle with her son, "Baby, we won't drink any more, ok? You are drunk already; drinking too much is very bad for your health."

This sentence she kept repeating over, and over. It was obvious that the son had closed his ears to her words. She wanted to say her son was her flesh and blood who had frolicked happily in the past at her breast. Having suddenly lost a leg he was now the decadent one and lays on the Kang crying, but her heart feels more pain than her son's does. The son had been back for one week, subsisting only in order to get drunk all the time; his mother was just a simple housewife with no education, and could not talk about major issues or principles.

"My leg! Wine..." ZhangYong screamed.

"You lost a leg, but you will continue to live, all right?" The mother answered.

"What is there to live for? Let me die!" he said wailing.

His father ZhangXianmin said: "You know you are just being pessimistic, you know that Beethoven was deaf, and became a virtuoso, and another Chinese, Mr Wu, who lacked a leg like you..."

ZhangYong interrupted his father hollering. "Shut up:"

Zhang's wife said: "Baby, is that any way to speak to your father? He is your father do not be so impolite."

ZhangYong said: "What I suffer today is all his fault. wu...wu... wuwu..."

ZhangYong was an only son and their heir. The parents had no child for many years after they got married, and they went to the hospital picked up an illegitimate child; a boy that looked skinny, so they called him Thin-cat. The couple cherished this Thin-cat and took him home. In three months the Thin-cat had recuperated, and gained weight on his body and face; when they went out, everyone admired the boy. The child was blissful, having had the good fortune of falling into the Zhang family, but just six months later Zhang's wife got pregnant and gave birth to a son. There was less than two years of age between the children, and the couple had no child raising experience, so they were very hard pressed looking after two little ones. ZhangXianmin had proposed finding a home for the Thin-cat but his wife would not hear of it. She had been raising the Thin-cat for two years and he called her "mom, mom" sweetly, making her feel like he was her own. She disagreed and said, "I want to keep both of them."

Then they underwent a lean year with food in short supply and limits were imposed on the quantity they could receive. The thin-cat was used to having the family giving him food first, now the younger brother came first, and the Thin-cat was not willing to watch what had been his, being given to his younger brother, despite his parents many lessons this did not change. When ZhangYong was only two, Zhang's wife was in the kitchen baking flour cakes, and the boys were on the Kang; (a bed built of bricks and clay) drooling waiting to eat cake. When the first cake was put on the table the brothers both tried to grab it, but it was quickly in the Thin-cat's hands. Little Zhang Yong's crying and screaming made the walls and ceiling tremble. ZhangXianmin called out from the study room telling the Thin cat to give the cake to his younger brother first. Oil flowed from the hot cake emitting steam, making the Thin-cat grimace, but he would not let go.

Zhang's wife shouted from the kitchen: "Another one will be ready soon".

ZhangXianmin wanted to change the Thin-cat's selfish behaviour so he held a whiskbroom, pointing it at the thin cat and ordered: "You give to your younger brother first." The Thin-cat was crying too, but still holding the cake in his hands. ZhangXianmin became even angrier, and asked: "Put down the cake. Do you dare not obey?"

The younger brother grabbed the cake and stuffed the whole cake into his mouth, and then started choking, his face turned red, then couldn't breathe, and was declared dead in the hospital two hours later.

Afterwards, Zhang's wife had been pregnant twice, and gave birth to a boy and a girl, but they both died young; ZhangYong had been doted on by his family.

Zhang's wife pushed her husband into the other room, and said. "What can we do?"

"Who knows? Let him cry. Let him act crazy!"

ZhangXianmin had been an outstanding student at university. After he graduated, he began working in the city government; and when after many years he had still not been put in a high position, he thought that his talent was going unrecognized. He had placed all his hopes on his son; he had objected to his son falling in love with YingLi, but only because he thought it best for his son's future. The son had demobilized back and now knew the truth; it was not YingLi that ceased to be faithful, it was his father who was responsible for the tragedy. Relations between Zhang Yong and his father had reached the breaking point quickly.

"It is easy for you to talk. You might like to see him go crazy, but I don't!" Zhang's wife said angrily. "We only have him, maybe you do not care, but I do. You must think of a solution, you just look at him and he goes crazy, but you are still his father."

ZhangXianmin shrugged helplessly and said: "I say if he wants to be crazy we cannot stop him; his psychological problem he has to solve himself. You have seen and heard him, when I say anything he just thinks I am full of shit."

Zhang's wife heaved a deep sigh of grief and said: "If you had not separated him from YingLi, his mood at this time would also be better...it's all because you were too snobbish."

"How was I to know that my son would be crippled today? Certainly I wanted to create an opportunity for him to be able to have a meteoric rise."

Zhang's wife nodded, she had thoughts that she had suppressed for quite a while, and still hesitated to speak, then said: "Otherwise, we must ask someone to do a match making..."

ZhangXianmin could hardly wait for her to finish speaking, and said: "Your idea is good."

"But..." Zhang's wife asked: "But who would want him now?" She had changed her question but was thinking : "May be, he still can't forget about YingLi."

"Oh! Yes? Go and ask him! If he still wants her, we could help them."

"What did you say?" Zhang's wife could hardly believe her own ears; she wanted him to repeat it again.

"If he wants her, I will speak to the government. They can arrange it, we don't need to care about what she wants, we only need to know what he wants."

"How can the Party organize these things?"

"It has been common practice since the national independence, lots of old cadre's marriages are organized by the party... It sounds like someone is knocking on the gate:; will you go and have a look?"

Chapter 13

ZHANG'S WIFE RUSHED INTO the courtyard with quick short steps, asking in a hoarse voice. "Who is knocking on the gate?" When she opened the gate, she stood speechless with astonishment.

YingLi felt embarrassed and muttered: "Hi! Aunt Zhang."

After YingLi had left her elder sister she returned in the direction she had come; midway, her legs began to disobey; she wanted to see Zhang Yong immediately. The news of ZhangYong being maimed ripped and tore at her heart.

Without her mother's problem, and without his father's pushing…so much, things would have turned out different and she felt she could not complain about him. She knew he had loved her very much, and in her heart, she still loved him, that had never changed.

She no longer had dreams about being with him, because of her mother's problem, plus the fact that she had lost her purity, dignity, and virginity.

She just missed him, and wanted to see him once more, and say: "hello!" that was all.

She knew from her own experience that people who were in his plight, needed others to come and console them. Even a person who was just a common friend with him should do that much.

Zhang's wife acted as if she had forgotten the last visit when she denied entrance to YingLi. She ardently held YingLi's hands, and walked to the door with her saying. "ZhangYong, guess who has come to see you?" She sounded like she had just found a long lost relative who has been away for many years. "Look, we were just talking about her and she has come." she said to ZhangXianmin when they entered the living room.

"You were talking about me?" YingLi asked in disbelief.

"We were not really talking about you. It was just...just...your name came up during the conversation."

YingLi was ushered into the familiar sitting room and seated on the sofa that she was so familiar with.

ZhangXianmin saw YingLi come in, nodded, and slipped away into his study room.

YingLi turned her head to Zhang's wife. "I heard that Zhang Yong was sick." She said sick to introduce the topic; in fact the question in her mind was answered when she entered the door, ZhangXianmin and his wife were not acting arrogant like before. Though she had a smile on her face, Zhang's wife's upper eyelids were red and swollen; any fool could see that she had been crying. YingLi felt her heart sinking.

"Oh, thank you, thank you, he is not ...oh... yes..." Zhang's wife was incoherent.

Then the hoarse bellowing voice flooded into YingLi's ears: "Wine...Wine..."

YingLi bounced from sofa quickly asking: "Can I go to see him?" She didn't wait for Zhang's wife to answer, she was already headed directly for ZhangYong's room but the door was closed.

"ZhangYong!" She called gently from behind the closed door.

"Wine... Zhang, give me wine."

Zhang's wife opened the door saying: "ZhangYong, look who has come."

"Go away, all of you go away!"

It was true as she had expected; YingLi saw him lying prone, there were two trouser legs, and one of them was empty and flat from the hip. Her face was covered with tears immediately; she was so repulsed she felt sick, and had to fight the urge to vomit.

"ZhangYong, it is me YingLi" she said softly.

ZhangYong recognized YingLi's voice, but his face was still facing down. In a subdued voice he asked: "Why did you come?"

"I came to see you."

"To ridicule me?"

"No." YingLi said very decisively.

"No?" He saw her feet on the floor, and his body convulsed.

"Did you come to tell me the major principles? That Homer was blind but wrote an epic, that Beethoven's was deaf but he wrote the destiny symphony, that Pavel Korchagin was paralysed...blah, blah. If you want to talk like that, it is better to shut up. I'm not from an educated class like that. I just wanted to be an ordinary person, get married and have a child."

His words "marry: and "child" made Zhang's wife's heart ache, she had already guessed her son's desire.

And the words made YingLi think deeply too. What was his meaning? Did he want to make up? Perhaps they were not just ordinary friends. She thought she had better go home and ponder her feelings carefully first, so she said: "ZhangYong, I will go home now."

Hearing that she was going to leave, ZhangYong was upset and struggled to turn over and sit up, but his body didn't obey him; he was laying on his side lacking a leg. YingLi went forward and supported him; he was in YingLi's arms like a child saying: "Please, don't go."

YingLi's eyes were moist, and she said choking with sobs: "Ok, let me wash your face."

Zhang's wife said: "You are a guest, let me do it"

YingLi pushed her hands away taking advantage of the situation; hinting that she should leave YingLi said: "I will do it."

Zhang's wife knew she should leave them alone and left.

YingLi brought the washbasin from the under the dining room table, and carried the kettle from the stove in her hands. She poured the water into the basin very capably. Steam rose and ZhangYong reminded her to: "Add some cold water."

"I know." She answered happily, and added cold water to the basin, tried the temperature, and then carried it to ZhangYong.

YingLi took a soft towel, put it into the hot water, soaked it, and then twisted it half dry using both hands, and carefully washed Zhang Yong's face. ZhangYong blushed, and YingLi's face felt like it was burning. Though they were once lovers, and their past happiest times were spent hand in hand, it was the first time they had ever been in a situation like this.

YingLi finished washing his face, and they sat silently.

YingLi struggled for words in the awkward silence that followed and then asked: "Are you hungry?"

"A little." he replied.

"What would you like to eat... noodles?" She knew this was what ZhangYong liked eating most of all.

"Oh, yes."

YingLi went to the kitchen to boil the noodles, and Zhang's wife came close and asked quietly. "What is going on? Is his mood getting better?"

"Yes, better."

Zhang's wife said in amazement: "You are very competent! What have you told him? I tell you since you are not a stranger, when this spoiled brat of a boy was wilful, his father used Chairman Mao's words but they did not work! But you..."

YingLi said: "I didn't tell him anything; I just asked him if he was hungry."

"Really?" Zhang's wife was confused.

The noodles were the kind pressed in a machine. YingLi rinsed the noodles in cold water after they were boiled, fried two eggs and added a little spoon of yellow been sauce, when the egg sauce was mixed with the noodles, it made a delicious meal.

"Take your time." Watching ZhangYong gobbling up the noodles, YingLi said. "You look like you haven't eaten for a month."

"For six months I have had no appetite for food."

YingLi thinking: Six months would have been the day that she claimed to break off her relationship with him. Her heart began to beat furiously, her eyelids drooped, her eyes were fixed on the bowl of noodles in Zhang Yong's hand. The bowl was shaking, with his right hand Zhang using bamboo chopsticks was shovelling noodles into his mouth and with his left hand guiding the bowl up gradually, covering the nose first, until it covered his face, and the slurping sounds stopped. As soon as he had finished the first bowl, he had another.

When ZhangYong had finished the noodles he said: "Thank you for still coming to see me when I am like this."

"Don't say that." YingLi said, turning her face to the side.

"I was unfair to you." he said.

"Don't say that." YingLi turned her face back, and looked into ZhangYong's eyes.

He said: "But I can't forgive myself, I can never forgive myself."

YingLi had been moved deeply by Zhang Yong's self-accusation. She plucked up her courage and said gently: "Let the past be forgotten, we can make a new start."

It was obvious that Zhang Yong had received a strong shock; he pulled the joint of his finger hard, the sound of his knuckle cracking was clear. Silence filled the room and only the spring breeze against the window could be heard. Zhang Yong's eyelids drooped then obviously very upset he said.

"Oh, that was in the past."

Zhang Yong began to feel sleepy, and YingLi helped him to lie down in his bed and covered him with a quilt; she withdrew from the room when he began to snore. Zhang's wife took hold of YingLi's hands in the living room, and asked.

"Why are you in a hurry to leave?"

"He is sleeping." YingLi looked sidelong at ZhangXianmin and his wife, and said: "He can't stand the advice you give, when you speak, it would be better not to irritate him."

ZhangXianmin took half a cigarette into his mouth, exerted himself to take several large drags in succession, then he nipped and killed the butt. The ashtray on the tea table looked like an anthill. He threw the cigarette butt on the tea table while it was still smouldering, and then used his thumb to role it several times ruthlessly killing it.

Zhang's wife cast a look at her husband and asked: "We get scolded, when will we get a chance to speak?"

YingLi said: "He is... He is quite resentful of your interference. "

Guiding the topic, Zhang's wife said: "The matters between the two of you were his father's fault, and he regrets what he did. But his regrets do not help, we were just talking about this when you came, I said, if ZhangYong and YingLi still have a good relationship, I will swear that YingLi did not leave of her own free will. But now, how do we talk to her again?"

YingLi bowed her head and Zhang's wife thought that she was being shy. Patting YingLi's shoulder, she said: "Silly girl, we don't care about your mother's problem now; if it makes ZhangYong happy, we will approve of anything."

YingLi thought for a minute and said. "I will go home now."

"You come back tomorrow, and I will cook you and Yong's favourite stewed fish."

"Oh..." YingLi wondered what to say, she wasn't sure if she would come again or not.

Zhang's wife sensing her indecision said: "Oh, you can come any time, this is your home too."

Chapter 14

YINGLI HAD CALLED AND asked LiuJiahuai on the telephone many times, and he always said: "Don't rush, I will take care of it." His promises sounded weak since she had heard her elder sister' advice. For a long time she had remained undecided, but her doubts grew as time progressed like a big stone on her heart. She decided to go to and get advice from Qing.

"Continue going." Qing said.

"How many times have you gone?" YingLi asked.

"Me?" Qing laughed and made a face. "I have not even gone once."

Hearing that, YingLi was very angry, and wanted to slap her face because she had told her: "A woman's body can solve problems better than Chairman Mao's words." This was her own experience... she raised her hand to slap her and then put it down again. She gnashed her teeth and said: "You just wait." and got up and left.

Seeing how angry she had made YingLi, Qing began to have regrets and called after her: "Wait, you listen." Qing had said, she went there because her mother was locked up too. Her mother and a Russian expert loved each other and gave birth to Qing. Later, Sino-Soviet relations turned cold and the Russian expert was withdrawn and left his lover and their daughter in China. In the beginning she had gone to his office in the daytime. In the office alone with him, she had made eyes at him, and moved her chair closer to him, so that she could touch his legs. She found, his eyes had an invisible hook that could take off her clothes, and that he wanted to get into her pants. His eyes stuck to her partially exposed bosom like glue and she knew what he wanted. From her experience with men, she decided to come back for a visit late at night. In their first night time meeting they had sex. There was no question of who seduced whom; Qing had clearly taken the initiative.

Internally half her blood belonged to White Russia, along with her yellow hair, blue eyes, and light coloured skin; the remaining half of Chinese origin was overshadowed. She didn't know who she should give her hymen to. After the Cultural Revolution began, she had led an aimless existence with boys, she first enjoyed being sexually excited, sexual contact led to promiscuity. Graduating from boys to a man of LiuJiahuai's position gave her a feeling of empowerment and prestige. Since she had rescued her mother at the same time she felt exhilarated with her power and had bragged to YingLi and another girl. However LiuJiahuai having experienced the forbidden fruit was like a cat who liked fish, one smell and he was salivating.

Qing caught up to YingLi, panting and said: "You have to listen..." and she whispered her secret, then YingLi forgot her anger, became happy again and said: "Ok, I will see you tonight."

Chapter 15

EVENING ARRIVED AND FOLLOWING Qing's suggestion, YingLi stood in front of LiuJiahuai's office. She looked around then raised her hand and knocked on the door timidly. But no one came to the door. She knocked again, a little harder but there was still no answer. She became impatient, and kicked the door with her foot, until she felt her foot starting to hurt. She knew he had been living here, since he came to Long Shan city with the army. Where could he be, away on business? Suddenly the door opened, LiuJiahuai had a cotton-padded jacket draped over his shoulders and stood in the doorway.

"What do you want?" He asked angrily.

"You know what I want." YingLi said.

Qing hiding, standing in the shadows, was concerned about YingLi, and their plan... She seemed not to be going on the right course to be able to do it.

"Business is conducted in the daytime." LiuJiahuai said: "Official business is done according to official principles." he tried to push her away and close the door.

YingLi suddenly remembered her plan with Qing, she had to get into the room. She tried to hold on to the doorknob and said: "No, I want talk now."

Qing's plan had required her to be gentle, flirt with him, and use all the charms of a woman fascinated by this guy. . . However, she felt she could not do that. She knew her attitude and response had been wrong and she wanted to change it, but her throat did not follow her command. She stepped back to think, as long as she had an opportunity to enter into the room she must take the next step.

YingLi stood outside awhile thinking, it was still dark inside and the door was locked. Seeing that her plan was failing she picked up a brick and threw it through the window. This action really worked, LiuJiahuai jumped from in front of the window, and pushed YingLi into the room knocking her to the floor while a petite woman silently slipped out of the room.

YingLi realised that he had been playing with another woman.

"What do you want?' LiuJiahuai asked while knowing very well.

YingLi stood up by herself slowly, her mouth was bleeding, and her heart was bleeding too. She forgot the purpose which she had come for; seeing that petite woman she was thinking about herself, thinking of the night he had stolen her virginity, she was burning with rage.

"I want you to give me an answer!'" She said trembling with rage. Her older sister's words and the woman quietly slipping away made her bad premonition even stronger.

"Answer what?' His expressionless face revealed his real feelings very well for the moment; he appeared to have forgotten his promise and how nice he had been to her before. Now he looked like a policeman who would beat his own father, in dedication and entirely out of public interest.

"My mother's case."

"I will answer you tomorrow."

"No, I want you to answer right now."

"If I don't say yes?"

"I will not leave."

"Oh? You want to sleep with me again? Did you miss me?" LiuJiahuai laughed lasciviously and grabbed her in his arms.

She was already in his arms, following the plan was just a step away, she just needed to tempt LiuJiahuai to lay on the bed and flirt with him, then, Qing would break in as YingLi's witness. . . human testimony and material evidence...would make him listen to her. But, because for the moment she was too angry, she forgot their plan. She struggled and bit his hand, making him yell.

"Oh, oh, you are a mad dog!" he said. His pulled his hand free and saw the teeth marks and blood oozing there.

She said: "Yes, I'm a dog, loyal to my host, and bite bad people"

"You are saying that I'm a bad person?"

"Yes, you are."

"YingLi, do you know the consequences of what you say? Can you shoulder the responsibility for your words?"

"Responsibility? Do you know what responsibility is? You do not know! You promised me, but you just lied, you were deceiving me."

"I have not deceived you."

"You rape women, and..."

"Hold on, who rapes women? Evidence? Evidence?"

YingLi remembered her plan suddenly.

Terrible! She thought. If she had become soft, the plan could have worked. But, YingLi was too stubborn and her personality had showed through again. Why do I have to react that way? I am justified, and I would like to convince people by reasoning

Regret was useless now; she became more determined and boldly said: "My hymen was broken, that is evidence."

LiuJiahuai laughed. "You are really a mad dog, your hymen is broken and you blame me; what about your mother's hymen and all other women? I am to blame for all of them?"

YingLi had not only failed in her plan, she also suffered great humiliation, she was frustrated and said: "I'm going to sue you!"

Chapter 16

T HE NEXT MORNING, YINGLI was still immersed in her anger.
Marriage customs required that on the day of marriage the
groom would check the bride's virginity; if blood appeared from
the rupturing of the hymen the bride was considered to have been
a virgin. If there was no blood the bride was inferior goods, subject
to cursing, beating, and or abandonment.

Twenty years later, China was open and things had changed,
including some hymen culture stereotypes. Advertisements for
mending the hymen would be seen everywhere, the advertisements
made it sound as if it was as simple as repairing a flat tire on a
bicycle. The value of the hymen went down in price. The standard of
judging chastity became a purely ethical one. Men no longer judged
women by their hymen, and women did not have to experience
the fear of rejection. However in the present YingLi had to endure
insults of both spirit and body.

She had been awake all night. The room felt like an icehouse;
the Kang was cold with no fire in it. She stayed under the heavy
quilt wearing a cotton padded jacket and cotton padded trousers
until nearly noon then she went to the courtyard and got a handful
of wood to start a fire in the stove. As she was lighting the fire

YongHong came rushing in the door and asked: "Did you go to ZhangYong's house?"

"Yes" YingLi said, with swollen eyes.

"Is he lame? Really lame?"

"Yes, like you said, his leg was gone from the hip." YingLi said.

"Tell me everything that was said."

"We only talked a little, he was in a bad mood." YingLi said

"Did he say that he wanted to get married?"

"Married? With who?"

"Did he say...does he still like you?"

"What is wrong with you?" She asked loudly and impatiently. YongHong already did not recognize their family. Today she had come back all nervous, just to ask about Zhang Yong; and if he was really lame? It was baffling!

"He wants to marry me! I will die soon." YongHong said as she pushed YingLi into the bedroom, and followed her in tears.

"I don't think so." YingLi said doubtfully.

"Yes, it is true." YongHong said fearing that her younger sister heard without comprehending. "The leader of our organization talked to me, he was very serious and told me that the government wants me to marry him, and to take care of him."

"This is not the Party's business." YingLi said confused.

"Some things you do not comprehend even when I tell you." YongHong was shaking her head, and sighing deeply. "My heart is in a mess; and you say I don't have to marry him."

"No one can force anyone to marry. We have been liberated. We live in a socialist country now not feudalism." YingLi said.

"My political future will be finished if I disagree. My Leader said that to test me...if... I can't withstand...I will be...I..."

"Which is more important?"

"Both." YongHong said: "It was not easy to go from a student with no reputation to my position today. That was not easy, you snubbed me, mother did too; nobody understands me. Even when I walk on the street, I hear people talking about me behind my back. I was born for the revolution, I can not give that up and go back; I would rather be dead."

"Then...you are going to obey..."

"To obey? Do you know what my ideal of a dream lover is? An army officer, tall and handsome wearing a uniform looks wonderful. ZhangYong, with one leg; he does not even wear an army uniform.!"

"Don't talk with such malevolence."

"I'm being malevolent?" YongHong jumped up in front of YingLi, "He is the one who is malevolent, there are lots of girls in the city, why does he want me? What does it mean? Why me?"

YingLi had the same question, she recalled when she was with him, she had not been able to guess what he was thinking.

"I have an idea...can I talk?" YongHong asked with pleading eyes looking at her young sister probingly.

"Yes, go ahead!"

"I will say...what...I'm thinking..." she said hesitantly.

"Hey! When did you become like an old lady?"

"Will you ...marry...him for me?"

"Me?" YingLi couldn't believe her ears and said to herself "Are you joking, what kind of thing am I?" She felt her elder sister was being so funny she burst out laughing.

YongHong continued: "Yes! I'm not joking I swear, if you do it, I will help you in your daily life! That is why I ask you, I am not being selfish, I just want to continue to do more revolutionary work. I am not like you, I couldn't stay at home being a wife; if I had to stay home and take care of him I would die tomorrow!"

"I believe that."

"Will you say that you will help me?"

"No!"

YongHong stubbornly continued: "You could say yes! Anyone else could not do it, but you can." She saw the question in YingLi's eyes and said again: "I remember the day I told you repeatedly not to go to see him. Don't go, but you went that proved to me that he is still in your heart. Young sister, if the shoes are comfortable or not, only the feet know. He lost a leg, but he is hero, the leader of Long Shan City has very great respect for him." YongHong imitated her leader's voice; the last syllable was drawn out long and thin. "If you have any problems in life you can ask for anything." Afterwards she returned to being serious. "Have you thought about it? You could go any where and you would receive flowers and applause isn't that great?"

YingLi looked like her interest had been aroused. "I must find out what ZhangYong thinks."

"I don't care about him. I only care about you and me." Hong Yong said. "I just want to slip out of a bad predicament; if you don't want to marry him you can use delaying tactics later."

"You and ZhangYong need to decide it first." YingLi said.

"Ok, I will go and talk to him now."

In the evening,: YongHong came back crying.

"Zhang Yong has a mental problem, he only wants me."

YingLi was silent.

"Will you go and tell him yourself? That you love him and you would like marry him." Yong Hong was begging now her voice was no longer arrogant, and her eyes were filled with hope as she pleaded with her sister.

"How can I go to talk to him? 'ZhangYong, will you marry me?' like that? Every body would think I'm crazy!"

"Tell me you still love him, don't you?"

"Um…if he got disabled after we were married I really couldn't divorce him for that reason."

"You act as if you were married and he got disabled, you go and tell him, you love him! Please! Please!! I'm kneeling to you."

Chapter 17

WALKING TO ZHANGYONG'S HOUSE, YingLi felt like she carried countless little rabbits in her stomach making her heart agitated and uneasy. She felt her shoulders heave too. In her mind, that day when she showed she would like to make up with him it was an impulse of the moment, as a friend only. She had not wanted to get married yet. Marry him? She also remembered that after she said "restart" he had become silent. She thought maybe it was ZhangYong's strategy, to disappoint me because it was not easy for him to speak bluntly. Maybe he was going in a circle to let me in? With this thinking YingLi's steps became lighter she would like to be in.

Seeing ZhangYong, without preamble she said: "Zhang Yong, if you need a woman by your side, we will marry. Is that Ok?"

"No." ZhangYong said coldly.

In his heart and mind another voice was saying: "YingLi, I love you but we can't share this life, if we have another life I will marry you. You are good girl, marrying you was my dream for years. My happiness was only with you. You are a beautiful girl; you are soft, kind, and smart. In high school everybody liked you because even though you were from a special family in Long Shan, with your mother in a high position, you never used your mama's prestige to gain any special treatment. In comparison, YongHong was domineering, and acted superior. At school most male classmates said behind her back: twin sisters, YingLi is fit for a good wife, YongHong is only fit for good business partner.

He stopped thinking, glanced at her quickly, recalling when he received the dear john letter, he had cried all night, he really wanted to go back to her side to make up, but he also had a letter from his father that said: If he didn't break up with YingLi, the family's relationship with him would end.

"Why?" YingLi asked ZhangYong, she guessed he had said "no", because he had broken off with her so she said: "The past is over. We can start again, is that OK?"

ZhangYong's heart was in turmoil, he really wanted to pull her into his arms, and say: OK, OK! I am sorry what I did to you. Let us make a new start, I will take this opportunity to make up for my fault for the rest of my life! We will have lots of children...children? My god! His heart ached and he broke into a cold sweat. He couldn't marry her, he was a basket case, he was no longer a real man! If he could not give her happiness, it was better not to add new pain and suffering on her, it would be unfair to her. He loved her, and wanted her to be happy, he could not be selfish.

The words were very hard for him to speak, he opened his mouth several times, then said unwillingly: "You don't need to know my reasons why. Our relationship was ended."

He surprised her and turned his face to the side to avoid YingLi's eyes and hide his guilty conscience.

That day he ate the noodle soup YingLi made for him and then he slept, and had a strange dream: He saw a white light in the sky splitting open, a middle aged woman wearing an ancient costume leading some young girls came floating down. Zhang Yong gazed in wonder with his eyes wide open, gazing steadily at the middle aged woman; he thought he recognised her, but couldn't remember where from. While he tried to remember she came to him, and said kindly. "I will help you get a wife." The seven young women behind her moved to the front, every one of them was beautiful. He had never seen women so gorgeous, were they fairy maidens? Then, a melodious voice said. "Wang Mu (Queen of heaven) I like this man."

The woman speaking had cheeks that looked like rosy clouds, and eyes like deep dark waters in a lake. As his dream became lucid Zhang Yong closed his mouth tightly, to keep his heart in his chest. "Wang Mu" only smiled, and the fairy maiden moved straight towards him. Her breasts were moving freely under her silk shirt like a cicada's wings arousing him and filling him with desire. He felt his body getting hot, and then begin to shake and ejaculate. Meanwhile, the two snakes on her breast were writhing their heads in a wrenching movement with open mouths and venom dripping from their tongues...now he was shaking and running...and fell heavily from the Kang (bed) to the floor in his wet dream.

His mama told him, he had been sleeping for two days already. And then she said: "Yong, we have organized support for you, to look for a partner in marriage, there will be no problems; you can have whoever you choose just say who. The organization will take care of everything for you." She said with a smile.

"I don't want a wife" ZhangYong replied.

"Yong, you need a partner; in your present condition without a partner how can you manage your life? While your father and mother are alive, we can serve you, when we die how will you carry on? Don't be wilful. Have a woman, have a seriously live woman, and give me and your father peace of mind."

"Who would want me?"

"What is wrong with my son, he only lost a leg; that is a national honour. The leader said, you could marry any woman you want, "just name her, they will arrange everything for you."

"Mom, I don't want anyone." ZhangYong said firmly.

ZhangXianmin hollered from living room, saying, "I can tell you, if you don't want to marry now, you will not be able to later."

Zhang's wife saw her son's face getting dark suddenly, she gestured to her husband not to chip in.

ZhangXianmin carried on as if he had not seen anything, saying. "You lost a leg, but life will continue. We need a family tree; getting married is not only your business, it is the families business too. Who does not want descendents, they are good for the future too."

Descendants? He laughed. "Ha, ha, ha, ok I will marry; I will make a child, I want YongHong. Go ahead, I will make a fine revolutionary variety for you."

YingLi was reviewing ZhangYong's, words once again, for his unrequited love and regret. Her mood plummeted and swept away her beautiful and romantic love fancy. Maybe...she thought: What am I? Like his father said: the daughter of traitor; and even though her older sister was also, she was now a prize revolutionary. A popular saying was: "You can not choose your family, but you can choose your road". She had to stay by her mama's side, and had never wanted to join the revolution, maybe that is why he refused her, and maybe only her older sister was a match for him. He was a hero of the revolution now.

The long awkward silence made YingLi uneasy she wanted to say something to break this embarrassing situation but she can not believe what she had said: "I swear if we get married I will take care of you all your life." As soon as she spoke she realised it was a very poor choice of words, they were not about love, more like duty or position.

"I know you very well." Seeing YingLi smile Zhang Yong continued. "I do not want to involve you YingLi, you are a good girl. For sure, very good! I'm no longer a match for you in this life; that is all."

"You want to marry my elder sister, does that not involve her?" this was YingLi's final argument.

ZhangYong took a deep breath, and said: "Maybe not, she wants to rise in the Party and get a promotion; together we can help each other."

"My elder sister didn't think about that; she was angry and in agony, do you think your decision is right?"

"I know it is not right but this has been organized and arranged, and I don't have a choice." He said: "I have thought conscientiously too, if a woman can't have anything from me, I am guilty. With your elder sister, it is different because, this is an exchange..." he said.

"Exchange?" When YongHong heard his reply said had screamed: "I will make a plan to make him angry everyday and hope he dies soon.

Chapter 18

LuDongChun had been locked up in a room in a dilapidated bungalow. The room was in darkness, a rusty iron stove stood in the centre, and the only way to get warm was by getting as close as possible to the coal fire. The building had gone without repairs for many years, and the walls had chinks missing from neglect. Through the widest cracks one could see the sky and see if it was night or day; is was a relatively private room, with only one door that opened to a hallway. A single window faced the walled yard, the walls were not high, young people could cross it easily. After LuDongChun had been locked in, the window had been covered with boards, and the light on the ceiling was only 15 watts, so even during the day the light had to be on.

When winter set in YingLi brought a few pieces of plastic hoping that she could block out the wind and snow, but it didn't work. LuDongChun could still see some sky through the cracks and could tell if it was windy, snowing, or the sun was shining. An old disease from frostbite that LuDongChun had from before the liberation, was back again with the cold; both hands were ulcerated, and the medication was not working well probably because the room was so cold.

LuDongChun was an optimist about the revolution; she had joined the peoples' liberation army in the north, and fought against the Japanese. After the national liberation, she left the army and went to work in local government. In the army she had become used to suffering and casualties, and thought her hands were not a very serious problem, no need to make a fuss.

But to Ying Li they were very serious, and she cried when she saw them. Whenever she thought about her mother confined in this place, her heart ached. She just wished that her mother could go home soon.

YingLi came to see her mother again.

"Mom." she called with a voice like honey.

LuDongChun raised her hand high, rapped her arm around her and hugged her a long time, then she asked: "Why did you come so much earlier than scheduled?"

Though this was not a regular jail, the schedule for visits was very limited; usually only twice a month. More than two visits were only for a special situation; and then it depended mainly on the mood of the guard. If one met the guard in an understanding and reasonable way, spoke nicely, and indulged in pleasant idle talk, one could come in more often. If one treated the guard like shit, they would be refused entry. YingLi had come only three days before and LuDongChun felt something must be wrong.

Because visiting time was limited, YingLi wanted to make the best use of the little time they would have.

"I asked you first, did anyone come to talk to you about representing you?" YingLi asked.

"Oh, yes." LuDongChun answered quickly.

YingLi was happy for a moment, and then asked. "What did they talk about?"

"They told me to explain my case."

"Was there not anything else?" YingLi was a bit disappointed, and said: "That is strange."

She thought that night even though she had not completed her plan with Qing to pressure LiuJiahuai, she believed that he would have heard the alarm bell; if he continued to not give her the answer she wanted, he must know what she would do. Though that day she had failed with her evidence about her hymen; if his affair with her were to become known, he must be more worried than her. He liked her elder sister, and he realised his political future was more important than life; she thought that raising his hand high for a traitor would be better than ruining his political future.

"What is strange?" LuDongChun asked.

"Nothing." YingLi said as she tried to think of something to say: "One of the neighbours was released; I think you will be too soon."

"There is no hurry; you see, I'm here and I don't need anything. I just eat and sleep like a pig, I am getting fat."

"Mama! That is not fat, you have oedema." YingLi said, tears dropped on her nose, and her mother used a ulcerated hand to brush them away. YingLi held her mother's hand lightly, and continued: "Mom, anyone can see that your hand is swollen. Just press on it with your fingers, your flesh does not spring back like anyone else's hand. Mom, someone told me that your swollen hand is a big problem." YingLi said feeling even sadder, and she started crying.

"Don't cry baby! Don't be afraid. Your always maudlin, you're not like your elder sister."

Mention of her elder sister suddenly reminded her why she had come.

She dried her tears, and said: "Yes, I came to talk to you about her, she is going to get married."

"Oh? That is fine!" LuDongChun sounded happy, and asked: "who is she getting married to?"

"I don't know." YingLi lied.

LuDongChun was deep in thought for a while, then she said: "Now that everything old has been destroyed and the new established, there will be no dowry but we will have to buy some suitable thing for her."

"No, don't buy anything for her." YingLi interrupted.

"Don't be stubborn, listen to your mother."

"After how she has treated you?"

LuDongChun laughed and said: "Even vicious tigers do not eat their own children, and we are human."

YingLi was still unwilling; she tried another reason to persuade her mother.

"We don't have any money." It was true, since LuDongChun had been locked up there had been no pay cheques just a living allowance of 12 MRB a month. YingLi spent very little for herself, most of it had been spent on food and her mother's medication.

"No money...hmm...yes..." LuDongChun's face became perplexed, deep in thought but she still didn't have an idea. After awhile, LuDongChun's expression changed as she thought of a solution: "We have some things in our home that we can sell for money." she said.

"What, our property was almost all confiscated; we don't have anything of valuable left to sell for money." YingLi replied. "Is that copper basin still in the house, the one we use to wash our faces?"

"Yes but it is so old...who would want it?"

"The waste products purchasing station, will buy it."

"Every body is busy with the revolution, who works?"

"What else can we do? I have no other ideas."

LuDongChun lowered her head in dejection, in helplessness and said: "Your elder sister will be mortified." LuDongChun insisted on a gift for YongHong, not for prestige, not to show that she was high and upright in character; but as a mother for her daughter, to treat her daughter's marriage as best she could as her mother.

A guard came rushing down the hallway saying: "Visiting time is over! It is time to go! You must leave now!"

"Mom, I have to go." she suddenly felt sad again, how short their time together was, tears dropped, as she started to go "Oh, wait!" LuDongChun's eyes suddenly brightened, she had remembered a person who was doing waste recovery that would help. YingLi was already at the door, and turned her head to listen, her mama said "You must find him, for sure he can help us."

"Find who?" YingLi asked, coming back to her mother's side watching the door cautiously and worried that next time she will have trouble if the guard got mad.

"Mr LinLin, who is in waste recovery, and also knows antiques. Tell him I sent you, he will help."

"Where do I look for him?"

"You ask around, not many people are doing waste recovery. That should be easy; anyway, you can ask anyone you meet if they will give you 20 RMB for it."

"What? 20 RMB?" at that time 20 RMB was a lot of money. YingLi smiled and shook her forefinger in front of her mother's eyes and asked. "Mama, you are OK? LuDongChun swung her hand and said. "Don't sell it for any less than 20 RMB."

Chapter 19

LONG SHAN CITY WAS not very big but not small either. Eight hundred thousand people lived in four administration areas. The Songhua River separated the city into two parts, from the south to the north, by bus straight going would take an hour and a half. YingLi was reluctant to begin a carpet type search for the person who her mom had recommended; she thought all waste recovery people would be the same. She didn't know how many waste recovery people might be in Long Shan city, she just asked people and then took them back home to see the basin; they all shook their heads and refused to pay the price her mom wanted. So she gave up and just followed her mom's wishes and went looking for LinLin, she could not accept failure. Finally she found an old woman who told YingLi that LinLin was treating her disease and gave her directions to his house.

At his gate she called out: "Is anybody home?"

When there was no answer she repeated her call. She realised there was no body at home, but decided to wait. Standing there for a long time gave her plenty of time to view her surroundings. She discovered the location was in a central part of the city; his house was only two blocks from a main business street; and behind the house there was a park. As the sun moved into the west, the noise from the traffic began to subside. YingLi was thinking to her self he would be back soon when a voice from behind her shouted out: "Step aside, step aside."

YingLi turned her head in hurry.

A bicycle was coming directly at her, and she had to jump like a rabbit to the side. The bicycle stopped less than one foot from her, and the man steadied his legs while still sitting on the bike. He was smiling, he enjoyed startling people and causing false alarms, he always did that and it gave him a sense of self-confidence and respect. His targets of fear were young people who always said: "Dare heaven and hell". The results verified that everybody fears death.

"Do you know how to ride a bike?" YingLi asked, she still had a lingering fear.

"Were you really frightened?"

"Of course."

"Wow! Little revolutionary heroes don't fear death do they?"

"I'm not a little revolutionary hero."

He looked at her left arm and she really wasn't wearing a Red Guard armband. His expression changed and with a serious face he said: "Sorry, I have some herbal medicine in the house, you can take some if you want."

"Who are you? Why should I trust you and take your medicine?"

"Oh, you do not know who I am? I thought...that is... OK! My name is LinLin, this is my home."

YingLi looked up and down at the man who was standing in front of her. He was more than 30 years old, not very tall, but strong, his clothes fit his body nicely and were clean. In her mind, she associated recycle men with dirt and grime or older senile people...but he was wearing good clothes and was in a laudable tolerant spirit.

"I saw you standing there from as far away as I could see my house; I thought you had come to borrow a book." LinLin said pushing the bike, with one hand, and opening the door with the other, as they went into the yard.

YingLi followed him and replied: "No. I did not come to borrow a book from you."

Passing through the gate, she discovered the yard was very big. Waste products were piled everywhere, he had a key in his hand, but did not make a move to open the door.

"You say you did not come to a borrow book, do you want to sell a waste product?

YingLi suddenly changed her plan and asked: "Where are the books? Can I see them?"

"They are just old waste product books but they make good reading, and young people can learn some thing useful. "

YingLi thought to herself, he is such an understanding person why is he doing a waste job? Curious, she asked. "Do you like reading too?"

"Knowledge can give life meaning so it does not pass by fruitlessly."

"But, now study is said to be useless." YingLi said.

"Useless? We are told to criticize feudalism, capitalism and revisionism, if you don't know what they are, how can you criticize them?" Another order says: 'Destroy the old and establish the new.' if you don't know which are old, and which things do not benefit the social development, what do you do? Without the theories and laws of social development, how do you go about setting up new things?"

LinLin guided his bike with one hand and leaned it against the wall; then he unlocked the door. Inside were two rooms one on either side. LinLin pointed for her to go to the room on the right. There were books on the wall and floor like a library.

She took a deep sniff and cheerfully said: "Oh, lots of books!"

"Go ahead, just remember to return them and you can borrow more."

YingLi looked out of the window, and noticed it was starting to get dark already. She said with soft voice. "Sir, Lin, I will borrow a book another day, today I want to sell you something first."

"Ok, what is it?" He saw her hands were still empty.

"It is at my home."

"Oh, you can bring it here tomorrow."

YingLi thought that if she brought that old basin and he didn't like it, she would just be making the trip in vain. If he went with her, maybe he could find something else he might buy. She said. "Can you follow me home?"

"No, I never go to a customer's home. Sorry, you have to bring the things to me, to show me."

"But, but, I don't know, really, I don't know what kind of things are valuable; my mom said you would know."

"Who's your mom?"

"My mom is LuDongChun." she said with a small voice like a mosquito.

"Oh, Mayor Lu!" LinLin said loudly.

"She isn't the mayor anymore." YingLi said.

"I know. OK! I will go with you." he said.

LinLin pushed the bike going out of the yard with YingLi. He wanted her to ride on the back of the bike, she remembered and was nervous about it, and didn't want to take the risk, and proposed it would be better to walk. They started slowly walking shoulder to shoulder toward YingLi's home. LinLin said: "How about you take the bus, and I will ride my bike?"

YingLi looked at the road, it was spring but there was still ice and snow, and said. "You must be careful."

YingLi got to the house and made a fire in the stove to warm the room, and cleaned the pan to boil water. She put the hot water in the old thermos flask, and placed it on the old dark coloured desk. She picked up a feather duster and brushed the dust off the desk and chair. Everything was ready, but LinLin was still not there; but if he was late or early did not matter, he said he knew how to get there. She sat, thinking about the books, she had liked reading since childhood; her home had many books before the revolution, but when her mom got in trouble, she was afraid that the books would cause more problems for her mom so she burned them. Maybe she had been stupid, but she burned them to protect her mom.

Hearing someone knocking on the gate, she ran out saying "coming."

She saw LinLin sweating, and led him in to the house. in a hurry, YingLi to give him a dish towel to dry his face.

LinLin pointed to a clean face towel and asked.

"Can I use that?"

YingLi's face flushed right away, in embarrassment and she hurried to explain that she had not intended to treat him as lower class because she knew he was a friend of her mom.

She gave him a cup of hot water and used a cattail leaf fan to cool it..

LinLin quickly looked around the room for anything of value, his eyes rested on a very old wall clock; he took it down and placed it on the table to examine it and said it is a really good clock it's just broken.

"That was broken by the Red Guards." YingLi said.

Noting the expression in his eyes, it appeared that there was nothing of interest to him.

YingLi took the old basin to him, and said. "This is what my mom wants to sell."

LinLin took it and turned it over in his hands several times very carefully, and said with approval. "Good, very good!"

"How much will you give me for it?" YingLi's heart was beating like a drum, when she asked, and she glanced at him, hoping to see a change in his expression, even little bit.

"How much does she want?" LinLin seemed to be thinking deeply.

"My mom said...20...RMB?" YingLi said, like a thief, who taken a number out of the air. She looked at his face without moving for a long time, trying to guess his answer. She saw him nod, and she felt triumphant; but that feeling was gone quickly when he said.

"Yes, but it is not enough."

The Chinese word for "not worth" and "over worth" were the same. Therefore, YingLi had misunderstood his meaning.

YingLi said. "I thought it was not worth much... but, my mama..." YingLi was disheartened and ready to give up, she would sell the basin, for any price he offered.

"I will respect your mom's wish and give you 20 RMB."

YingLi was very happy again that her mom really had a big face; and thinking that he was helping out of charity, she must remember that they owed him, and pay it back later.

"How much do you think it is worth?" YingLi asked.

"I don't know." LinLin said.

"Then, how can I know how much I owe you to pay back?"

"What? You owe me? You don't owe me anything"

"This is not worth 20 RMB, but if you give me 20, you will have lost money" When she said that, he laughed at her misunderstanding.

"No, no!" He said: "I meant 20 RMB was not enough, it is worth much more than that; do you understand now?" LinLin saw YingLi look at him with wide eyes, and very kindly he said. "Sorry, I confused you; but I thought you had more knowledge... you really need to study more. Today it is late, the next time you can go to my house and pick up some books to learn from if you like. "

LinLin took money from his pocket for her, and counted out twenty one dollar bills, and then he counted them again because the money was old and difficult to count.

"The money is for you to use, I will just keep the basin for your mom, until she wants it back." LinLin said.

In the dim light of evening, YingLi followed him with her eyes, as he rode off on his bicycle until he disappeared in the dusk.

Chapter 20

T HE NEXT DAY, YINGLI took the 20 RMB to her elder sister's office.

Sitting opposite YongHong, she said in a very cold voice: "My mother is giving you this money, so you can buy something for your wedding."

This was quite unexpected and YongHong was very surprised: "Mother wants to buy something for me? Really?"

"Yes, the world only has cruel hearted sons and daughters, it never had heartless parents."

YongHong's face turned dark right away, she asked. "Did mom say that?"

"No, I said that."

YongHong took a deep breath and said: "I don't need anything." She stood up, moved to the filing cabinet, and took out many beautiful things. "You see." she said smiling bitterly. "Doesn't this quilt cover look good?"

YingLi wanted to leave, but, she was fascinated by her older sister's gifts, bedcover, bed sheet, embroidered pillow...all those things in a time of a shortage of supplies. Most people could only dream about having things like these. YongHong took out a shining green brocade to show her young sister.

YingLi had never seen anything like it before, with envy in her heart, and praise in her mouth she said: "Oh, very good, a dragon and a phoenix, they are the best."

"It is said that the dragons and phoenixes are auspicious. Ha-ha." YongHong laughed coldly.

Taking out some white material for her young sister to feel she said: "This is quilt lining, doesn't it feel soft?"

"Yes! Like a baby's skin, soft and so white; I never saw anything like that before." YingLi was in awe of her sister for the moment, her eyes were dazzled; she knew it must be very expensive, and not available to common people.

"Of course these new materials are just for special people; do you think it is white enough?" YongHong used a finger to dry her tears. YingLi suddenly noticed her older sister had very red eyes, and that two streams of tears had been running unnoticed.

"What do you mean...white enough?" YingLi asked glancing at her older sister uneasily?

"White means love, loving until the hair turns white, on both us, lovers forever. Ha, ha, ha! "She laughed again, even colder, giving YingLi goose bumps.

Next YongHong took out a big red paper cut, opened it, showing two "Happy" words joined together, that were necessary only with marriage.

YingLi listened and watched her sister's face: "This is called the happy couple. Ha, ha, ha, ha..."

YingLi pushed it aside, and said: "Can you not laugh like that?"

"Why?"

"Your laugh makes me frightened."

YongHong with tears covering her face again said: "You take the money and use it for mom's health."

"I thought you had forgotten how to be human." YingLi said in tears.

"Will you come to my wedding?"

"Sorry, I don't want to do that, it will make everybody embarrassed."

"You must be come to represent the family." YongHong said.

"I will think about it"

"No thinking! Just come! Please!!"

Chapter 21

YONGHONG'S WEDDING AROUSED PEOPLE'S envy and stirred the greatest excitement in ten years. Later when she killed her husband and had to be dealt with according to law, the people felt sorry, sighed, and wondered what had gone wrong. Times and customs had changed; entering the new century, people suddenly realized what had happened, and what kind of wedding it had been.

The wedding was a mass assembly as was customary for important figures at that time. Many years later people who read historical books or researched the records might think the opposite was true for the occasion, and use the view of the descendants to do a calm appraisal. However, who ever does the appraisal will find that calm did not belong to that era; that era was crazy!

YingLi went to the wedding earlier than the scheduled time. The front of the municipal government auditorium was over crowded, and she had to struggle to enter through the disorder. People carried tickets to find their seats. Almost all the guests were smiling. YingLi also tried to smile and opened her mouth, pulling her face muscles to relax, to make a smile.

She stood on the last platform of the auditorium, the platform for the wedding. This auditorium could hold a thousand people.

When she was a child, sometimes she had been here with her elder sister to play when their mom had meetings. One time, they played hide and seek, she was just trying to find her sister, and forgot that adult people were having a meeting; she ran to the platform and knocked a microphone off the desk. Afterward she was very much afraid, and believed that her mom would hit her. Her whole body shook as she waited but her mom didn't hit, but she still shook. Mom said these were lost souls, when she fell asleep her mom carried her back to the platform again, saying her name softly. Her older sister was bolder and more talented than she was, and constantly lectured her. Her sister hated it when they had to wear the same clothes because they were twins. When they had to wear the same clothes, her sister cried and said they made her mouth look bigger. Actually, her mouth was just a little bit bigger, but not ugly, but it always made her unhappy.

Sounds coming from the platform drew her attention; a tall man, carrying a microphone was rushing on stage in a hurry, looking from side to side checking everything. A desk and two chairs had been set up on the front of the platform, wrapped in used red flannel. YingLi guessed this would be the bride, and bridegroom's place. Behind it was a long table had been formed from desks and covered with a white cotton cloth. The tall man was commanding two young men to put the chairs at the back of the table. When the chairs were in place, he counted them, and then signalled with his hand for the young men to bring two more up, but a minute later, he ordered them to move them back again.

Finally the tall man tried the microphone: "Hello, hello..." the microphone was not loud enough so he ordered a backstage supporter to increase the volume "more, more. Ok." Then speaking seriously he said "Comrades settle down"

Settle down? YingLi asked herself.

She saw the people around her all laughing and joking with each other. "Settle down, why are you still moving around?"

YingLi finally realised he meant be quiet. The man had a speech impediment, he did not pronounce the words clearly and he confused people.

"Settle down please." All the people understood now, and the noise began to subside.

"Every leader to the stage and take your seat please." Someone on the platform seated them one by one to their designated place.

"Let's give a welcome to the bride and bridegroom."

The music began and ZhangYong appeared in a wheelchair, wearing his army uniform without the red collar badge and cap. He was wearing medals on his chest, propelling his wheelchair with one hand, and holding YongHong's hand with the other. Like actors in a play, when they showed up, the audience responded with applause through out the whole auditorium, for over 20 minutes without stopping; because the young man had defended the national honour and dignity he was the pride of all the people of Long Shan city. The people were excited that the national leaders had acclaimed him and his companions' actions. The people of Long Shan city had something to be proud of and they looked like they were worshiping an idol; anyone who had approval from the top leaders had golden protection and was highly regarded.

YongHong wore an army uniform too. With a badge of a national leader, which was as big as an apple on her chest, her face was beaming with a charming smile, and it looked like she was smiling from her heart giving the impression that she was a very happy woman. A few years later, when she killed ZhangYong and was arrested, she had the same smile she wore today.

YingLi had a seat number in the first row; but when she discovered that LiuJiahuai was seated close to her, she moved back with the people who were standing by the side without tickets.

She heard the tall man say: "We will start now..."

And then another man rushed up in a hurry and whispered in tall mans ear, and the man with the microphone loudly asked: "YingLi. Is YingLi here?"

"I am here." She answered unwillingly from a distance.

"Come up here please"

She did not dare to hesitate, but was extremely unwilling, went slowly, and took her place.

Shortly afterward, she followed the crowd standing up to sing the national anthem and when took her seat again she discovered

Zhang Yong's parents by her side. The Master of Ceremonies began to introduce people from the rostrum. "This is..." and following his introduction, a big square headed man stood up and sat down, and on and on; then YingLi saw LiuJiahuai lift his hand to salute. Her mind began to wander to another world, and when she was introduced, she didn't stand up because she was not listening.

The master of ceremonies out of respect came to her, and pulled her up to introduce her. "This is the bride's penis (delegate)."

The Chinese words: DAI BIAO meant delegate; and DAI DIAO, was slang for penis, with DAIO the meaning became "bride's penis." The people erupted in uproarious laughter. The Master of Ceremonies had a hard time being heard above the din even with the microphone. People were laughing so hard they had tears

YingLi almost cried with laughter herself, she wanted to leave but saw her elder sister's eyes earnestly pleading with her: "Please don't leave."

The master of ceremonies had a red face that looked like a boiled pig's liver; but he raided the microphone speaking in a low voice and stammering a little he announced.

"The wedding witness will speak."

The people slowly quieted down again then a short man took the microphone,

Everyone applauded.

He announced loudly. "Zhang Yong, male, age 20, revolutionary demobilized soldier, and YongHong female, age 19, revolutionary cadre, are willing to be married as we witness this day March, 1967."

Applause rose again.

The bride and bridegroom spoke next. ZhangYong made a short speech thanking the party leaders. "We will not disappoint our leaders and the people of Long Shan city; in the future we will be together until the end of the revolution."

As he finished speaking, his gaze turned to YongHong and he saw that her face still wore a beautiful smile; he did not understand why she hated getting married to him but still looked so happy. He did not understand, and would never understand how such a beautiful and strong woman could be joined to his devilment, and still smile.

YongHong spoke next saying: "Our emotions, with our leaders help, are going on the road to health, and will grow vigorously. As time passes we will understand each other; take care of each other; and help each other. We have embodied the principle of equality and mutual benefit; our love trend is good. I believe in the future, we will develop our achievements, overcome our shortcomings, and go forward hand in hand. We will live in harmony based on our love for each other in the spirit of the revolution."

YongHong's speech won a warm round of applause.

No body could know that only during this moment, she forgot her burning hatred for ZhangYong.

Chapter 22

SINCE SHE HAD FELT insulted and cheated, YingLi had been unable to find peace day or night. She had asked herself many times in her heart: what could she do?

The words of LiuJiahuai repeatedly rang in her ear: "Where is the evidence?"

Yes, she didn't have any evidence; it seemed that no one was as stupid as her in the whole world. She had been raped, and her mother was still in detention, she wanted to make a complaint, but had no evidence. She hated LiuJiahuai and the people who had locked up her mother. For the past eighteen years, she had been happy, her future on the road of life was to follow in a straight line, university, and job, get married, and have children... Instead now she was at the mercy of people beyond her control, and she was filled with bitterness. Why was she so unlucky at a time like this? For death one needs courage; for life courage is needed too, but even more so.

At the wedding, sitting on the platform LiuJiahuai appeared to be a man of moral integrity; such a woman destroyer in human clothing, receiving applause and respect. If the people, knew his true nature would they applaud him? She believed in justice, but there was no justice now.

At home after the wedding, she suffered deep depression; she didn't comb her hair, wash her face, cook or eat.

Two days later LinLin was passing by and stopped to see her, he was shocked and concerned at her appearance and asked: "What happened to you?"

In his eyes, YingLi was a child.

His son seemed to be the same age as she was.

Thinking about his son, he felt deep regret and wished he could apologize to him. For more than ten years, he had not seen his son, and do not know where he was; at the same time, he remembered his friendship with LuDongChun, said that she was his saviour. He had promised LuDongChun long ago that he would live thinking positively and helping others.

He felt he had a duty to take care of her daughter.

YingLi smiled pathetically. "Nothing." she said.

"Nothing? Then why do you look like this?"

"I don't know."

"I just feel that your condition is abnormal."

"I...was...worried about my mom."

LinLin learning of LuDongChun's disease said: "She should be treated as soon as possible; if she gets an infection it would cause a big problem. When are you going to see her? Let me go with you."

"Can we go now?" YingLi asked.

"The sooner the better." he said.

YingLi didn't want to wait a minute, and she was not sure if they would be allowed to see her mother or not, because this month she had been there twice already. Today they would be pushing their luck. However, Chairman Mao said: "Real knowledge happens in practice." She would go and practice at once.

LinLin stopped at his house for a few minutes to pick up some herbal medication, and then they went on to see LuDongChun.

They were really unlucky today.

The face of the guard looked a hard as a sculpture.

YingLi had very good intentions in her heart, and she spoke to him kindly saying: "Good morning comrade..."

Her speech was interrupted. "Who's your comrade?" The guard asked sternly.

YingLi had been reprimanded and was very embarrassed. She was thinking to herself: you son of a bitch, how can I be nice to you?

LinLin saw that YingLi had caused the guard to bristle, so he tried to smooth things over.

LinLin fumbled a cigarette out from his jacket pocket, and offered it to the guard courteously. "Please take one." he said.

"That is a sugar coated capitalist trick. Do you realise that?" The guard said sternly.

LinLin thought for a moment, and said: "Young Revolutionary hero." He said watching the guard's face carefully. When he saw that the guard accepted that address, he continued. "You are right, I am sorry. But, I am a just a recycle man, and belong to the proletariat, she is my student"

The guard was beginning to laugh and said: "A recycle man has a student? What bullshit"

"It is because I know herbal medicine, and she is learning from me. Now, she knows some things like checking pulse, and preparing prescriptions...for talking, she understands very well. But, for practice, she doesn't have any experience. She wants to serve the people and that is good for the revolution. But, will you give her a chance to practice?"

The guard looked closely, examining YingLi, and LinLin, after awhile, he said: "You just want to get in."

"Yes, your right." LinLin said without mincing words.

"That is serving the capitalist class. Do you know what kind of person her mother is? Don't you know who she is?' The guard pointed at YingLi, as he reprimanded LinLin.

"Yes, I know." LinLin said nodding.

"Oh you know! Then why do you still try to sell your bullshit?"

"That is..."LinLin tried to find the right words to explain..

"That is what?" the overbearing guard asked menacingly.

YingLi tugged on LinLin's sleeve urging him to leave.

Chapter 23

IN THE HOTEL ROOM, ZhangYong was angry, and threw his walking stick in the corner, he sat on the edge of the bed and took off his prosthesis, saying.

"Why is it always painful?" The prosthesis had been adjusted many times, but it still felt very uncomfortable.

YongHong who was sitting on the sofa reading a newspaper, heard him said and without looking away from her newspaper answered. "Why are you so picky."

The prosthesis had caused trouble from the beginning; it always seemed to not fit right somewhere. Many times later, his impatience and was progressively becoming angrier, and more anxious.

"Hey!" He ordered YongHong: "Send this back and tell them to fix it again."

YongHong was reading her newspaper, and glanced at him, and said in coldly: "It is not necessary to change it again. Go straight to the Party and demand a real leg."

"You're a bitch." he retorted angrily.

YongHong continued reading the newspaper as if nothing had happened. Then shifted her sight from the newspaper to ZhangYong's stump, she took pleasure in his misfortunes.

Coldly she said: "If you truly want things to be better you will go along with the Party Organization. You are an able person, you can want me, and your leg is a small thing."

Her words hit his sore spot and made Zhang Yong almost fly into a rage, he threw the prosthesis in the corner, and roared loudly: "Shut up."

But YongHong was not going to shut up, she said smiling at him: "Do you think I want to talk to you? Saying, she carried on looking at her newspaper, and on the surface it appeared to him that she was calmly continuing to read, she was very happy because she liked to make him angry.

Since being totally ignored the night they were married, she had been in an extremely contradictory mood. She had planned in the beginning that if he wanted to have sex, she would oblige him; but when she saw him go to sleep quietly, she felt lonely, and humiliated. Even though Chinese people did not talk about sex, they had practiced it as the birth of babies showed. YongHong had a revolutionary mind, but, her renal gland and pituitary still played their parts inside her body. Her hormones and lust produced curiosity and expectations. When she was in high school the class had gone to the countryside to support agriculture, and there she saw a horse's penis, and had fantasized about it many times since. She knew that marriage was not smooth and easy, if he had sex with her roughly on their wedding night, she should curse, bite, fight back, and cry. A lot of things between woman and man were strange. In married life she was still confused about what she wanted or didn't want.

ZhangYong said hatefully: "All you Revolutionary heroes are no good. You just want promotion no matter how unscrupulous!"

His platoon leader had taken them to the border area and shouted Mao Quotations at a Russian patrol causing a misunderstanding with the Soviets and they began shooting. As a result of the incident ZhangYong lost a leg and his platoon leader had got a promotion.

YongHong found his words very irritating, threw down the newspaper, stood up, and walked towards the door, but came back again after taking a few steps and pointed at Zhang Yong and said: "You should say clearly who wanted a promotion and was unscrupulous?"

His words had struck a nerve. "Unscrupulous?" Since she had written the big character poster against her mom she knew that her younger sister, ZhangYong, and all the people around her looked down on her. Many times she had seen people chatting and buzzing with activity, but when she joined them everyone quit talking. This made her feel very awkward.

She had a complaint too, she turned toward Zhang Yong, scorning to even glance at him and said: "Were you not unscrupulous when you picked me to marry you, what it is that? What son of bitch chose my name for marriage?"

"I chose you, I did not push you. I just said in a fit of rage with my father. Seriously, I really don't understand why you said yes? You could have said no. Nobody pushed you to say yes."

"You shout like an idiot! I could say no? I did not have any reason to say no. I made a vow when I joined the Party that I would give my all to the Party. I could not refuse. Do not pretend you are a good person. If it were not for you, I would not be like this. I...I...my life is like death. Do you know that? Do you know that?" She repeated with her voice rising higher and higher.

He knew it; ever since he married her he had felt very guilty. To remedy his conscience he had made two resolutions to himself, first to help her to rise in her career; the other was to be forbearing and conciliatory with her. Now, because the prosthesis was not comfortable, he was enraged all over. With the added stimulus from YongHong, he flew into an even greater rage.

"If you want to die it is very easy." he said, "The river is not frozen over, you can jump off the bridge; or I will buy a rope for you so you can hang yourself."

YongHong stamped her foot in anger and said: "Fuck your good dreams! My career in the revolution is like the sun at high noon, my future is brilliant. Death.? I never think about even in a dream."

ZhangYong suddenly had to go pee, but he had thrown his walking stick away in a fit of temper. He couldn't reach it by himself. Now, he needed help and said to YongHong, "Pass the walking stick to me." His voice sounded like he was issuing an order. .

"Don't you have two hands?"

"I, I can't reach it. Did you blink? "

"Oh! Ha-ha! I did not blink! I'm very well! "Will you get it or not?"

"No I will not!"

ZhangYong became really enraged; he seized an empty cup and threw it at her. She avoided it and the cup hit the tea table knocking over a thermos flask full of hot water that flowed on the floor. His eyes were red and his hand, which had thrown the cup, was still poised in the air, like a statue.

This made her a little nervous for a moment, but she regained her composure very quickly.

She knew that he couldn't walk without his stick. Even if he wanted to strike her in anger there was nothing he could do. She felt very good about having two legs, she danced and jumped up and down in front of him just beyond his reach, saying with a smile: "I won't help you, I am quite determined not to, no, no, no. Ha-ha, ha-ha. How wonderful it feels to have legs! Ha- ha! "

"Get out." He roared.

"Thank you." YongHong said as she put on her shoes, and then walked out slamming the door.

ZhangYong felt like his bladder would pop, and started calling: "Waiter, waiter..."

Chapter 24

LINLIN CONTINUED GRINNING AT the guard, and said: "It is like this, to learn medicine, practice is very important. I can't let her practice on the revolutionary masses, because it would be a case involving human life, which must be treated with the utmost care. Here she has a chance; the traitor LuDongChun had a frozen hand, we can let her practice on her mother, if she succeeds then we can let her use it on other people in the future, if it is not successful, it is only her mother and no body will care."

YingLi, couldn't help wanting to smile.

LinLin's story made up on the spur of the moment sounded very convincing. At the same time, she felt puzzled that he understood Chinese traditional medicine; and could value antiques, why was he going to waste as a trash collector? When her mother recommended him to her, she had laughed at her thinking she did not have anybody to help that is why she thought about him. But, since she had met him, she felt he was a very unique person; his thinking and behaviour were exceptional. She was deep in thought when she felt him pull her arm, she awoke from her thoughts, and asked: "What is it??"

LinLin led her sight to the guard, and she saw him rolling up his sleeve. In confusion she turned to look at LinLin again. LinLin just wanted to explain to her, when the guard said: "Ok, I will let you check my pulse, you can tell me how many years of life I will have."

LinLin motioned for her to go and check his pulse. Facing the guard, she couldn't expose the lie by saying no, and couldn't go up to him saying yes either. She didn't know anything about checking a pulse. My god, she thought: how do I check it, where do I start?

"Check his pulse as I taught you." LinLin said lifting his right hand and raising his forefinger, middle finger and third finger, one by one on his left wrist to demonstrate. She understood what he was showing her but when she touched the guard's wrist she felt very nervous. Following her left three fingers on the guard's right wrist, but she could not feel any pulse, she pressed her fingers down more firmly but still didn't feel anything. Oh, my god! She was feeling dizzy, as she fainted on the floor.

When she woke up LinLin was applying pressure to the "RenZhong" point on her top lip, and the guard was speaking to LinLin: "You look like you understand medicine, today I will let you go in, but don't try this again."

LinLin still greeted LuDongChun as mayor Lu.

LuDongChun corrected him: "Call me elder sister Lu." and told YingLi. "You call him uncle-Lin."

YingLi curled her lip, hearing this and asked: "How old is he? He calls you elder sister?"

LinLin turned his head to her. "How old do you think I am?"

"Thirty?"

YingLi estimated that he was thirty-five years old, but she intentionally said younger than that. LinLin was laughing and LuDongChun joined him.

YingLi tried again: "Thirty- five?"

"Similar this time." LinLin said.

YingLi smiled and said: "See! He is only sixteen years older than me, he is not old enough to be my uncle? I'll call him brother."

"I said similar, not the same, similar can be up or down. Thirty-five add eight, I'm forty-three, do you think that is old enough to be your uncle?"

Everybody laughed after he said that.

LuDongChun said: "You do not really look like forty-three. How old do you think I am?"

"Forty:" LinLin said recalling the year he had met her.

LuDongChun shook her head and said: "When a man talks about a woman's age he does not like telling the truth, Lin, you are the same."

LinLin said: "Mayor Lu, Oh! Sister Lu, you are not the same as ordinary people, look at how many things you have to be concerned about in a day. All Long Shan city is a big family. You were the master of this big family. You look older, because you have worked too hard."

The conversation was not going as YingLi had expected; she saw that LinLin showed great respect for her mother and expressed sincere feelings from his heart: "Mom, now if you would just relax; you would rejuvenate soon."

LinLin spread the herbal medicine on LuDongChun's hand, and then bound it well with gauze, and adhesive tape, and said: "This is a terrible disease if you don't take proper care it will return again, and again."

"How can she take care of it?" YingLi said: "This place is like a dog house."

LuDongChun reprimanded daughter, said: "Be quiet you speak too flippantly."

LinLin smiled lightly, and said: "The medicine, you must remember to change the dressing every two days. Keep it clean so you don't get an infection, I will leave this medical cloth and rubberized fabric with you too."

"Thank you so much! My daughter will give you money later." LuDongChun said.

"No, no!" LinLin said: "I did not come for money."

"But, all these things are products that cost money." LuDongChun said.

"The money is nothing. Compared to what you did for me; I owe you my life."

YingLi was confused; she did not understand what they were talking about.

Before leaving, YingLi held her mom's hand, and was reluctant to part from her.

LuDongChun felt YingLi's hand was very cold, she looked at her face, and asked: "Li are you ok? Do you feel ok? Your face is very pale."

YingLi shook her head, and said: "Mama, don't worry about me, I'm fine."

Chapter 25

THE BOOKS IN LINLIN'S house transported YingLi into a new world. When she read, the pure, and the romantic made her forget her worries. YingLi believed that LinLin had many such books, and that he would have a lot of knowledge too. However when she asked him questions he never answered them, he just said: "Go to the books and you will find it." She quit asking, and when she came back the next time she just went looking through the books.

A week after LinLin treated LuDongChun, YingLi came to borrow books again, and when she started to leave, LinLin told her to wait a minute, and asked her.

"Do you feel Ok?"

"Yes."

"You don't feel anything is wrong, like...feeling dizzy, or that you want to vomit?"

"No."

"Have you had your period on time?"

This was a girl's private affair; you are a man, why are you asking about it? YingLi thought, she was shy, and her face blushed.

She did not want to answer, but because he helped her mother, and out of respect for him, she said: "It has been awhile." When he asked, she counted the days and realised that it was late, but that was not a big thing, it was always irregular. She looked down at her foot, and said shyly.

He asked? "How long since your last period?"

"I don't remember."

"Let me check your pulse." LinLin said with sigh.

"I have no disease; my period has always been irregular." YingLi was extremely reluctant.

"I hope so. But..."LinLin said seriously, he had started to speak and stopped again.

"What?" She pushed him to answer.

"When you were dizzy when we went to visit your mother, I found your pulse had a problem. I'm not sure, that is why I want to check it again."

YingLi stretched out her wrist and LinLin placed three fingers on it for around ten minutes: she saw his fingers sometimes pushed together, and sometimes he lifted one in the air and left two on the wrist, and then changed again, and again...pushing heavily or lightly...after he finished checking both hands he said. "You are pregnant."

"What?" YingLi said loudly and jumped up.

"You are pregnant." he repeated.

"It is impossible!"

YingLi was stunned by the terrible news, she didn't remember how she got home, and she had forgotten to bring the books that she planned to borrow. "Pregnant" was such a strange and terrifying word, it meant that she would wear the scarlet letter on her face?! She would have no place in the sun. She would be like human waste... LinLin's words kept resounding in her ears. "You are pregnant, you are pregnant..." Her mind broke down. When she got home, she had a splitting headache. She started opening drawers hoping to find some medication to take; she found nothing and laid down to rest. The Kang (brick and clay built bed) was very cold, but she was too lazy to get up to light a fire in it.

LinLin came to the house the next morning, carrying the books she had planned to borrow. Inside the room, his eyes were evasive, and he looked ill at ease. Neither of them spoke, and then he asked: "Do you want me to accompany you to the hospital?"

Chapter 26

YONGHONG WAS VERY ANGRY after she left ZhangYong, and got on the train to Long Shan city.

The carriage was crowded, and stunk. The seats were all taken and she had to stand in the aisle. She let her body lean against the back of a seat. The sound of the train wheels made her want to sleep, and she dozed off and her head moved from side to side. The man sitting in the seat was sleeping too, but he woke up when he felt his neck and face itching, and when he opened his eyes he found a woman's long hair brushing over him. He lifted one hand and moved her hair to the side, but a minute later it was back again. He moved the hair again a little roughly and she woke up angry, but when she saw him she transformed her scowl into a smile, the guy was laughing.

"I wondered if it was you." she said.

They were from the same high school; he had been two grades higher than her, and joined the army when he graduated. The man got up to give his seat to her, and said: "Yes, I was just thinking about you, and here you are."

His name was WenJun; he was six feet tall and looked very handsome in his military uniform.

YongHong turned around to take a closer look at him, and said in surprise: "You have four pockets, you are really something."

At that time, the only difference in uniforms between a soldier and an officer was the number of pockets; a soldier had two, officers had four, and she regarded him with special esteem.

He replied: "You are very competent too. Your reputation resounds through the whole province now. In Long Shan city probably every step you take sets the whole city shaking." He said in adulation.

WenJun had returned from the field forces to the provincial military region office for a few months; and since he had been back, the name of YongHong had reverberated like thunder. Just before he got on the train he was thinking that after he finished his business, would like to see her and talk to her. He had long hidden his feelings for her and this chance meeting seemed to be predestined.

She replied happily, but modestly: "I'm just a small case."

"Were you in the provincial capital on business?"

She did not answer but replied by asking: "Did you come back for a family reunion?"

"Yes and no."

"What do you mean by that?"

"I came back to select new recruits; I will go home for a visit in passing."

"It sounds like you will be here quite awhile."

"Perhaps a month."

"Ah, when you have time, how about going back to the school to meet our classmates? I haven't been to the school for a while either and I miss them." She said.

"Yes, that would be great. Just let me know when!"

They talked continually until the end of the trip and the time passed quickly; it made YongHong temporarily forget her unhappiness too. At the last stop, after they got off the train, they both stood in the station square, and continued talking.

WenJun decided to make his move, and asked: "Do you have a boyfriend?"

YongHong asked back: "Do you have girl friend?"

"Not yet! Do you have one to introduce?"

"Need I introduce you to someone? You are a great officer now, handsome and good physical condition; you must have many women chasing you." YongHong had hit WenJun's sore spot. The daughter of his military commander was in love with him, but he thought she was very ugly to look at. He was hoping to find a suitable wife while he was at home in order, not to have to marry his commanders' daughter when he returned.

"Yes, someone like you." WenJun said.

"Why?" YongHong asked.

"You were the school flower; do you know that 99% of the male students wanted to write letters of love to you?"

In the dark he could not see her face, but heard her breathing get deeper.

After a brief awkward silence, she asked, "Who was the other one percent?"

"That was me!" WenJun said rejoicing. "I did not write to you, I married you in a dream!" He said laughing, and when he saw YongHong laughing too, he continued saying, "I knew I was not a match for you then."

YongHong looking at him, thought: before he was really no match for her, but now, he was an excellent prospect. She realised that if she had a boyfriend before, it would not have been Zhang Yong either.

WenJun continued: "I wrote a poem for you, but at that time I did not dare to give it to you! Let me recite it for you." WenJun cleared his throat, and began reciting,

"I do not wish too high,
Just that you look at me,
The smile in your eyes;
Is like love's touching;

I do not wish too high,
Just that you look at me,
With that sweet look in your eyes,
Is love dreaming;

I do not wish too high,

Just that you just look at me,
That fire in your eyes; is ..."

YongHong interrupted him, saying disappointedly: "I am married already."

Chapter 27

AFTER YONGHONG LEFT WENJUN, she began to think about where she could stay. Since her fight with ZhangYong she had decided to leave him so she could not go back to his family home. Her only option was to return to her mother's house that she had not regarded as her home since the beginning of the revolution. She had broken thoroughly with her family, and had stayed in the school or at a classmate's home, after she was married she stayed in ZhangYong's home. But, now, she didn't want any body to know she had a problem with ZhangYong, so the safest way was to go home. Mom was not at home to make her feel guilty, and facing her young sister would be easy. YongHong came to the gate but was stopped by the big lock, and she had thrown away her key already. She stood there thinking her younger sister was not in the habit of often leaving the house, perhaps she was visiting with a classmate for while and would be back soon.

Spring nights in Long Shan city, were often cold because of the air coming down from the mountains. Standing outdoors she soon became chilled, and her teeth started to chatter. She had left just wearing a sweater jacket after her fight with ZhangYong, she had been so angry she forgot to wear her winter coat. Travelling on the crowded bus and train, she had not felt cold, but she could not stay outdoors any longer so she headed off to her office.

When she entered the government compound she saw that there was only one light on and she knew that it was LiuJiahuai's office. He had a room in the dormitory, but it looked like he always stayed at the office to work. For this reason, he had received a notice of commendation from the city government. To go to her office she did not necessarily have to pass his, but tonight because ii was so dark with no moon, she felt afraid to go around. As she passed his door she could hear something like arguing, but she didn't mind, because even during the day time it happened often. Every body wants their own case cleared, and people try to persuade officers to agree with them. She had just passed by his office a few metres, when suddenly she heard a woman's loud voice.

"Don't even think about it, you can not deceive me any longer!"

It was her young sister's voice.

She turned back quickly, and saw a black shadow run out, and another black shadow trying to catch it and pull it back into the room.

YongHong called out. "YingLi!" and both of the black shadows stopped moving. YongHong went over and put her hand on her sister's shoulder and asked. "What happened?"

YingLi only cried.

When they got home, YingLi told her elder sister the whole story, and saying. "I went there, to ask him about mom's case and ask if he was helping or not? If he wasn't, I would sue him."

When YingLi learned she was pregnant, had become afraid and nervous, but after she had settled down. She had an idea and decided to show him the laboratory test report from the hospital.

"What did he say?" YongHong asked.

"He said mom's case would be very difficult; but he would marry me."

"What did you say?"

"I said I didn't believe him."

"What did he say?"

" I ran out and didn't hear."

"If you sue you can't win"

"I have evidence."

"What kind of evidence?"

"I...I...am pregnant" YingLi said barely audibly with a burning red face, in a voice lower than a mosquito.

"What? Are you sure?" YongHong exclaimed.

"Yes."

"Did you have a pregnancy test?"

"Yes."

"Let me think...sue... where do you want to go? He is a serviceman; he no longer comes under the local government."

"Can you ask Zhang Yong?" YingLi said. "He was in the army, perhaps he will know."

YongHong did not want to talk about him and said "We will talk tomorrow." Then her growling stomach reminded her that she had not had dinner yet, she asked: "Do you have any thing in the house to eat?"

"Are you not going back to your home?"

"This is my home too, isn't it?"

"I mean..."

"I will never go back his home."

YingLi glanced at her older sister, then went to the kitchen to find some food for her. She guessed that she must have had a fight with ZhangYong. If it had happened at another time she would have asked about it, but today she was not in a mood to get concerned.

That night, was like a woman with small feet, moving very slowly. And the twin sisters tossed and turned sleeplessly, and occasionally moved about aimlessly. The twin sisters did not sleep all night, but they didn't talk to each other either, they just lay there thinking to themselves.

Chapter 28

THAT NIGHT LIUJIAHUAI LIKE the twin sisters could not sleep either. He really didn't understand how she could have got pregnant because he always took birth control precautions. He took out the tape recorder from under the bed and placed it on his desk, put in the tape and listened carefully. He dismissed them all; since he had Qing, and had tasted the pleasures of a woman, he had researched women too. What kind of woman could he use safely, and what kind would be better not to touch. LiuJiahuai believed that a woman who wanted to transact business with her body, and was a virgin would be relatively safe. They didn't have experience at being coy, and if they suffered a loss they would be too ashamed to talk about it.

He had recorded having sex with YingLi so that when he felt horny he would be able to listen to it and relive the experience. But now he wanted to see if he could use it to prove that he had not seduced her.

He tried to find something to prove: YingLi had lured him, she was a sugar-coated bullet of the capitalist class, and you were too slack, you were lured, you are innocent...No! This could show that he shirked his responsibility. You are a communist, you studied Mao, wrote as an activist in the army, you were trained to target

Capitalist Roaders especially...where was your awareness? Were you so weak that you couldn't withstand the sugarcoated bullet? If you act like this, how can your leader continue to believe you and put you in a higher position? He had come to support the revolution in the city; that was a signal to the leader of the army to pay attention to you, and promote you.

He wanted to stay in the army forever; he didn't want to go back to the countryside and his home village. He had spent 26 years living in the country and didn't want to ever go back. Compared to the city, country life was not even human life. It was not easy to get out, and when you did get out you did not want to go back. He needed to have a very good reason for getting involved with this woman. Singing love songs together...yes. When a man and woman fall in the love it is natural to express their love this way; yes it was love, they were making love together.

He got excited about the prospects with this solution; he could marry her anytime. But on second thought, he felt that getting married was not a great idea because YingLi was the daughter of LuDongChun, and her identity would affect his political future. But, comparing the two options, getting married looked like the best idea; get married, wait for the baby to be born and get a divorce. A woman who was so easy to go to bed with he didn't want for a wife. He spent all night thinking about it; his thinking wandered back and forth, he believed the possibility she would sue was small; that the threat was only to pressure him to release LuDongChun, but the possibility that she might sue was also strong. He wanted to fulfill his promise, but the case of LuDongChun had multiple problems; she had a very complicated background; in this situation, if he let her out, he would be taking on a very great risk. He didn't want to take a risk for anyone; even if it were his own mother he would weigh the advantages and disadvantages before making a decision. He was thinking that to marry her was being lenient, let her be happy now and cry later.

The tape in the recorder began whirring, the man was talking, and he was promising something. That was no good; that would prove he was seducing her. Next in the conversation the man said: "You will say you like me." The woman said: "You like me." Could that be regarded as love? Although it seemed somewhat reluctant, it was better than nothing. Afterwards, she was singing, oh! Yes! He could take out the other parts, and only leave her singing, that would be enough. He thought this was all the proof he needed, and tried to get his nerves to relax.

The next day, LiuJiahuai took a chance and went to the office of YongHong to make a deal with her.

"You are aware of your younger sister's affair, aren't you?" He said.

"Yes, I know, what do you want?"

"I think we need to open the window and have a talk."

"What do you want to talk about?"

"I want you to know that we love each other."

"Try to make your story sound like its true. Go ahead, continue making it up, who would believe you?"

"I will play a section of a recording for you to listen to."

LiuJiahuai put the recorder on the desk, following the sound of the switch a voice said: "YingLi you will say you like me...can I sing for you..."

"Pass the word on to your younger sister, not to do anything foolish; that will be best for everyone."

Chapter 29

YONGHONG WAS NOT REALLY interested in meeting with the alumni association just now; but as the promoter she was scheduled to be there, and she was already half an hour late for the appointment.

She planned to walk from the compound of the city government to the school; it was not far but there was ice on the streets. Spring had come very late this year, but when it arrived it had been irresistible, most of the snow had melted in just three days under a blazing sun. During the day rivers of melting snow flooded the streets in search of the river, and at night the streets were covered in black ice.

YongHong had considered going by bus but it made a big loop and wasted a lot of time, if she walked and took the short cut, she would get there faster. From the office gate she headed west but soon heard someone behind her; it was a public street and people were off work that time of day, so she didn't mind for awhile. But the person following her kept getting closer, she could clearly hear someone's breathing. She stopped suddenly, and they collided; she had no choice but to turn her head and look, and at that moment the person following her began laughing.

"WenJun?!" YongHong scolded him: "Do you want to frighten to me to death?"

WenJun stopped laughing, and asked seriously: "Why are you so late, were you busy?"

"Don't say I'm late, your still on your way also."

"I was there early, when I saw that you were not there, I came back to pick you up." WenJun had his bicycle in hand.

"You didn't need to pick me up I know how to get there."

"I'm just to be your escort, is that all right?"

They were walking shoulder to shoulder, and she asked: "Did you find your flower (woman)?"

"Yes."

"Who is it? Would I know her?"

"It's a pity that flower already had an owner."

"What are you saying? Find another one! You are an officer in the army; any flower would be easy for you. Tell me, what kind of flower do you want?"

"One like you."

"Don't talk nonsense."

"No nonsense, it's true."

"Don't annoy me." she said.

"I know your situation now, you married him and you look like a flower in excrement."

"Don't be so nosey, my leader organized and arranged everything, it is unnecessary that you be concerned about my situation"

"But it is because, I love you!"

He had said "I love you" very softly. But for her it felt like a heavy hammer striking her heart. She stopped in amazement, and her body started shaking uncontrollably.

WenJun stopped too. They were looking at each other in the dark, they could not see into each others' eyes, but their breathing revealed they both were experiencing a rapid heartbeat.

YongHong turned and continued to go on, WenJun followed, saying: "My words are from my heart, I do not lie."

"You are too late."

"You can divorce him, I will wait."

YongHong did not answer.

He said: "I don't care that you have been married."

"I care."

"Do you really love him?"

"Yes." she lied.

WenJun was silent.

He didn't believe what she said, he believed that she was trussed up in a marriage arranged by others, how could she possibly love him? It was like his own situation with Ming, he wanted to throw up when he thought about having to be married to her. The few days he had been back in the city, he hadn't done anything else, just made enquiries about her, and he concluded that her marriage to ZhangYong would have been a tragedy, even if he was not disabled. What kind woman was YongHong? According to his understanding in the school, she was a beautiful looking woman whom was extremely wild at heart. In her heart, was hidden great vanity and self esteem. That kind of woman was very difficult to handle, he didn't have any qualifications in the past, but now, he believed that he could tame her.

He thought about Ming, who was an ugly looking girl, a daughter of his military commander, and her rush to marry him. With so little time he had to move fast and find a woman with personal or family standing higher than Ming's. YongHong was the ideal candidate.

"Don't spout your heroic revolutionary spirit to me; do you think I don't know you? You have a smile on your face, and your are crying in your heart." WenJun said. "I love you, if you are happy, I am happy, that is love."

YongHong was taken aback, love, did people really have feelings like that? She had never experienced love, didn't understand that it felt like. Love in her mind was a man and a woman sleeping together, and making kids. This was the first time she had heard that love was about missing, and caring; how invigorating it felt, the rush of unexpected feelings beginning to stir from within. She really wanted to experience that mysterious and novel feeling of love,

But, she said to him coldly: "Don't talk nonsense, we are both Party members, don't mess things up."

Chapter 30

THE ALUMNI ASSOCIATION GET together was not very successful. They were all happy for a little while until students started asking WenJun which group he belonged to and who they supported. Talking about groups the atmosphere suddenly changed, and the school was divided into two groups, the army only supported one group, the other group felt like bastard children, who had been hurt and wronged very much. The groups had been constantly arguing and fighting with each other, but today for the important appearance of WenJun, they had sat together amicably for awhile. Some believed they were bastard children of the revolution, and used the opportunity to ask WenJun, why they couldn't get army support? What was wrong with them? WenJun had no answer and, the two groups started arguing again.

After their schoolmates left, WenJun took hold of YongHong's hand with a very strong grip, but she pulled her hand free, and he stubbornly caught it again.

"So, you don't love me?" WenJun asked.

YongHong's hand did not struggle any more. "Love", this word was like a heavy hammer beating her heart. About love between a man and woman, YongHong was not sure. Her love was selfless, she loved the Party of China, and she loved Chairman Mao. From childhood to adult, lots of male schoolmates had professed love to her; she never took any of them to heart.

Getting married she was confronted with a husband who expected her to love him before anyone or anything else; they slept in the same bed, and the man's breath made her hormones begin to secrete. For this reason, she became two personalities inhabiting the same body: one was YongHong (her revolutionary name), other one was YingHua (her real name); two totally different people, sharing one body, fighting with each other. Now, YingHua was coming out again. YingHua said to WenJun. "I...want to love..." and YingHua quickly replied to WenJun: "I want to love you too, and to be loved."

WenJun was surprised when he heard that. He cuddled her and asked excitedly. "Can you say that again?"

"WenJun, don't push me" YongHong said suddenly becoming agitated.

"I will talk to your husband tomorrow!" WenJun said happily, he couldn't hide his excitement and didn't want to wait even a moment.

"No! It will be best if I talk to the Party first." YongHong said; but she did not sound very convincing.

"Well then, I will wait for you."

WenJun finally went back to the provincial military region alone but his body temperature, words, and promise remained in YongHong's memory. She began to like these memories, often thinking about them over night and they left her feeling warm, and fuzzy.

Chapter 31

AFTER LISTENING TO LIUJIAHUAI'S tape recording, YongHong became discouraged for her young sister.

Originally she had a different idea that it was better not to sue.

The people lived in an environment of socialism, but how many people were still carrying a head full of feudalism who knew. People here were simple and honest, clear about what to love and what to hate; if it was clear that her young sister had committed adultery with LiuJiahuai, she would lose all standing and reputation. She and her younger sister had grown in the same placenta; but she had emerged first and was half an hour older. Her years of experience in the revolution and society, had made her feel that she had an obviously superior intelligence than her younger sister. Somehow they were not the same as time passed, she had rose to government and held an important position. She just sensed her superiority, did not express it to her young sister in words.

When she got home, she said to her young sister: "It will be very difficult for you to win."

"Why?" YingLi asked, she was now determined to sue him.

"He has your...your..." Then YongHong with a red face in embarrassment for her young sister, paused for a moment, and then continued and said: "He has a tape recording of that night, and he let me listen to it."

"He...has made a recording?" YingLi asked; feeling very shocked.

" I never thought he was so sly." YongHong said.

"What can I do?"

"He said he wants to marry you."

"Marry?"

"Yes, that is the best way."

"I don't want to marry him"

"I know you don't, but hearing that tape, with you talking and singing, who would agree that it was rape?"

YingLi remembered Qing's story and the sight of another little girl running, and she said angrily: "It was not only me he injured, and I will try to prove it"

Chapter 32

YINGLI DID NOT HEED her sister's advice. She wrote a letter revealing her affair with LiuJiahuai and his involvement with the others. She refused to get married to marry a rogue who was such an unscrupulous man.

YingLi finished writing the letter and took it to Qi-Sanhai who was the leader of the committee for members of the military in control of Long Shan city.

As he read it he acted like a sausage in a hot pan, fidgeting and sputtering. Such an importance matter, he couldn't decide by himself. He told her he would write a report to his leader, and other higher authorities; and that he would give her an answer as soon as possible.

What the letter he wrote said no body knows. People just knew that the government officers had an emergency meeting that very night.

YongHong attended the meeting and presented three points: 1, Offer good treatment for LuDongChun's medical problem; 2, Increase manpower to investigate the case of LuDongChun; 3, place army cadre LiuJiahuai in protection.

Her proposal was justified, reasonable and hard to find fault with.

Her indignation about LiuJiahuai's behaviour resonated in the ranks of the revolutionary council.

Official meetings always started and ended with consensus: if someone presented a motion, everyone would speak their view on the motion, there would be a vote for or against, and the outcome would be the meeting's resolution.

The Conference Resolution, was as YongHong expected, LiuJiahuai's position would substituted by ZhangXianmin (YongHong's father in law. Other content, in full accordance with the recommendations of YongHong: to offer medical treatment for LuDongChun and send her home temporarily for treatment) order a special investigation group to be set up to check out the accusations against LuDongChun.

After this meeting, YongHong's image was elevated to a more mature stature.

Chapter 33

LuDongChun was in a fever caused by the inflamed ulcers on her hand; and when she got home she was confused.

YongHong representing the revolutionary committee brought a western physician to treat her; YingLi brought LinLin.

Western medicine and Eastern herbal medicine were two very different treatments. The doctors wanted to work along both lines; using Western medicine primarily, and Eastern medicine as a complement.

"Don't fail the trust that Party and Chinaman Mao have put in you." YongHong told the western doctor.

"I will do my utmost." The doctor said.

Two days later, the fever was gone with Western medication, but the hand with the ulcers appeared to be the same as before. During this time LuDongChun remained in a lethargic state of sleep. LinLin brought Chinese herbal medication to treat the ulcers and, YingLi asked: "Are you sure that will help?"

"Yes, I'm sure." LinLin said and sat down in front of LuDongChun to check her pulse.

"Don't experiment on her if you are not certain." Yong Hong said not very nicely.

"Who's talking?" LinLin asked. He knew very well who YongHong was, in Long Shan city who didn't know her?

But, YongHong didn't know LinLin; she had only received a little bit of information from her young sister recently, and her younger sister treated him like a supernatural being.

LinLin was sitting in front of LuDongChun teaching YingLi how to check her pulse.

YongHong was amazed that someone didn't know her, and said: "If you don't know me it doesn't matter, I don't know you either. But, the law will know if you treat her with something wrong, and then you will be in trouble."

"What did you say?" YingLi said. "He is a friend of mom's."

"I never saw mom with such a low class friend as him."

LinLin did not know why, but when he saw YongHong he was overcome with a nameless anger. He was aware that both the doctor and patient needed peace and quiet so he said: "You'd better leave."

YongHong roared back: "Who do you think you are? You get out."

YingLi said: "If he leaves are you going to check mama's pulse and make up the prescription for her?"

They were now in a deadlock, but just then LuDongChun opened her eyes and asked: "What happened? Who is fighting here?"

"Wow! You are awake mom!" YingLi's voice was happy and surprised.

LuDongChun saw a lot of black spots moving in her line of vision that made her feel dizzy. "Don't let them move, stop them, stop them." she said.

The people in the room were all confused; they didn't know what she was talking about or what she was seeing.

"What do you see?" LinLin asked.

LuDongChun did not answer the question, she just asked: "Where am I? Why do you have to fight when I am trying to sleep? I want to sleep, don't fight please." And she closed her eyes again.

YingLi leaned close to her mom's face and said: "Mom, you are at home, you are at home, and do you know? Your daughter and your friend are both here."

LuDongChun opened her eyes again for awhile and looked around, then she said: "Oh, I am at home? Am I free?"

YingLi's tears fell on her mom's face. "You were very sick; you are at home for medical treatment."

At the time, YongHong standing behind her younger sister said: "The city government leader said to let you stay at home until you get better."

LuDongChun saw LinLin, was gratified, and spoke to him: "I was just had a dream, I was talking to Yanwang (devil), please do not hold me here, I want to go back to the human world again, LinLin will be happy to treat me, he doesn't care that I'm accused of being a traitor and Capitalist Roader'."

"It was the Party who brought the western doctor that helped you." YongHong said from behind her young sister.

This time, a familiar voice caught LuDongChun's attention, certainly the voice was familiar, it was her own flesh and blood. But thinking slowly and carefully she felt that voice did not belong here, and she asked YingLi: "What is she doing here?"

YingLi took the opportunity to push her elder sister to the front, and said: "Go and talk! Mom asked about you."

"I...I...came to ..."Yong Hong's words were very cold and hard, she tried to say mom but the word stuck in her throat and couldn't get out.

She was the first to revolt against her mama; she had believed her mom was a traitor, and also believed her mom was the No 1 capitalist roader in Long Shan city. Since she had entered the government of the city, her political consciousness had reached new heights, but now her former fervour was beginning to look more like infantilism and fanaticism. Since she began the revolution had changed, and some leaders who had been in trouble had been freed to go back to work, and she had started questioning her own actions. But, before LuDongChun's case was resolved, she would remain reticent.

"Tell her she can go back, I don't need her." LuDongChun told YingLi.

"Mom" During the past few days YingLi had felt, and believed that her elder sister was not really bad, and she attempted to explain to her mom: "You don't know that my older sister has done a very good thing to help you."

LinLin had the herbal prescription ready for LuDongChun, and he told YingLi. "To go to drug store and buy these things, then make a soup for her to drink three times a day. You must remember to give it to her three times a day."

"I will, thank you Doctor Lin."

"Don't call me Doctor, call me uncle, as your mother told you."

"Uncle Lin, thank you." YingLi said softly. After, YingLi used her elbow to touch her elder sister to hint that she should thank him too.

"Thank you." YongHong said unwillingly.

Until evening, LuDongChun felt that YongHong was still moving in her sight, and asked YingLi: "Why is she still here?"

"She came back to live, mama."

"She's married, isn't she?"

"Mom..." YingLi didn't know how to explain.

LuDongChun said.: "We have only one Kang(bed), how can a revolutionary sleep with us?" Her meaning was bright and clear, YongHong should leave.

YongHong felt grievous in her heart, what was to happen to her? On the surface, she had a reputation, and people clustered around her, but in private, she didn't have any friends; not even family? She had never considered that she was part of her husband's family, she had abandoned her parent's home, but now she looked to it as her haven. Her mom was making it clear that she was not welcome and very clearly it would be very difficult for her to stay. Had she really done wrong? What kind of wrong had she done? Revolution was not wrong, why did no one understand her. These thoughts made her very sad and she began to cry; her tears moved her mom, LuDongChun said no more.

Chapter 34

AFTER THE NIGHT MEETING, the military control leader Qi-Sanhai was very mad at LiuJiahuai for having a problem with YingLi to begin with, and if the evidence was conclusive, he could not be lenient, that would breed more corruption. When he followed up on YingLi's letter and found Qing, she denied everything. That left Qi-Sanhai feeling uneasy about punishing LiuJiahuai. Affairs between a man and a woman could develop for many reasons. The tape recordings of LiuJiahuai only muddied the picture. He wanted to believe LiuJiahuai's story.

Qi-Sanhai had neither family nor friends related to LiuJiahuai; his only concern was for the Party and the people.

Qi-Sanhai went to see LuDongChun and talked to her for almost two hours. If love was really the reason for this problem a marriage was the answer. After he left, LuDongChun told YingLi: "The important thing is that when the man and woman, are married having a child is normal. Every body supports that; how about you drop the law suit?"

"I will not marry him." YingLi said very firmly.

"If you don't marry him, your reputation will be ruined and, will be with you all your life, have you thought about that?"

"Mom, let me ask you one question, you must tell me the truth."

"Go ahead."

"You need to swear on Chairman Mao first."

"Ok! I swear!"

"When you were with the Japanese, why didn't you escape, why did you wait until after you killed them to leave?"

"I felt I would never be able to live with myself if I didn't kill them

"Mom, then why don't you don't understand me?"

Chapter 35

YINGLI HAD BEEN OUT searching for Qing for several days, her hatred for her had reached a peak of rage.

But, Qing was shacked up with a man somewhere and no one seemed to know whom it was. If YingLi could have found her, the least she would have done would have been to give her a face a severe slapping.

YingLi met LinLin on the street.

"Your mom told me everything:" LinLin said, he sounded depressed, and he asked YingLi: "Why are you so stubborn? Your mama was just trying to help you."

"Help me save my name? I'm fearless, no man is any good."

YingLi saw LinLin touch his head and begin to smile, suddenly she realised that her words had been off base condemning all men. She said: "I am sorry, I talked without thinking."

"Your mom knows a lot more than you; tongues can kill people."

"A dead pig is not scared of boiling water! I am just following my nature."

"Whatever you decide, I will respect your wishes; but you should have an abortion as soon as possible."

"The pregnancy is evidence that I want to keep for awhile."
YingLi said.

LinLin said emphatically. "Listen to me, after an abortion you
will still have evidence." Let me go with you, we can go tomorrow,
ok?"

"Ok."

Chapter 36

SINCE YONGHONG HAD MOVED back to her mother's house she had received no information about Zhang Yong for over two weeks.

She hadn't caused the problem so that she could be with WenJun, and she had entertained the idea of getting a divorce even before they were married, but she didn't want to risk her future in the Party. She had listened to the Party and thought that if they were married and their lives were both unhappy, that divorce would be the natural course.

One bright spring day in all its brightness and charm she was summoned to the office of Qi-Sanhai; who asked in a voice as cold as winter.

"What happened?" His finger was pointing to a story in the city newspaper that she had already read and had been very happy to see. Sensing QiSanhai's displeasure she immediately began crying; it was a notice of divorce that had been placed by ZhangYong.

QiSanhai took her to the ministers of the Organization's Office, and held a very long meeting with YongHong about her future and her relationship with ZhangYong.

"Who proposed divorce?"

"He did of course, the notice is from him." The notice in the news paper said: "As of today, I am no longer married to YongHong, our marriage is over.

"What is the reason for divorce?"

"Reason?" She thought to herself; we married without a reason, why do we need a reason to divorce?

"What do you think?" The ministers asked.

"I want to follow his wishes."

"We do not agree with you."

"Why?"

"You were a typical fine example for the city so we trained you; the leader of city put in a lot of effort. If you are divorced, that would be the same as if the Party had failed."

"You go back and do some deep thinking; you can't be having problems like this and be the women's leader."

"It was not my decision it is his, he is the one who wants a divorce that is not my concern." YongHong said with a red face, but her voice was firm, and her vision was sharp.

"Don't say that it is not your concern. I have been doing this job since the beginning of the national liberation. At that time, we had lots of revolutionary cadre who needed wives. Lots of women like you, got married when the Party's matchmaker arranged things. Some didn't love each other, and were unhappy in the beginning, later on there was no problem. You can make up and become closer after you're married. You and ZhangYong want a divorce because you never tried to know or understand each other."

"We were..." Hong started to speak, but was interrupted.

"Beginning now, you go home and make up, this is very important. Oh, yes, have you had a child yet? No? That is why you are having problems. A woman should give birth to a child, and not only consider her job; have children for him, the children will strengthen your relationship."

YongHong wanted to admit that they didn't have a sex life, so they couldn't have a child. But she was too shy to talk about it, so she just lied and said: "I can't have a child."

"Do you have a physical problem?"

YongHong lied again, and falsely admitted: "Yes, I do not have fertility that is why he wants to divorce me."

"That is no excuse either. Premier Zhou went without a child, you can see he and his wife have a good love life. You little Revolutionary heroes need learn from the elders of the revolution."

"I..."

"You're a Party member, your marriage is not only your concern, it is a matter of the working style of the Party, a matter of discipline in the Party. When you married him that was very big news and the provincial and national leaders are watching you."

YongHong tried to interrupt him, but he waved his hand to silence her.

"Don't interrupt me; let me finish talking to you; if your family has problems it would interfere with your work, you are in a leadership position, you are the women's model now, on how to lead the women of Long Shan in the revolution."

"Then I can't have a divorce and be free?" YongHong asked.

"That's right, comrade YongHong, you can't; you are not one of the common people, you are a Party member. Words like that show that you need to learn more about the Party program. You are free under the Party principle of unified leadership not your personal freedom."

"I understand, I belong to the Party of China."

"Yes, now go back and do some deep thinking; you are young and have a very good future ahead of you, don't disappoint your trainers and the beliefs of the Party."

YongHong went back to her own office and cried on her desk.

Chapter 37

A T THIS TIME THE special project group for LuDongChun
had dispatched one group of people to Beijing to find her
companions during the war with the Japanese and the domestic
period of the war of liberation; another group was sent to the
northern part to her hometown. From the research about her, a
detailed picture of LuDongChun's life emerged that went right back
to when she had left her mother's womb.

The father of LuDongChun had taken four wives in an attempt
to produce a son and heir but to no avail. LuDongChun's mother
was the fourth wife and had studied abroad so her thinking and
actions were very modern. After giving birth to a daughter, she
began researching how to have a boy through scientific principles.
Before she got pregnant she fed her husband acidic foods like,
beef, chicken, fish, and albumen, and she ate alkaline foods, green
vegetables, fruit, milk, tea, kelp, marine alga, iodine, and calcium.
It is said even the position used during sexual intercourse was
important, but these were secrets that only two people knew. A
servant in the family just remembered the abnormal food that was
served perhaps for six months, and then Ms Lu became pregnant
with Sir Lu. After she got pregnant, Ms Lu felt different, and made
every body else feel different too.

One day, when Mr Lu was not home, Ms Lu talked to wife number one about what she was thinking.

"Elder sister," In those days, in old families of China, the wives of the same man called each other sister, she said. "If this time it is another girl, what will we do?"

Wife number one was a very kind person who had never given birth but treated the other wives' children like her own. She said: "What do can we do? If it is a boy or a girl both are Lu's family, we treat them the same."

"I mean, the baby's father's health is getting worse day by day."

"Yes, and we are a family in need of a man. If god wants to cut our family tree, I don't have any idea what we can do about it. At this time everything depends on you; you must try to make a good showing, and leave a seed for the family of Lu."

LuDongChun's mother smiled, and said: "I want to, I really want to even in my dreams but I just worry...worry...what we can do if it is another girl and I had an idea."

She reached over and whispered in her elder sister's ear, her elder sister laughed with happiness.

They stayed in the elder sister's room until their husband came back.

Finally LuDongChun gave birth.

The day of the full moon, they had almost hundred dozen guests for the party because it was the first son born to the family of Sir Lu. The household was the centre of a large population and every body knew the Lu family now had a descendant.

During this period in China the situation was very chaotic, with warlords, new political parties, and foreign countries invading. Business became very difficult and Sir Lu decided to start a new business, and bought several hundred acres of cultivated lands, becoming a big land owner in a northern area. After the revolution, the property of Lu was given to poor people; and Sir Lu was only allowed to keep his first wife. LuDongChun's mother and Sir Lu's other two other wives were ordered by the government to leave and begin living independent lives.

What happened later is another story.

From the time she was a baby to an adult, LuDongChun had worn men's clothes, had a man's haircut, and been educated in an old-style private school for boys where the tutor taught the Confucian classics, and she practiced boxing. LuDongChun was a man in the eyes of the people and was called. "Young master Lu". When young master Lu was 20 years old, he was 5'8" inches tall, with delicate features, and considered to be very handsome. According to custom in order for a young man to marry, the man's family would hire a matchmaker who would go to the woman's family to make the arrangements. The family of Lu had been different; matchmakers had come to the gate of the Lu family to no avail. The Lu family gave no particular excuses for the rejections other than that picking a woman posed some problems. This failure to select a wife caused much anger for several years.

The local bandit Chief's family wanted to form an alliance with a rich family for their only daughter Jiao. The matchmaker for Jiao's family wanted her to marry LuDongChun.

Jiao being the only daughter in the family was a prize too, but because of her family background, it was hard to find her a suitable husband.

That year she became 26 years old, and her parents were determined that she should get married. They lived several hundred miles away but on learning about LuDongChun the father of Jiao was overjoyed. One day, the bandits came down and kidnapped LuDongChun and put up a notice of engagement and betrothal gifts for the exchange.

Faced with no choice LuDongChun could do nothing except go through with the wedding. The evening LuDongChun was married, after the guests had all left; LuDongChun kneeled to Jiao and told her the truth. At the time, even if Jiao wanted to blame and hate some one, she could not blame or complain about LuDongChun. It had been her family, which had rushed her into the marriage, and kidnapped LuDongChun. She lived with LuDongChun for a year, and then they adopted a boy, planning to keep this their secret for life.

Jiao's mother had become very sick and was in a critical stage when death could come at anytime, and had sent her daughter a message to come as soon as possible.

LuDongChun was in FengTian; now named ShenYang City on business, and would not return for another week. Jiao could not wait that long. She watched four strong family men who were confident bandits with excellent skills, and thought also about her elder brother who was a translator for the Japanese army commandant; that made her feel safe. On the other hand, her mother's life was only one step from hell, if she missed seeing her mother that would bother her for the rest of her life.

Jiao left a message for LuDongChun and started out to go and see her mother. Not long after someone reported that Japanese had met Jiao just after she left the village. Eight Japanese had raped her even though her brother was with them. After she was raped, Jiao could not stand up to walk, so she crawled to the river and went over the bank; that was in 1934.

When LuDongChun returned he (she) went to the river for a memorial ceremony, and afterwards she joined the army in the war of resistance against Japan.

A few years later, in 1938, she was promoted to detachment team leader of the anti-Japanese allied forces of the north. One day on the way to a meeting, she passed a village where she decided to stop and spend the night; just after midnight Japanese troops suddenly surrounded the village. Being hopelessly outnumbered, and to reduce the bleeding and dying of the common people of the village, LuDongChun decided to hide her gun and go with the other people to the vacant lot as the Japanese ordered. The officer ordered the men and women of the village to be separated standing each on one side. The officer was wondering why the village was without young people and there were few women who were mostly very old. The officer ordered the men to take off their clothes, and a woman who had dressed as a man along with LuDongChun was discovered. Two Japanese officers had ravaged LuDongChun for 24 hours. This was the basis of her being accused of being a traitor during the revolution. When at last the officer had exhausted his energy and fell asleep on the Kang (bed), and started snoring

LuDongChun took his sword, and killed him. Then she killed the guard standing outside, took their guns and made her escape. LuDongChun led her detachment back to attack in retaliation; the Japanese troops left without a leader were like flies without heads, and they were able to kill all of the Japanese with little difficulty.

By 1947, LuDongChun had been living as a woman for several years and had married a man who had also been in the anti-Japanese war; during the following year she delivered twin daughters, YongHong, and YingLi.

How to judge if LuDongChun had been raped was viewed differently by different people, the main point to be proved was that she was not a traitor. To go back and find LuDongChun's companions who helped her kill the Japanese was a problem, because many had died later in the war and even the village no longer existed. The war had left the country changed beyond recognition with people drifting about aimlessly. Trying to find someone from this village who was still alive was like looking for a needle in a haystack.

LuDongChun's story and her legend were just too difficult to reveal during this period of time. This case had not only baffled LiuJiahuai, but also those who followed him. Until the National Government came under a new order, LuDongChun would remain in trouble for this case; there were also other factors such as her family being landlord class, and the fact that after the liberation she had held the position of leader of Long Shan City but without any notable achievements.

Chapter 38

I N THREE MONTHS, LuDoNgChun had been home twice: her first time back home was to treat her disease; the second time was due to a special pardon. LiuJiahuai was finally demobilized from the army, his punishment was very light but for him it was very heavy, because he had dreamed of staying in the city forever.

Some things that should have ended were now over.

The first thing that LuDongChun discovered was that their dog had disappeared. YingLi could not escape from leaning the truth about what had happened. Since the dog had showed up at the meeting to denounce LuDongChun, and defended her; it became a target. People wanted revenge and they seeing how fat he was he was slated to become a delicious meal.

One day, YingLi left the dog in the yard as usual but when she got home the dog was gone. YingLi recalled before that there were usually two or three men walking in front of the gate like people on patrol, but she never saw them again either.

Both YingLi and her mother shed many tears at the loss of their loyal friend.

YingLi told her mom one day that she had started learning traditional Chinese Medicine from LinLin and mom said in encouragement. "That is very good."

The month that LuDongChun was at home flew by quickly.

The whole month, LinLin had used LuDongChun as a model to teach YingLi how to check a pulse and make up prescriptions. He checked her work, and sometimes added or took out some herbs. By checking LuDongChun's pulse, she learned what was ailing her and what caused the abnormal pulse; which herbs would work on that condition and which ones would have the best effect. When she answered correctly she would laugh and jump up and down, when she was wrong, she would shyly hide her face in her mom's chest like a baby.

LuDongChun's health improved day by day; the ulcers on her hand scabbed over and the swelling had gone down, only her feet were still a little oedema.

LuDongChun had no job and YingLi had not graduated they stayed home mending their emotions and a relationship that had been neglected for nearly ten years while Lu was the mayor of the city.

Chapter 39

ONE DAY SOON AFTER, LinLin had a traffic accident at an intersection near his home; it happened on one of YingLi's study days, and when she got to his house he was not back yet. She waited what seemed like a long time and impatiently went to the gate to see if he was coming; she saw a big crowd of people gathered across the street and she went across to see what was going on. She saw some blood, and a person lying beside a bicycle wheel; she couldn't see clearly but felt she wanted to throw up at the sight of the blood. She moved out of the crowd and waited while the injured person was loaded into an ambulance. When the ambulance had left, she went back and saw the bicycle unintentionally, but the sight took her breath away: Oh! God! It was LinLin's bicycle, looking closely she saw the cover on the bell that she had made. She asked the militia nervously about his condition and where they had sent him. Then she went to the hospital as fast as she could.

Waiting outside the emergency room, she didn't' know how long she waited, or how many people she asked for information.

She just waited patiently with tears in her eyes thinking that he had the accident because he was rushing to get back for her lesson. Yesterday he had said he would go to the north of the city to do some business, and her lesson might be a little bit late. She asked him what to do and he had given her his spare house key and told her to just go on time and wait. He said: "I will try to be back as soon as possible..." An attendant wearing a white uniform came out and called out: "Is there a relative of LinLin here?"

YingLi rapid jumped up and said: "I'm here." When she answered, she felt her heart leap in her throat, after she was clear the attendant emphasized family member. She said: "I'm just his student...he is single..." The attendant looked at the form in his hand, and said. "Single? Who will sign this?"

"Sign for what?" YingLi asked.

"For the surgery." The attendant answered.

YingLi felt great relief, LinLin was alive he was not dead. Oh, wonderful. Immediately she asked. "Can I sign?" The attendant looked at her for a moment, handed the form to her, and said: "If you sign you will have duties and responsibilities."

YingLi asked what kind of duties and responsibilities. The attendant replied:

"You will have to take care of him while he stays in the hospital and pay his expenses." And the attendant said a lot other things that YingLi did not hear clearly at the time. She thought only of signing, she knew that time was critical to saving his life, and even if she signed there was a lot of risk but it still gave him a chance to live. When she signed her hand was shaking so bad that her name on the paper was almost impossible to read.

After she signed she had to wait again.

The waiting was unbearable. All afternoon she stayed there.

It was evening when LinLin was moved out of the surgery. She got close to him, as he was moved down the hall and saw that he was still alive but sleeping. She began to relax and just felt exhausted. Now he looked like he would live, but his body looked like his life was being supported through tubes with oxygen and intravenous.

Chapter 40

YINGLI WENT THE HOSPITAL counting the days: 1, 2, 3... ten days passed, and he was still unconscious.

The doctor said he had become comatose.

YingLi asked what the word comatose meant, and the doctor explained comatose was between death and life, people have breath but otherwise are like the dead. YingLi cried and complained to the doctor: "What kind treatment did you give him? Why did you let him end up like this?"

"We talked about this before, you agreed and signed the paper." the doctor replied.

Ying Li remembered, she was the one who allowed him to become comatose, that made her feel worse, she was even sadder, and cried harder. Seeing how upset she was the doctor said: "Some recover and return to normal."

YingLi stopped crying, and thought to herself: maybe he does still have a chance. When LinLin was moved into a public ward, the nurse told YingLi: "We just give patients injections and medication, everything else must be done by the family."

YingLi asked what kind of things the family had to do. The nurse said: "Turn the body over, wash him in the bed, shave him, and clean up his shit and piss."

YingLi acted like she didn't have any idea about what the nurse said and asked the nurse to show her.

"Ok, go and get a basin of hot water." the nurse said.

YingLi got the water and watched the nurse soak the towel in the water for a minute, then lifted it up and twisted it lightly; the cloth was still wet but not dripping. She began washing his face and with her other hand she moved the bed sheet and then began washing his body. When YingLi saw LinLin naked, her face flushed red right away. She looked at the nurse who appeared to be about the same age as herself but when she faced the naked man her face looked like wood. She wore a big gauze mask, and both her hands worked on Lin's body. She rubbed a bar of soap in the towel, and continued washing, when she had lather on the body from his neck to his pubic area YingLi got shy and shook just watching the nurse. But the nurse carried on like nothing happened, and when she reached the penis she washed it like a cucumber, cleaning it carefully and gently. When she turned him over to wash his back the nurse told YingLi to do it. She told YingLi that keeping his back clean was crucial to the patient's life; if he was not kept clean he would get bedsores. YingLi didn't understand what a bedsore were either, and the Nurse to explained it to her. Finally YingLi took the towel and tried to copy the nurse's demonstration but her hand was very stiff. The Nurse held YingLi's hand to try relaxing her a little; and then she saw that LinLin's skin was red where she had washed.

Because she was full of respect for him she was willing to do these trivial things. However, out of curiosity, she had asked her mother why he had been divorced?

"Because he was a rightist." LuDongChun answered.

"He had a lot of knowledge and he was a rightist too?"

"The rightists almost all had good educations; their understanding of the situation gave them a different view than the leaders."

"Whom did LinLin have a different view with?"

"With our Political Party."

"Very unreasonable."

"The Party is reasonable but also capable of making mistakes too."

YingLi had held another question in her mind since her mom had been locked up and LinLin had told her that he owed his life to LuDongChun, she had been curious and now she wanted to know and asked:

"Mom LinLin said you saved his life, how did you do that?"

"That is an old story, don't mention it."

"I want to know. Please, please."

"The year that LinLin became a rightist, he had lost his family and his job, he was very depressed, and wanted to die."

YingLi had experienced the feeling. "Oh yes, when people feel there is no way to go on, it is very easy to think about dying. Did he want to commit suicide and you helped him?" Li asked excitedly.

"No, he tried to kill me."

"Wow! Why?" YingLi asked wide eyed.

"I was the mayor of Long Shan City, I was a woman too, and easy to kill."

"After?"

"After...of course he didn't kill me I'm still here." LuDongChun said with a broad smile.

"Did he get in trouble because of you?"

"No."

"Why?"

"He did not hate me, and he did not hate anyone else either. When he understood politics and history, he knew how to be peaceful."

"But, what reason made you become friends?"

"That is a long story..."

Chapter 41

ONE DAY, THE DOCTOR told YingLi, that there was a new medication that could help LinLin, but it was very expensive.

Ying Li went home and discussed it with her mom.

LuDongChun said: "Are you sure the doctor was being honest? I agree to try it, but where will we find the money?" LuDongChun asked.

YingLi said: "He has a lot of iron and copper in his yard, I will try to sell that."

She went to LinLin's house to find which things might be sold for money. She picked up some things and put them on a small push cart, and then went to the waste station to sell them. She only got a hundred RMB but she was delighted. But when she went to the doctor, she discovered it would cost 15 RBM for each shot. It was not enough money for one cycle of treatment. She was unwilling to give up but had no choice.

When she reached home it was evening and LuDongChun was sitting on the Kang with a small box in her hand. She asked.

"Did you get some money?"

"Here." YingLi threw the money on the Kang, and said sadly: "The Doctor said, it was not enough money for one treatment cycle so it was no help."

"Baby." LuDongChun asked smiling: "What kind of friends are you and LinLin?" closely examining her daughter's face.

"Oh, mom, you are imagining things. Do you forget he went to see you, and helped you?"

"I didn't forget."

"He has...he also donated blood for me."

"When? Why wasn't I told?"

"I ...I...had an abortion...of course you didn't know, at that time you were having serious health problems, I just didn't want you worrying about me so I didn't tell you."

"You needed a blood transfusion for your abortion?"

"I don't know what happened. I had a lot of bleeding and felt dizzy and I couldn't stand up...the doctor said I needed a blood transfusion. LinLin had type O blood and he gave me 400 ccs."

LuDongChun held the box in the palm of her hand, and said: "This is from your grandmother; she left it on her deathbed. It has been hidden in the flue of the Kang all the time. I don't know what is inside, but I know it will be valuable for sure. Today I dug it out to look; maybe we can help LinLin after all."

YingLi had very vivid memories of her grandmother; before she died they had lived together for a while. She was dying during the national food shortage period, and like YingLi's father's problem, she was dying from malnutrition from hunger. Since the national liberation, grandfather had left her under government care, she was unhappy, and always weeping. Grandfather had angina and died in 1958. Grandmother felt sad and said she wanted to follow him. LuDongChun had only one elder sister who shared the same mother and father, and she lived in the countryside had a very poor life. LuDongChun was much better off and took her mother from her elder sister and brought her to Long Shan City. YingLi remembered that her grandmother had many stories to tell, and could speak other languages too. Grandmother had a lot of knowledge about many things, she seemed to be the most intelligent woman in the world.

LuDongChun opened the box very carefully, there was a small pocket of satin, and from the pocket emerged a jade bracelet and a gold finger-ring. The jade was of very good quality and the gold was pure. YingLi didn't need to ask to know the history and story behind these treasures. To sell these heirlooms would be a shame.

YingLi said: "Mom, you must keep them."

LuDongChun put the heirlooms in the palm of YingLi's hand. After awhile, she returned to this world again and said: "Sell them."

YingLi stopped her and said: "No mom, you keep them."

"People are worth more than things. If your grandmother in heaven knows these things will help LinLin, she will be happy too." LuDongChun said.

"My grandmother knew him too?"

"Yes."

YingLi was full of curiosity and wanted to know what had happened between her grandmother and LinLin, she said: "Tell me about LinLin and grandma, please tell me. Please, please..."

"I had set him free and he felt he owed me. He came to apologize and express his gratitude; but, when he came, he told me that I had a disease, and talked about it as if it was true. He said he had a secret prescription handed down in the family from generation to generation, and wanted to treat me..."

YingLi interrupted her mom and asked. "Did you believe him? It was not poison was it." Ying Li's mouth was open wide, she was anxious for her mom to continue.

LuDongChun laughed and said: "I thought maybe he wanted to kill me again, like a plot in a novel. If one plan fails find another one. But, after a few days, I was in the hospital with acute exacerbation of chronic hepatitis. He came in to see me; I asked him how he knew I was sick. He said the colour of my face showed that I had hepatitis. I let him check my pulse, and his diagnosis was same as the doctors. Then I thought he was very intelligent, outstanding people like him shouldn't be wasted. I give him a recommendation to the traditional Chinese hospital, and because he had medical education in both eastern and western medicines they gave him a position as an intern doctor."

"Then, why did he not continue there?"

"The hospital was accused of malpractice, and they said he was to blame."

"Did he do it?"

"I don't know, but I thought maybe not."

"Why didn't you send someone to check? Why didn't you help him prove he was innocent?"

"He gave up, when he saw me, and we talked he reminded me of two sayings that I had given him."

"What two sentences sayings?"

"A gentleman has a big heart, and a villain always has sorrow."

"A gentleman has a big heart, and a villain always has sorrow." YingLi repeated the words deep in thought.

"After, your grandmother got sick, she didn't trust anybody except LinLin. Your grandmother lived in the country at that time, and LinLin went there often to take care of her. Ha! Many people believe that he is your grandmother's son with an unknown father..."

YingLi felt closer to LinLin than ever. Suddenly she felt her face burning with embarrassment. .

Chapter 42

YONGHONG HAD RETURNED FROM Beijing, and set Long Shan City in a whirlwind again. Chairman Mao had held her hands, and she had become the heartbeat of the people of the Long Shan City revolution. Wherever YongHong went she had a sea of hands around her, many hands waving to her and cheering her. It was very inspiring and exciting for her to have the people holding her hands like Chairman Mao had held them. The people acted like they were drunk and crazy. An old woman held her hands in tears, and said Chairman Mao had freed her from a life of slavery and bitterness. A young red soldier held her hand a long time, and said he felt the revolutionary power from Chairman Mao, he would follow the revolution and go on to more and greater victories.

YongHong was greatly surprised that her hands carried such an honour and she got carried away following the people's crying and laughing. Marrying ZhangYong had elevated her image even higher with a colourful ring of lights. Her smiling face was brighter and glossier. Her public life made her feel great! The flowers, admirers, honour and praises... but at home she and ZhangYong were still fighting with each other.

WenJun, who was under the power of the military Area Command Chief of Staff, was married to his daughter Ming.

YongHong hated ZhangYong more than ever, and blamed him for her losing WenJun. In her heart she was asking which were more important, flowers, and applause, or WenJun. She had no way to compare. The Party did not give her a chance to compare. It seemed she was predestined to live with Zhang and she did not have any other choice.

One evening, ZhangYong was washing his foot. The water in the basin got cold and he wanted to soak his foot some more so he called YongHong to help.

"Get some hot water for me."

YongHong went to the kitchen carried back the kettle of hot water and poured it all into the basin. ZhangYong felt like a scalded pig and yanked his foot out; the skin was already scarlet. He cursed her. "Mother ###!" Then, he took a vase from the tea table and threw it at her.

YongHong jumped to one side, and the vase broke on the floor.

The sound of his voice made ZhangYong's parents nervous. Zhang's wife pushed her husband ZhangXianmin to go and see if he could calm them down.

"When I talk, no body listens." ZhangXianmin said.

"It is better to talk than not say anything. Go ahead."

"No, just let then fight." He said.

Zhang's wife took a deep breath, and asked. "What's wrong with their relationship, how can we continue to live like this?"

ZhangXianmin said. "Let them move out, then we won't see them fighting and won't hear the cursing." He was very mad at his son now. ZhangYong had wanted to get married and he had many women to choose from, but he chose YongHong. Ha...revolutionary women, a soft woman after she joined the revolution developed a hard heart, and bad temper. If the woman is too hard, the man will lose his confidence, and a man without confidence is not a man.

ZhangXianmin had recently been raised to the position of Long Shan City's Economic Commission Director. He discovered that the past prosperity had been lost with the revolution; goods and materials had become deficient. The rations for each person per month had been reduced and even so, the State Grain Depot was nearing depletion. The people were busy with the revolution, and not working, the economy was collapsing. He did not know how to reverse the situation; he only knew that people said Chairman Mao's theory is food, which seemed a bit ridiculous. Moreover, the whole situation was much worse than when LuDongChun was the leader. In the past, he had opposed LuDongChun and was happy to see her overthrown by the revolution. Now, he changed his mind and wanted her returned as the leader Long Shan city again.

Chapter 43

SOME SAID THE COLOUR red symbolized enthusiasm, sexuality, authority and self-confidence; others said red symbolized blood, violence, jealousy, and control. In any event, this year was the red year of the nation in the revolution. Political power was now in the hands of the people. Long Shan City turned red in colour too.

This was the autumn of 1968. The scenery in autumn was always glamorous when nature painted the countryside. It led people to think about the colourful mountains gathering in the crops, and lots of food to eat. In those days, the revolution gave autumn new meaning making it even redder. An enormous red carpet of red maples without end stretched from the city into the country and up the mountainsides. The movement of educated youth to the countryside must begin, and YingLi was on the list of those who were ordered to go.

LinLin was still lying comatose in the hospital, and the new medication that cost 15 RBM per each shot, had been used for 20 days already. LuDongChun had used her mother's heirloom jewellery for the money to pay for it and in a few more days it would be all gone. YingLi knew they did not have any thing else of value to sell.

YingLi was washing him as usual with her hands rubbing his genitals copying the nurse's method; she lifted the penis to rub around his testicles, and washed his crotch. While she was doing this, she heard a voice: "Oh, it is itching too much."

Not only YingLi heard him speak, some of the other ward patients heard him too. They all got up and gathered around to look at him. LinLin tried to use his hand to reach the bed sheet to cover his private area. After checking him the Doctor was happy to confirm the news and said: "He just needs time now."

YingLi was so delighted; even though they didn't know how long it would take, perhaps a year, two years, or more; YingLi could see a future.

When YingLi told her mama this good news; LuDongChun said: "You must go to the countryside that is imperative. Aunt-Yu stopped me on the way here."

Aunt-Yu the community cadre had the duty to push young students from city go to the countryside. The educated youth were going to the countryside; the first batch and the second batch had already left. YingLi didn't go, she not only because of LinLin, but also she feared life in the country. Her grandmother and her aunt lived in the countryside, and she knew that life there was much worse than the city. There were many things that she could not stand, like being sick from snakebite, when she had stayed in the countryside with her grandmother. Her innate feminine nature made her fear that strange and inhospitable environment. Even though the students were sent off like heroes; with drums beating and gongs, their chests swollen with pride; YingLi became like sand after a heavy wave, and made aunt-Yu very frustrated.

Mother and daughter both knew YingLi had to go to the countryside; early or late she could not refuse. LuDongChun wanted YingLi to go as soon as possible, YingLi was very unhappy: "Mom, you are not in the cadres any more, why are you still so active?"

One day, the community cadre aunt-Yu met YingLi on the street and stopped her to pressure her to make the decision to go to the countryside as soon as possible. When she got free from aunt- Yu it was noon, and she hurried on to the hospital, saw a lot of people around LinLin, she elbowed her way in and found LinLin talking with the doctor.

"What is your name?" the doctor asked.

"My...name...is LinLin." He answered very slowly.

YingLi used both hands cover her chest: My god, he can talk! Will he know me too? She heard doctor ask him:

"What is your wife's name?"

YingLi's face turned red, she knew that every body had mistakenly thought she was his wife.

LinLin said: "Wife...no...wife..."

The doctor pointed to YingLi in the crowd and asked. "Who is she?"

LinLin and YingLi's eyes met.

"My...student."

Student? The doctor and the patients were wide eyed..

YingLi moved to his side crying and laughing, calling him. "Uncle Lin." And throwing herself into his arms

LinLin touched her head and said: "Don't cry." But his own tears dropped beyond his control.

A few weeks later, when LinLin finally got back home he found his Kang had been broken and asked YingLi: "Who did that?"

"I did." YingLi said: "I was trying to find money to pay for your medication." Then she told him the story about when he was sick and he laughed.

YingLi said: "You just know how to laugh; you don't know how sick we were worrying with no money."

LinLin fixed the Kang; and then took her to the back yard where he moved some copper and iron, and scraped the soil away, revealing a little door of wood. He opened the lock, and entered into a steep, dark and gloomy passageway. YingLi was afraid, her heart was pounding, and the flashlight he had given her shook in her hand.

She followed LinLin very closely, clutching the back of his shirt with one hand.

After going down about ten steps, he stopped and said. "You stand here, don't move, and just hold the flashlight for me."

She nodded her head and said: "Ok." But she did not feel ok. She was deathly afraid of the dark; after her mom was locked up she had slept with a light on all night. She believed there were ghosts in this world, and knew they bullied the weak and feared the strong. When her mom was home, the ghost never came out, but when she was home alone, she always heard noises in the kitchen in the middle of the night like someone was cooking in there. When she had the light on, it was quiet. Thinking that ghosts feared light, she lifted the flashlight higher; the wall was cement, wet and mouldy, with a suffocating smell. She suddenly felt something moving in her shoe, soft and wriggling. She screamed in fright, and dropped the flashlight on the floor. LinLin helped her take off her shoe, and he found an earthworm. For her that was the worst kind of ghost because it was a ghost without an image. She was scared and feared many things; she told Lin she wanted to go out, and LinLin said: "Ok." But YingLi was shaking with fright and LinLin had to carry her out, he started to put her down beside the door but she was holding on to him so tightly that he just held her. His hand was still on her lower back, and being together they didn't feel time passing. Much later they just felt their body temperatures had increased and their hearts were beating quicker. YingLi had worked hard for him, been sad for him, taken care of him, and all that was being conveyed and appreciated in this moment. Because she was with him her world was now sunny; that is love. Love with a man was something she had never known. When she was hurt and lost her chastity she locked her emotions deep in her heart, like a Buddhist nun. She couldn't remember when she had began to love him, perhaps it was when his blood started running through her body; maybe it was their first meeting when he talked about the basin. She laid against his chest without moving, feeling like she was in a dream that would end if she moved.

At the same time LinLin felt time stop running; her soft body was shaking and that told him that she loved him. He had thought there would not be another love for him in this life, but misfortune and good luck were interdependent. He felt they were predestined to be together in this life. He knew she would not yield to evil, he had a student who was a sponge thirsty to seek knowledge...they hugged tight. He kissed her softly, kissed her face, her mouth, her chin and neck...his tears dropped on her face, mixing with her tears running down her nose, blending, becoming a river of warmth, in the season of love, and running forward to the future.

Chapter 44

FEELING IN LOVE MADE YingLi fly like a little bird, in an imaginary sky dreaming about marriage.

LinLin and YingLi were busy preparing to get married and wanted to surprise LuDongChun.

LinLin took out all his resources to give to YingLi. They ransomed YingLi's grandmother's ring and bracelet, the balance was for marriage expenses.

YingLi was recalling that her elder sister got a lot of beautiful things for her marriage.

She went to the stores to shop and look, but after she had run through all the stores in Long Shan city, she couldn't find any goods like her elder sister's. She resigned herself to seek something less attractive than her original objective. She found a twill with some flowers but it was very poor quality material and crude, but she still couldn't buy it, she also needed enough ration fabric tickets.

She went back to ask LinLin for the ration tickets.

LinLin said: "City residents get tickets for two metres a year. What can I do my baby?"

She went back home to ask her mom. LuDongChun asked. "What do you want the tickets for, you're not getting married?"

YingLi chuckled and thought to herself. Who said I'm not getting married? I am getting married. She lied to her mama hiding her happy mood with a serious look on her face and said: "My friend is getting married, please give me the fabric ticket."

"You have to go to the countryside. We need a new quilt for you to take, it is much colder there than in the city." LuDongChun said.

YingLi was deeply touched by her mama's words and almost told her the truth.

But even two peoples' fabric tickets would still not be enough. Getting married had a lot of traditional mores, the revolution had taken most of them away and all that remained was the benefit to make a new quilted cover. The lucky number had doubled, and that is why she thought about the proverb that said: "If the Kang has a beautiful cover; the family will have a golden future." She knows she is just a common girl, and it is unrealistic to compare herself with her elder sister; but she just wants the symbol, not something luxurious, and wonders if she is entertaining hopes beyond her ability. She wants her elder sister to help, but YongHong was very busy during the day with a talk show providing extravagant and baseless talk.

That evening, YingLi took LinLin to ZhangYong's home.

As before Zhang's wife came out to open the gate, seeing YingLi holding a man's hand she was surprised at first, and then smiled and let them into the house. In the living room, YingLi explained that she wanted to see her elder sister. Zhang's wife did not reply; and then she heard the arguing going on in the next room. Zhang's wife took a deep breath. YingLi and LinLin understood what was happening, and looking at each other, saw their minds were the same. YingLi said: "Aunt Zhang, we will come another day."

Zhang's wife carried on as if nothing had happened, she pushed YingLi to the sofa and motioned for LinLin to have a seat, and said: "Sit down please! My husband has a meeting tonight."

YingLi said: "Aunt Zhang, you misunderstood, we came to see my sister."

LinLin was quiet for a while, and then he asked. "Were they fighting?"

"Every day."

"What about?"

YingLi remembered her elder sister had said: "I will make a plan to die in a rage at him."

"You must try to persuade them that when a husband and wife fight often, they will injure their emotions." LinLin said.

"We can't persuade them, they will not listen." Zhang's wife shook her head, she looked helpless and upset, she continued: "I have lived with my husband for many years, we were never like that; fighting is like eating for them, it happens every day. Since they were married, my heart has a disease because of them...I can hear it pounding.

YingLi called out: "Elder sister."

Soon YongHong was facing YingLi with a big smile on her face. YingLi looked closely at her face, and saw clearly that she had been crying. YongHong was composed and affable now; if they had not heard the yelling and crying, no one would believe that she had just been fighting.

YongHong looked at LinLin and said: "Oh, we have a visitor here."

YingLi held LinLin's hand, and said quietly: "We are getting married!"

YongHong was startled but Zhang's wife even more so.

Zhang's wife looked very happy, and said. "Congratulations! YingLi is a very good girl, the man who marries her will be very lucky."

YongHong had a dark face.

LinLin said: "Dear wife let me meet our brother in law."

YongHong asked: "Have you registered?"

YingLi answered shyly: "Not yet."

"Not yet? Are you sure he will be good for you?"

"Yes." YingLi nodded happily. She said: "We came here to ask how you got the fabric tickets when you got married; we need one"

"I...that was special."

"Can you help me?"

"I don't think so, the government for did that for him." She said referring to ZhangYong."

ZhangYong's mother asked: "How many do you need? We have some for them if they have a baby. You can use them now and when we need them we will let you know."

YingLi been had a big wish when she came, after hearing what her older sister said, she got depressed and did not accept Zhang's mom's offer. Zhang's mom was not going to accept refusal, she kept insisting.

Then LinLin and ZhangYong came out together. YingLi noticed that ZhangYong had gotten thinner. The artificial limb didn't help him very much, he walked very awkwardly lifting his body with every step, and when he lifted his body, his face showed suffering. YingLi's eyes got wet for a moment. This had been one vigorous and enthusiastic centre on the basketball court at the school; this was the handsome graceful tenor who performed with her on the same stage. She did not dare to look again.

ZhangYong stretched out his hand wanting to hold YingLi's hand, when he saw her turn her head to the side, took his hand back and said: "Congratulations to you!"

YingLi turned her head and seeing his smiling face, thought both he and her older sister had performer's talents, they had just been fighting on the back stage, now they come to the front stage and they looked like nothing had happened...they sat down in the living room and chatted awhile.

When they were leaving, ZhangYong followed them out although everyone wanted him to stay; he insisted and stood up, and with his body shaking made his way to the gate, to hug YingLi for a moment and say again: "Congratulations to you." YingLi shed a tear like a pearl breaking yarn unrestrained it dropped down. She had many words welling up in her throat, but could not speak a single one.

Chapter 45

Y INGLI'S PLANS FOR MARRIAGE did not go as smooth as she had imagined; in addition to the trouble of obtaining material, she could not find her HuKou. (Chinese ID). She had wanted to hide her marriage plan until she registered; now she would have to tell the truth. Her mother said the community cadre had taken the HuKou. This was a hard measure for the any of the educated youth destined to go to the countryside; their HuKou would be held for them, if they refused to go, it would be cancelled. A city person could not live without it because they were dependent on food rations from the National supply.

YingLi did not believe her mother and said she thought her mother made the decision on her own. Since she was old enough to understand, she knew that her mama not only obeyed the party, she also expected her daughters to obey her. That had been family policy for many years.

YingLi has angry at her mama.

She laid down on the Kang (bed) and covered her face with a bed cover, when lunch time came she didn't get up, and it looked like she was fasting. Her mother called her to have lunch, but she did not reply.

Since LuDongChun became unemployed she had become a housekeeper. For many years she had lived like a man even after she went back to being a woman. She had always been busy and never learned much about house keeping, so she was not a good cook or a good housekeeper. Thinking about her life as a wife and mother LuDongChun felt guilty and now she could only try to make it up to her daughter. Her mother and husband had both died and left her feeling sorry but with no chance to fix things. She was used to being busy, with time to relax she felt like she was losing her mind every day. When she went out shopping, she always forgot one or two things. Today, she found that she needed to buy soy sauce, but when she got home she realised she had forgot to get garlic.

LuDongChun heard someone knocking at the gate, and said: "Maybe it's LinLin, I will see, if it is him, I will not open the gate, he can go home."

YingLi jumped up from the Kang, and ran to the gate; the person that had come was the leader of communications, aunt-Yu. She had a strong body and voice too; her voice boomed from the gate into the house ahead of her.

"Hi, you won! You don't need go to the countryside." Still talking aunt-Yu passed through the door way. She put her fat hand on the YingLi's shoulder, and was talking in high spirits and said. "Hi, it's so silly, if I had known you didn't need to go I wouldn't have always been catching you and your mom. I felt like a cat catching mice, it is so funny, very funny..." She smirked to herself.

Mother and daughter were both confused about what she was laughing about, but they smiled to show aunt-Yu respect.

"You have a seat please." LuDongChun said.

Aunt-Yu sat down, and asked: "Do you have any water to drink?" Even though it was winter, her face was sweating.

YingLi made a cup tea for her, and when she finished, she said: "I have a document." She putting her hand into a pocket drew out a piece of paper, "This is a letter from the educated youth office."

YingLi took it and asked: "What does it mean?"

LuDongChun moved beside YingLi and said: "Read it to me."

YingLi looked at the letter, and answered: "This is a letter that LinLin wrote to the government, asking for permission to go to the countryside with me so we could be together."

"Look down the page." Aunt-Yu said still excited.

YingLi's sight travelled down the right side, and found a few words. "The policy says, each family can keep one child in the city, YingLi can stay."

She was so excited and happy she just ran out with out a word and disappeared. She couldn't wait to tell this good news to LinLin, and they would get married.

YingLi and LinLin had no wedding ceremony. There were no guests, no best man or bridesmaid, no fireworks, no candy, and no cigarettes. In the evening LinLin came riding his bicycle to pick up YingLi and they left.

LuDongChun went to the gate with them, and watched them go shoulder to shoulder in the sunset's glow. Their shadows grew longer, and longer from the sky to the ground, in front of her. She wept if she still had her former position, her daughter's wedding would not be so shabby.

Her daughters were now married and they had their own lives and roads of life to travel. The road of life was not smooth and flat. In the future, they would have luck, or troubles, they would be happy or sad; anything could happen. This is life. From the mother's side, LuDongChun gives them her prayers. She prayed that her YongHong and YingLi, twin sisters had come into this world together, and even if they had different roads to travel, their blood was thicker than water. Their relationship was sisters; sisters forever.

This simple wedding, and did not cast a shadow over the love.

LinLin and YingLi went back to their bridal chamber. LinLin carried his new wife lightly past the doorframe, and in his mind he stepped onto a red carpet with wedding music raising; and around them, guests' benedictions; fresh flowers, and name brand wines... in truth; only a single candle was flickering. The melting red candle had red tears flowing maybe it was happy for them! Two loving bodies under candlelight, starting to meld together.

Chapter 46

THE NEWS OF YONGHONG'S promotion, made WenJun very excited.

YongHong had a new position and had been transferred to the city where WenJun was; when he found out he started pining for her again.

When YongHong had failed to get a divorce, he had been compelled to marry Ming-the daughter of his military Area Command's chief of staff. Ming was just not very good looking; otherwise there was nothing really wrong with her, but WenJun saw her as disgusting, his heart still belonged to YongHong.

For YongHong the fire of love that WenJun had lit in her had been extinguished by her leaders in the Party. She heard that WenJun had married and when she moved to the city where he was, her heart was quiet, and she never considered contacting him.

The job of Leader of the Women's Federation of the province was to manage five cities and thirty-six county towns. On the surface, the job looked like a heavy load but, the work was the same; she just needed know the names of the leaders and basic city or county town information. The times she was living in were earthshaking and literally everything was changing; government was not restricted to promoting cadre, a peasant could rise overnight to become a national leader; and an ordinary soldier could be promoted to a general. This was a very beneficial time for her, and she returned to continue her outstanding work for the Party.

Private emotions became negligible with the revolution, and marriage made WenJun even more disillusioned. He often regretted not taking YongHong to bed first and then let her decide on divorce. He believed that she had not divorced because she cared more about keeping her name and position. Any way it was too late for what might have been he was stuck with the pig Ming and what had been done couldn't be undone. Now, he can't change reality, so he needs to change his attitude.

People said men came from butterflies, in a multi coloured world no man liked to spend his whole life with only one woman. Even if WenJun had not met his wife Ming, and married YongHong or some other woman, he would tire of her after awhile. People said: "Dumplings are delicious, but if you eat them every day you will get tired of them." The truth was that he wanted to taste YongHong not spend the rest of his life with her. WenJun began calling YongHong and eventually she agreed to meet with him.

Then one day at last WenJun succeeded and took advantage of YongHong and fulfilled his desire; for him it was the Himalayan Mountain in his life, his life long dream was now coming true. He was excited with his life and thrilled that he had experienced his fantasy in reality. He praised her like a beautiful jade that had been chiselled and carved, but he believed that in his hand she would become more perfect. That body actually colder than ice and snow; was now transformed into one that was hot and fragrant. The wild and intractable one like a rose with thorns had not hurt him; she was sleeping soundly, passed out in a drunken stupor. He was feeling euphoria from the wine but he was not too drunk to function and take advantage of her. With a pounding heart he mounted her; it made no difference to him that she lay there like a corpse and made no response.

He was aroused just taking off her clothes and allowing his imagination to run wild. Afterwards as he lay beside her like a spent athlete he noticed blood on the bed and thought that she was having her period. Alcohol had left YongHong helpless in a world where she had been manipulated and ravaged; for two hours she had been like a noodle helpless to resist WenJun having his way with her body. When she woke up and realised her situation she did not move, and remained silent. WenJun broke the awkward silence and his embarrassment pointing to the blood and saying:

"Your period has started."

YongHong still remained silent.

WenJun nudged her and repeated what he had said. Suddenly she rose to her knees, grabbed hold of his hair, lifted his head, and pushed his face into the blood stain. Then she yanked his head up and slapped his face with all her might, the force came from deep in her heart leaving her fingers imprinted on his face with a red seal. Then again she pushed his face into the bed and forced it down. WenJun did not resist, maybe he was afraid of her anger or maybe he just wanted to pacify her. Then like a dog eating shit he crawled on the bed until his tongue reached the blood, he closed his lips tight but YongHong said:

"Lick it."

WenJun like player in love guessed that she was angry because she was shy. Women were like the weather, sometimes sunny and sometimes cloudy and hard to predict if they would rain. Therefore, he crawled and accepted her punishment. Later, when he heard her crying, it sounded like a storm with thunder, and lightening he understood, that bright red blood, glittering, and pure was not her period. That blood was a woman's wedding gift to her husband; overwhelmed he stretched his tongue to reach the blood, wetted it and licked it.

Chapter 47

LATE AUTUMN CAME, YINGLI, as a new housewife was busy roaming the streets looking for her choice of potatoes, radishes, and cabbage to prepare for the coming winter.

Long Shan City winters were very long, almost six months of ice and snow. People, who lived here, were accustomed to preserving a big winter food supply. Every family had a vegetable cellar, but most of them were very simple. A typical cellar was a one and a half meter deep hole in the ground with a wooden roof with a small window, for light when a person went in to pick up things; it was also opened some times to change the air.

LinLin was busy building a large vegetable cellar about two square meters with brick, and cement walls; he was preparing the extra large cellar so he could store his mother in law's vegetables.

Newly wed marriage life made YingLi smile all the time. She came to LinLin who was working hard and said:

"Oh my dear, you've working so hard!"

"Yes, do I get paid now?" LinLin's hands were covered with cement; he was holding a trowel in one hand and pallet in the other.

YingLi knew he wanted a kiss, but deliberately pretended to not understand, and asked: "What kind of payment do you want?" laughing, like a bird in spring.

Lin came up and kissed her cheek and said: "My darling wife, I'm hungry."

"Well...I will go and cook now!" She kissed her husband and went to make dinner.

When dinner was ready YingLi watched lovingly as her husband washed his hands came to the table; sat down, picked up a piece of corn pancake, took a bite, and a drink of egg soup. Suddenly he stopped, and looked into her eyes and asked: "My dear wife, why are you not eating?"

YingLi thought for a while and said: "I just want to hibernate."

"Oh? Do you have such a special ability? I don't think so, give me your hand."

"No!" YingLi said laughing. She guessed his thoughts: he was suspecting she was pregnant.

LinLin put down his pancake, and reached for her hand, YingLi pushed his hand a way, and said: "It is not like your thinking, my menstruation just passed."

The following spring YingLi really was pregnant. She had very bad morning sickness, and was craving to eat pork.

LinLin took all his money to buy high priced pork without a ticket, and made a delicious meal for her. Looking at the meal, YingLi saliva was drooling, but she could not eat it all by herself, she made reasons for him to eat some too.

Then sounding angry he said: "My little Aunt, you can not abuse my son; you do not want him to suffer from congenital malnutrition, do you?"

YingLi was surprised and said: "The party always says that the revolution would lead people to a better life, is this a better life? No good food, no...nothing! Who can carry out a revolution on an empty stomach?"

"Shush!" LinLin quickly covered her mouth, and said: "My dear wife, we just eat, we do not talk about such a profound question."

YingLi said laughing: "I can tell you are nervous since your ex-wife caused you trouble, you don't dare to talk freely. I'm sure I'm not like her, you can discuss anything you want with me. Keeping your thoughts to yourself will just make you sick."

"My wife, I am not afraid to talk to you, I am worried that if you are used to talking like this at home, and went out side talking the same way you would get yourself into trouble!"

"So is it really so serious?"

"Yes, it is really very serious!

"OK, let me repeat my last sentence. You say, we do not have enough to eat, our clothes are not warm enough, and so how are we to liberate all of mankind?"

"That a question, you need to ask Chairman Mao. Will you please stop talking about this now?"

YingLi went to see her mother, and asked her: "Mama, when you were pregnant, did you want special food?"

LuDongChun answered: "Oh yes! The country was much poorer than it is now. Your father saw that I wanted to eat good food, but we couldn't find any anywhere so he went hunting on weekends. Wow! That pheasant and wild rabbit was delicious!"

"LinLin has said he wants to go hunting too."

"Does he know how?"

"He said that where he grew up, he knows the forest."

At this time, YingLi and LinLin were both immersed in a happy marriage with immense joy and looking forward to the birth of their child.

They never expected that LinLin would end up in trouble again, and that their lives would suffer great change.

Chapter 48

IN LONG SHAN CITY, #1 primary school there were two brothers, the elder one was named LinHu and the younger one LinXiao. LinHu was ten lbs when he was born, the base of a burly man. His father was delighted and gave his son an appropriate name "Biao", it was take a word from bruiser. And combined with the family name "Lin", he would be called: "LinBiao". But when his father went to register him in the HuKou, the officer told him that name belonged to a national leader already, therefore, finally, the boy's name became LinHu.

LinHu was a good student in school, when he was in the second grade, he had a good reputation as a young vanguard team member. At the ceremony for the citation he was standing on the stage, and got so excited that he pissed in his trousers. When LuDongChun representing Long Shan city put the red scarf on his neck, he made a salute to her with hot steam rising from his crotch. In his young mind he deeply remembered the female mayor very well.

From the fourth grade, his school was changed. Some teachers joined the revolution, others had problems, and they couldn't continue teaching. Some factory workers without education who had support on the political level started to do teacher's jobs. And smart factory worker teachers, started using higher-grade students to teach lower grade students that led to the story that follows.

LinHu was one of those chosen to teach. From fourth grade, he went to first grade teaching arithmetic 1-100.

His younger brother LinXiao, was very naughty and a trouble maker. He liked to put water into other students pockets from behind when all students stood to respect the teacher; and he liked to stand up to say hello to the teacher too; so he could move the chair of the student in front of him back so that he would sit on the floor.

LinLin was a recycle man who by chance came to meet a student teacher named LinHu when LinHu's class had some old waste paper to sell. LinLin always treated the little teacher special and went to the class room to pick up the old papers from the young teacher.

They both had the same last name Lin that indicated a common family if distant family relationship.

LinHu, like many other young boys was very interested in the war and history stories. When LinLin came to the class this day he was asked to talk about one of the leaders in the war.

That afternoon after he received the scrap paper, LinLin took a seat in the class room and told a national leader's war story whose name had been denied to LinHu.

During in the talk LinLin wrote the national leader's name on a sheet of paper. Later the school leader discovered the sheet with the national leader's name had "bastard" words also.

To say a national leader was a bastard was anti-revolutionary.

There was an investigation of the school and a policeman was involved. Even though they discovered LinXiao had added the "bastard" word; they believed that a class struggle was taking a new direction, and that LinLin had cleverly used a child.

At the time only LinHu could say that the story was wrong. LinLin had written the national leader's name, but the younger brother LinXiao had written the libel. LinXiao was a little boy, who really did not know how serious it was, and not something to joke about. He thought that the joke was on his older brother, because he only recognised the last name "Lin", and thought it was his brother's name. LinHu tried many times to talk to the adults at the school to clear LinLin's name but no one would listen to him. The revolution had made people very sensitive about class struggle; they were not about to let the facts about LinLin's crime to be changed by the words of a child.

Chapter 49

LINLIN WAS IN TROUBLE, and YingLi looked like an ant in a hot pan. Heavy with child near the end of her pregnancy YingLi went to the provincial capital to ask for her older sister's help.

She believed that is was a mistake. Anybody would know that it was a game that children played. Even in her childhood, sometimes with a classmate they made these kinds of jokes about each other. Sometimes they made a little poster and put it on someone's back, saying "bastards" or "son of bitch" that everyone saw and laughed about with out him or her knowing.

LinLin was too old to do something childish like that.

The Provincial office had been last emperor's palace. Since then it had changed residents many times: when Japan invaded and occupied the north of China, this building had been their headquarters. After Japan surrendered it became the army of the KMT's administrative base; when the KMT retreated to Taiwan, the Communist Party had set up the provincial government there.

YingLi had never been here, after she got off the train, she had to keep asking directions. The people all knew where the government offices were, and YingLi had no problem finding her way there. But getting inside was another matter; the doorman was a soldier with a rifle guarding the gate, to go in she would need to register and to do that she had to have an invitation from someone inside. YingLi didn't know her sister's phone number, and the guard didn't let her in. People would come with all kinds of stories in an attempt get in to make a complaint about their own problems and interrupt the officer's scheduled work. Therefore the policy was very strict, now anyone without a pass could not go in.

YingLi stood outside for more than two hours, until the guard changed, but she was still refused entry. Soon after she fainted and fell on the street in front of the guard. This behaviour worked; the guard called his superior, and two people came to check on YingLi, one of them had stethoscope on his neck and checked YingLi's chest and back, then he pressed on her upper lip, the pain caused tears to come to her eyes. "You need to be careful, don't try to play tricks with me."

YingLi reached his sleeve and said: "Help me please. I have to see my older sister."

He swung his arm and said: "If you are looking for your older sister, you don't need to pretend that you are dying"

"They won't let me go in."

"You can go to the door room to phone her to come out to pick you up."

"The problem is I don't know her phone number. Can you help me?" YingLi kneeled with her big belly protruding to him; the sight made him feel a little compassion. He shook his head and said: "There are so many offices and thousands of officers, how can I find one for you? Which department is she in, and what is her name?"

"Her name is YongHong, which department... I don't know yet; but she used to work in the Women's Federation in Long Shan city."

He took her to a room beside the gate, and made a few phone calls. Finally, when YingLi heard her older sister's voice, her body felt like jelly. She had gone since this morning without food and water, now more than nine hours, she was hungry, and thirsty... almost dehydrated.

YongHong came out to get her and took her to get something to eat first.

Then YongHong said: "If you have evidence, I believe the government won't indiscriminately kill an innocent person."

Yong Hong's words were like a shot of heroin mustering YingLi to have more confidence to go back and look for evidence.

Chapter 50

AFTER YINGLI LEFT, LUDONGCHUN could not stay home either. She had been thinking a lot, and remembering that YingLi had gone to the school to ask the teacher what had happened, and been kicked out by a revolutionary teacher. She thought about the people who had been under her when she was the leader and realised that no one could help. She clearly understood people under these circumstances would not want to endanger themselves; self-protection was a natural human instinct. Hmm...if this was the case, LinLin's predicament would be very hard to clear.

Her daughter, who was heavy with her pregnancy, had been shaking all day since she learned that LinLin had been arrested. She had not eaten either; poor girl! The new life had just begun, and the romantic dream was already broken.

She saw YingLi crying without tears, eyes that were dead...her heart was aching.

How to help clear him; she had asked herself that question a thousand times, and still did not have a good idea.

The #1 school was close to her home, but she could not go there because she was not the mayor, she was a Capitalist Roader and traitor. A light wind was blowing her hair causing it to stand up, she patted it down, and some hair had stayed on her palm, when she opened her palm the hair was gone with wind.

She was walking down the street, and saw students who had finished classes on their way home; this made her think of her future grandchild, if his or her father's death was a case of anti-revolution, he or she would have a miserable life. Oh, poor baby!

She was walking deep in thought, and did not see a rock front of her, and tripped and fell in the street.

A boy come to her and was helping her to get up.

Suddenly, an idea popped into LuDongChun's mind and she asked: "are you #1 school student?"

"No." the boy shook his head said.

This answer did not make LuDongChun disappointed. She realised that children were very naïve; and she also believed that since a child had caused LinLin's trouble, it could be cleared up by a child too.

But, how to contact those students was the big question; she spent several hours searching for an answer. Then she got an inspiration: children loved illustrated books. LinLin's house had a lot of books; she decided quickly and not wanting to waste a minute she took a hand truck, and moved the children's books on to the street, to let children look at them for free.

Unexpected good news was waiting for YingLi when she got home. LinHu who was a substitute teacher at the No.1 School had told LuDongChun the truth. LuDongChun had taken lots of picture books from Lin's house and set up a stall near the school, and the students had gathered around the books and she had been able to talk to them. LinHu recognised LuDongChun and he believed that she could fix his mistake and he had promised her that he would witness and that would relieve his feelings of guilt. Ever since LinLin had been arrested, YingLi hadn't wept, didn't have time to weep; but, in this moment, she began crying. They decided that LuDongChun would go to Beijing to make the appeal, and YingLi would go to the provincial capital and send letters.

In the evening, just after LuDongChun went on the train, YingLi heard someone knocking at the gate.

YingLi went out to open the gate, but she didn't know these people. She saw a woman and a man that looked like a couple each holding onto a boy. The two boys were looking up faint-heartedly at their parents who were holding their hands. The woman spoke first asking: "Is that her?"

The little boy nodded and said: "yes" very timidly.

The big boy was struggling to get free from his father's hand; he pushed the little boy on the shoulder and said: "You talk nonsense that is not her."

YingLi guessed it was the boys LinHu, LinXiao, and their parents; she had learned the boys names from her mother. Her mother had already written a letter based on information provided by the boys. She shifted her gaze from the adults to the boys, as the big boy said continued: "It is certainly not her."

The man said: "What are you doing, who asked you? Keep quiet."

The little boy was crying and his mother was bent down comforting him and drying his tears. She said: "Don't cry, dad and mom are here, don't be afraid. Ok?" Then she turned her neck to glare at the big boy, and asked YingLi. "Are you LuDongChun?"

"She is my mother." YingLi said, she was sure now who they were but did not know why they had come. The big boy looked delighted and said: "I told you that it was not her! Hey! You did not believe me!"

YingLi kindly invited them go in the house and said: "How can I help you?"

"We want talk to your mother." the man said.

"She is not home. Can you talk to me?"

The man continued asking: "Where is she? When will she be back?"

The woman moved in front of him and said: "That is fine why not talk to her? These two kids talked about shit to your mother! They are very young and don't understand anything! Don't believe what they said; they made up a story just to kid you!"

YingLi now understood why they had come and she felt heaviness sink into her heart; then she heard the big boy say: "I did not make up a story, it is the truth."

The man silenced the boy, and the woman asked again: "When will your mother be back?"

"She went to Beijing. She will be back..." YingLi had not finished answering, and was interrupted by the woman. "She went to Beijing? Was she carrying these two boy's stories?"

"...Yes."

The couple made her nervous, but the big boy gave her self-confidence.

"Your case is not relevant with our boys." The man said with a red face and his eyebrows screwed up vertically. "The kids didn't say anything; and we don't know any thing!" The man's voice was very firm.

YingLi felt like cold water had been thrown on her head in winter, a chill swept threw her body. Since her mother found the two boys, she had held high hopes, but now all hope seemed to be gone. She knew they were afraid of being involved in the case; who wouldn't be afraid? Yes, anybody would. If it had happened to her, she would have to consider very carefully before getting involved too.

She kneeled on the floor in desperation, and made her final plea: "Elder brother and elder sister, it is said, to save one life, is better than building seven pagodas."

She said in a tearful voice. "I ...want you help my husband."

The baby was kicking her belly from inside the womb, and YingLi pointed to the baby saying. "My baby has knelt to you too. I have a complaint; poor are parent's hearts who don't want a child to have a good future. I'm having a baby soon; I want my baby to have a father too. If you pity my baby, just be fair, and let them tell the truth. Even if the truth does not benefit my husband, I will not complain. Just tell the truth."

LinHu helped YingLi get up supporting her with his little soft hand.

His mother lifted YingLi up from the floor too, with her mood of contradiction.

YingLi continued, and said. "Chair man Mao leads us to be honest. Don't you listen to him? Isn't that right?"

"Yes." LinHu said very loudly.

The little boy followed his brother and said: "Yes." His hand was pinched, and he asked, "Mom, why did you pinch me?"

YingLi said: "My husband only wrote the name, the little boy wrote the other words; by investigating carefully, the police will discover who did the writing, and that it was not my husband. Handwriting can be checked out."

"Did you write it?" The woman asked the little boy. The boy only looked with blank eyes and did not answer. Then YingLi continued: "The evidence is in the hands of the police, they will not kill the wrong person."

When they heard YingLi say this, the couple realised then that they could not break away from their responsibility.

The man asked YingLi: "What is your plan?"

"We have a document that describes what happened. It clears my husband of the crime and your child is so young that he can not be guilty of a crime either."

"Are you sure he will not die?" The man asked hesitantly.

"Mom, I don't want to die." The little boy said.

LinHu held his head high, straightened his chest and said: "Coward! I want to be a hero, and die like a martyr bravely!"

Chapter 51

YING LI WENT TO the provincial capital again; YongHong had not been willing to get involved before, but now she changed her mind. She thought if this was a case of an unjust verdict and she fixed it then she would benefit from both sides. Her job was not to handle cases against the revolution, but she could intervene through the Women's Federation department to help clients. Clients could bring her their problems if their cases were difficult; it depended on her experience to decide if her intervention was appropriate. LuDongChun had gone to Beijing, and in addition there was evidence supporting the appeal; she decided to accept the documents and expected that she would be called to appear. YongHong's attitude gave YingLi hope, the turmoil that had embroiled her for many days began to abate.

She came back from the provincial capital feeling a little more relaxed.

In the mid-autumn season the smell of potatoes, cabbage, turnips, and garlic permeated the air in Long Shan city. YingLi wishing and hoping for the best took their HuKou(ID) to the market and bought 600 lbs of fresh cabbage, that would need a few days to of sunshine to dry; after it dried she would take off the rotten leaves and then put the cabbages in the root cellar to store for the winter.

After she bought the cabbage, the weather had turned cloudy so she put them on top of the yard wall, to wait for the sun to smile on them.

Last year, LinLin had built a larger cellar in back yard. YingLi went to look at the cellar often, looking at the cellar, she seemed to be able to see LinLin.

Time had passed swiftly, LuDongChun had been gone for almost a week and there had been no news. YingLi knew that the government always worked slowly, and she tried to relax. One day, the sun came out, and she was in the yard busy turning over the cabbages so that they would dry. In the afternoon when she went out to turn the cabbages again, two men showed up at the gate. She let them in, and one man asked:

"Are you YingLi?"

"Yes."

"Is LinLin your husband?"

"Yes."

"You sign here."

"What is that?" She asked, partly worried and partly delighted. She hoped this was good news, but she was worried that it might be bad news too. Her hand and voice both were shaking; she took the paper and didn't look to see what it said, she just asked. "What is this?"

"That is notice of your husband's execution."

YingLi was convulsed for a moment; her face turned pale, then got red, and she screamed: "You can't shoot him, he is not guilty."

"We are just carrying out our duty to deliver the message." the leader said.

"Why do you treat human life like cutting grass?"

"That is decided by a higher office, we don't have any idea about that; but you need pay money for the bullet."

"Bullet...fee? You want me to pay money for you to shoot my husband?"

The other one said: "After he dies, do you want to take the corpse back or not? You must sign here, saying if you want to take the corpse or not."

"My mom has been gone to Beijing for a week; can you wait a little while?"

"Sign here!"

Was this to be their destiny? When she heard LinLin would be executed, YingLi completely collapsed.

She decided then to die with her husband.

She went to the pharmacy and bought some sleeping pills and some painkillers to help her forget the agony of this world, and wanted to find a quiet place to rest. She felt helpless and incapable of carrying on; she was exhausted and had no desire to live without LinLin. In addition, she as the daughter of a traitor had become an outcast; after her husband was executed, the child would be an outcast too. Is it possible that she could let a child be born to live in this situation? No! She couldn't let him or her come into this world, for its own protection, because she would be unable to protect it.

LinLin was much like a child. When he had learned that she was pregnant, he cried. Who cannot be excited when life is extended? If they had not had this trouble, they planned to have two children, a boy and a girl. Their names had already been chosen. But, something unexpected could happen at any time; LinLin could go, and her soul would go with him.

Why should she live in an empty shell here, or to keep their child here for a life of misery? When she went to the hell or heaven to see LinLin, she would explain to him and he would understand. Life is suffering; Lin would not like her and their child to suffer. She decided that her fate was inevitable and all she could do was sit and wait until her mom got back so that she could see her one last time. Her mom was very strong and brave; and she knew that to stay alive in this life one needed to be brave, but she wasn't brave and that is why she chose to die.

She made a plan, when LinLin was shot she would go there and stay with him, forever.

Three days later, aunt-Yu with and an old skinny lady came to the house. Aunt-Yu told YingLi: "Your husband will be shot tomorrow." Aunt-Yu put her fat hands on YingLi's shoulders, and said. "Baby, if you want to cry you can cry; if you want to talk we will talk, we are just here to take custody of you, we don't care about any thing else."

YingLi went back into the bedroom. Aunt-Yu and the old lady were very surprised that she said nothing and did not even cry. Soon YingLi came out again wearing a pink cotton shirt under a faded old army uniform and headed straight towards the door.

The two women blocked her way and asked: "Where are you going?"

"I will go to the execution ground." This time, she heard the two old ladies say at the same time; "No way! You have been placed under control! And you can not leave the house!"

Chapter 52

THE EUROPEAN STYLE RAILWAY station had been built by the Russians, and was located in what was now the provincial capital near the Russian border. During the Japanese Russian war the city had been a battleground; and after the Russians had won the war they built this station to mark the boundary between two countries. The ownership of Chinese territory had been divided up between them, and the old rail way station had been upgraded since then, but the bloody history remained; many ghosts of previous wars still lingered here. It was said that if the ghosts wanted to come back in human form they would find a scapegoat, and when the scapegoat died they would be born into human life again.

Of life in the hell no one knew for certain.

But, following the changing times, the blood had dried up in the city and then ran again. When people are going to a killing, the air is always different. It is not only ghosts who have delights; humans have delights too. And ghosts' may be delighted to have the chance and to move into the new human life; one human delight for sure was winning class struggles.

The night before LinLin was to be executed YingLi was in the waiting room of the station at midnight. She had changed her appearance with a loose fitting man's jacket that made her belly look flat, and her face was dirty like she had just come out of a garbage bin; she had dressed that way to avoid attracting attention and to be as inconspicuous as possible. She walked into the station, and went to the ladies' room first to check her face and clothes. When she felt satisfied with her appearance she went into the waiting area; the big waiting rooms by this time were quite full.

The hard wooden chairs were all occupied but there were still some spaces to be had sitting on the floor. Between the chairs on the floor there was enough space for skinny people to squeeze in who were very tired but had come too late to get a chair. Sitting on the floor put their faces on the same level as the asses of the people sitting in the chairs and they knew that the air would not be fresh.

When YingLi went into the waiting room, there was hardly even a place to stand and she could not squeeze in between the chairs and sit with her big belly. She tried standing beside a chair to support her body but her legs felt numb. Oedema caused by the pregnancy and many days of running working on Lin's case had left her legs very weak, and she kept slipping down. Finally the man who was sleeping in the chair woke up and when he saw her belly and her face, he stood up and gave his chair to her. She thanked him and plopped her body down on the chair.

Outside the sky was beginning to get light, she didn't know what time daybreak came in autumn but she knew that it was still early. Her nerves would not let her body relax; she was thinking that aunt-Yu would be awake now or very soon, and she would go to the hospital and have an enema or get a shot. Three sleeping pills would not make her die, but could cause YingLi to have problems. If aunt-Yu told the government the truth, there would be people looking for her to arrest her. She knew that any minute she might see the militia in front of her, handcuffing her, then escorting her back to Long Shan city. Long Shan city was in this province and only a two hour train trip, it would not be hard to arrest her if they knew where she was.

When daybreak came, the things she had worried about had not materialised. She took a deep breath, got up off the chair and walked outside on unsteady feet.

Outside, the air was beginning to fill with sounds of the big event; the propaganda truck was making the rounds, and the speakers on the truck were blaring full blast. The announcers were not specialists or experts on what was to take place they just shouted themselves hoarse repeating the basics of what was to take place. The sun seemed to be scared by the commotion and had a very pale face.

YingLi followed the sounds on the street, looking for any trace of her husband. The first thing, she saw was the death court verdict: a big picture of a bowed head, the person's name, with a great red x on it, meaning that person would be getting killed. Under the picture, in smaller letters facts about the crime committed were elaborated on. Today nine people would go to the execution ground; each one was guilty of a different crime. LinLin's crime was anti-revolution, which was the worst possible crime.

At the time, an anti-revolutionary should die ten thousand deaths. Even death with ten thousand executions wouldn't atone for such a crime. However a human body could only die once, to the masses of the revolution it looked like they had suffered great losses and they were screaming in the street.

LinLin was an active anti-revolutionary. In China's history there were two kinds of anti-revolutionaries: Historical anti-revolutionaries and active anti-revolutions. The Historical anti-revolutionaries suffered from a lower political IQ and they made mistakes, usually the government put them where they "could be educated"; but active anti-revolutionaries were different because they had openly said things or done things against the revolution.

Like at the arena, the Peoples Proletarian Revolutionary Dictatorship looked like a superman on the platform against competition. Anyone who wanted to struggle against the revolution was doomed, let them try and then kill them. Only people who overrated their abilities were "active anti-revolution." At this time in history 700 million Chinese had the same belief that the revolution could liberate the whole of mankind; they felt they were lucky to have been born in China and have a happy life.

There were more and more people on the street, many with their mouths open eagerly shouting with hope in anticipation.

The muscles on many faces were shaking and looked like they were already chewing like they were at a party, and excited by the palatable foods.

YingLi stood in the crowd reading the notice with tears in her eyes, she looked at the LinLin's face that had been divided in four parts with the red mark, saying to him: "Dear, your wife is coming, your child is coming; we will go with you. Whatever happens, any where, life and death, end of earth, we will be together forever."

She saw him wearing a big smile, from his lips to his ears, his bright eyes shining, his wide forehead... her tears ran uncontrolled down her face...

"Lady, do you want a Pedicab?"

The old man's words interrupted YingLi's thoughts. He in ragged clothes with a face like a hickory nut was approaching YingLi looking for business.

YingLi stepped back to put more distance between them, and said: "No, I don't want a Pedicab."

The old man went to another person, and YingLi heard a young woman asking: "Will you take me to the bear mountain?" That was the execution ground and when YingLi heard him clearly say "yes" she suddenly regretted having told him no. From her past experience, the people who were to be killed received open justice from the masses of the revolution, making a circle tour of the city showing them to the people, and afterwards taking them to the execution ground to kill them. The truck was driven very slowly, so that people who wanted to follow could without any problem; but with her legs still weak, she considered following the truck but the going would not be easy. If she was in a Pedicab, she could save her energy, watch LinLin, and perhaps use her eyes to talk to him in his final hours.

She heard a young woman beside her, bargaining with the old man: "How much do you charge?"

"Three RMB."

The woman said: "Three, that is too much" In truth three RBM was enough money for one person to live on for half a month; most people would work two or three days to earn that much.

She saw a younger woman moving toward the old man who said: "One RMB?"

The old man said: "Two and a half."

But the young woman still said: "No one RMB! No more than one."

YingLi went over and said: "I will give you two RMB, is that a deal?"

She followed the old man to his Pedicab, but when she saw the Pedicab she began to have second thoughts; the condition of the cab was like the owner, really old.

She was hesitating when a young guy who seemed to know her mind came up to her saying: "Two RMB! My Pedicab is very strong and you will be safe." The old man was not angry he just held his hands together and kept quiet waiting for her to decide.

YingLi checked the young guy over from head to foot; he was tall with a strong body. Even if the Pedicab was easy to overturn, she believed that any Pedicab in his hands would have no problems. YingLi looked at the young guy's Pedicab, and decided quickly, but she felt pity for old man. She was thinking a moment, and then said. "I will give you two RMB and you can look for another costumer is that fair?"

The old man accepted one RMB and left.

The time for the execution was still hours away and it seemed like the young guy knew what she was thinking; he said: "If you trust me, you can come to my house to rest awhile, it is very close by."

YingLi asked him: "Who lives in your house?"

"My grandmother." The young man said smiling.

The house of the young man was really close by and it only took a few minutes to get there.

YingLi went into the room, and found an old lady sitting on the Kang(bed), her hair, teeth and sight had been taken back by god; she just had breath in her shrivelled mouth and chest. But her senses still worked well, when she felt the air change in the room, she asked loudly: "Who is it?" at the same time, she moved over to make room for another person to sit down.

YingLi sat down on the Kang and the young man gave her a dirty pillow that smelled very rank.

He said: "You can relax and sleep, I will wake you up. I have a few years experience, and know that people who spend big money to go the execution ground, have a special relationship. I don't care about politics; I just need to make money."

YingLi was very tired even though she saw the pillow was dirty she was not in a mood to be picky; she fell asleep right way.

Chapter 53

YINGLI FELL ASLEEP REMEMBERING the day before when aunt-Yu and another woman had come to her house to prevent her from leaving.

Aunt-Yu had turned to the skinny lady and said: "This afternoon you will stay here, I will come later. Don't be afraid, the militia is on patrol outside, if any thing goes wrong you just go to the gate screaming, and you will have people here to help you."

Those words had also been for YingLi's benefit.

YingLi felt that she only had the right to cry; though she knew crying wouldn't help anything. But now she really wanted to cry in frustration. She cried, like a headstrong child until her throat was hoarse, and her body only had enough energy left to breathe. Then she slept and had a dream. She dreamt that she used a knife and killed the skinny lady; the mummy had fallen down on the floor, and blood had started gushing out. YingLi was afraid to wake up, but she needed to pee, and she had gone to the bathroom in the corner of the yard. The skinny lady who had been sitting on the doorsill, now had to get up, she followed YingLi to the bathroom and watched her crouch before she turned her face to the side.

Autumn was nearing its end, the wind was getting cold and it felt more like winter. YingLi was shivering when she finished and when she went back into the house she asked respectfully: "Aunt-Wang, would you like to come in?"

"I'm fine here," The skinny woman answered. She looked a little nervous, because she knew a little of YingLi's history: she had seduced a revolutionary soldier...who knows what else she might come up with?

YingLi really was trying to come up with a plan.

YingLi sat on the Kang, watching the skinny woman sitting in the doorway, and scheming how to make her escape. She must keep the skinny woman quiet so no one outside will know what is happening or she would not be able to get away. However, how to keep her quiet, use tape to seal her mouth shut? The skinny little woman's beady eyes were continually following YingLi, as she sat on the doorsill blocking the only exit. YingLi didn't have any chance to get behind her; but as her eyes searched for something she saw the rolling pin on the table, and suddenly had a brainstorm. If she could use it to make her dizzy awhile, that would be wonderful; but could she make her dizzy with one blow? Last year, she was with LinLin when he hit a rabbit trying to kill it, he had to hit it many times before he succeeded. The key to the problem was he didn't know how hard to hit. She had no idea how hard she would need to hit this woman, just to knock her out or make her dizzy, if she hit her too hard the outcome would be too ghastly to contemplate.

Then she had received a telegraph from her mother that made her even more confused; her mama did not seem to know that LinLin was to be killed. Had the local government deviated from central government control? Thinking about so many questions given her a headache. She went to the drawer to find aspirin, and there she got the inspiration for her plan.

Having a plan at last she began to feel excited.

YingLi wanted to try anything to get outside and she thought that after dark would be the best time. She started cooking, washed the rice, put it in a pot, and covered it. When she saw she needed more wood for the fire, she said: "Aunt-Wang, I need to get wood for the fire, it's in the back yard."

"I will go with you."

While they were still in the back yard YingLi said: "I need to get some vegetables too."

"Let's go." The skinny lady was getting impatient. At the door to the cellar, YingLi opened it up and started to go down, the skinny woman grabbed her arm and pulled her back.

"I will go first." she said, she had good reason to be vigilant, who didn't know about tunnels? During the Japanese occupation many tunnels had been dug, some just to hide in and some to make an escape through. If YingLi escaped through a tunnel, she would be held responsible. Half way down the ladder, she called to YingLi: "You come now." She now had to be very careful that YingLi didn't try to run.

It was a very good cellar for that time; it had an electric light, walls built with brick, and wood shelves, the upper shelves for the cabbage were empty, but on the ground there were some potatoes and radishes. There was plenty of room for two people, and no sign of a tunnel.

They had just got back in the house when aunt Yu came to relieve the skinny woman. Dinner was soon ready, and YingLi called aunt-Yu to eat with her. Aunt-Yu said she had eaten at home.

"You have a big heart, that it is nice." Aunt-Yu said.

"What else can I do, I have to eat for my child." YingLi replied.

"You are right, how many months is the child?"

"Six months and ten days."

"Oh." Aunt Yu said taking a deep breath, and continued, "I know you are sad, you can cry and curse anyone or anything you want, you just can't go out. That is an order from a superior leader. In this room, I can decide what goes on. If you say bad things I will not report you to the authorities. Don't hide your emotions; every one has a heart."

"Aunt Yu, my tears have run dry, my head is numb."

"I believe that, during my many years I have experienced many different emotions; the greatest emotions were when people died. With all family members I believe that it is the same."

"Aunt Yu, it will be better if we have a talk; that might relieve my anxiety."

"Talk, talk, Ok today I will talk with you." AuntYu stood up to go to the kitchen.

YingLi asked: "What are you looking for?"

"The water dipper."

"Are you thirsty?"

"My dinner was too salty."

YingLi said: "Drinking cold water in the autumn can cause diarrhoea, especially if you are a little fat. The internal heat is strong, when it meets cold things it can make you sick." YingLi went to the kitchen and added some wood to the fire in the stove.

"You have a good heart, you are just unlucky."

"Aunt-Yu, I will make tea for you. What kind tea would you like, green or black?"

"It doesn't matter, either one."

"I will make you the black one, in the beginning it tastes a little bit bitter, later it tastes better and better." As soon as aunt-Yu tasted the tea she spit it out saying: "It is very bitter."

Aunt-Yu had to drink it, and YingLi started thinking. She had already put the sleeping pills in the tea. She felt guilty about it, but she had to go; LinLin was waiting for her. Three sleeping pills should just keep her quiet, and make her sleep. Later, even if a higher leader inquired about what happened and discovers that she was tricked, it wouldn't cause a big problem for her.

"Can I put some sugar in it for you?" At the mention of sugar aunt-Yu became very excited. During her lifetime she had always loved sugar, but sugar had always been in very limited supply. During those years, only a woman who was going to give birth could have a pound of sugar. She had given birth four times, those four pounds of sugar had given her a sweet tooth and then there was no more.

"I love sugar." she said.

YingLi added sugar to the tea; aunt Yu drank it, and asked for more. They talked and soon aunt Yu was nodding off to sleep; and she slept like a pig until the next morning.

YingLi learned later that when the skinny lady came to relieve her in the morning she called people who took Aunt-Yu to the hospital and had her stomach pumped out. Aunt Yu knew what had happened, but made no complaint, she just said she had taken the wrong medication at her own home.

Perhaps that way she thought she would be excused for her lack of vigilance or perhaps it was for YingLi's benefit, no one knows.

Anyway, YingLi had gone out in the dark to the train station. She didn't want to wait for the passenger train in the morning, and she convinced the train controller, to let her board a freight train that was going toward the provincial capital. She arrived in the capital at midnight and that is why she was in the waiting room so long.

Chapter 54

IN THE SAME CITY but on the opposite side, YongHong's nerves were being stretched. When word of LinLin's impending execution reached her ears she flew into a flurry of action right away. At the time, the director of the Women's Federation of the province was biting her buttocks, and giving her a hard time. Everything depended on her daring. Though she could not move the Rocky Mountains to China, she would dare to go through the sky to the moon or go in the sea to find a turtle. She was a woman with male hormones and when aroused she reacted like a man; she wanted to do men's things and have a man's daring. In the heavy wave and strong wind of the revolution, she had begun to realise that she had made a mistake not sending the letter for Lin. She did not wait to ask her leader, she started to write a report to acknowledge a mistake to show who had to be alerted as soon as possible. But on the paper, she only had written: "Report to acknowledge a fault." she had run into a mental block and didn't know what to write. She felt amazed; usually her writing talents were excellent. She could speak or write an article, with no shortage of words criticizing someone else but was at a loss trying to criticize her self. To write about her self required very careful thinking, she didn't want to cause trouble for herself.

Really having no idea about how to go about it, she picked up the phone from the table and dialled a number; when she heard some one answer she said: "Hi." in a voice that sounded like an order. "Take time to come."

"Do you miss me?" A man, on the phone asked laughing.

"WenJun, this is proper business."

"Missing me is proper business too; the ancient's said food and sex had personality." WenJun said.

YongHong paused for a moment then said: "I have a problem." Then she was brief about what had happened.

"Are you nervous? Does it involve you?"

"No, No, just come as I asked." YongHong said simply: "I need you to come and help me write a report of acknowledging a fault."

WenJun thought he had heard wrong and asked YongHong to repeat what she said again; then he said hesitatingly: "I thought you were a lot better writer than me."

YongHong choked, and said: "Yes. Your right! But, the knife can't peel its own hilt."

"That I believe! You are just used to criticizing everybody else..."

"WenJun shut your dog's mouth."

WenJun was silent and the phone was got quiet then YongHong asked: "When are you coming?"

"In the evening of course."

"This evening!"

"Yes, did you see your second brother stand up to say hello to you?" Second brother in WenJun's language was his penis.

YongHong laughed and said: "That is your second brother."

Chapter 55

LuDongChun had gone to Beijing many times while she held her leadership position. The leader of a city at the county level rank was thirteen degrees. In the system of the official ranks in China, level thirteen was senior cadre. As a senior cadre she had travelled to Beijing many times, and always had a special car to pick her up, someone to register a room for her in a hotel, and a driver. This time she was travelling with the common people and in Beijing there would be no one to help her.

The direct express train was crowded with so many people that the carriage was like being in a sardine can. LuDongChun had to stand for ten hours then finally got a hard seat at midnight. She was very happy to get a seat and planned to sleep awhile so that when she arrived in Beijing the next day, she could go directly to the government office. She sat down and fell asleep almost immediately. It seemed like she had just had a little nap when she was woke up itching; she felt her legs and realised that she was being bitten by bedbugs, she reached under her seat and brushed a lot of bedbugs off onto the floor. Oh, my god. She cursed to herself, but the urge to sleep had left her. She looked across at the guy sitting opposite to her who was killing bedbugs in his fingers; and giggling foolishly. She smelled something stinking like blood, then saw his hand was black and red. LuDongChun was concerned about his hand, there was no water on the train; how could he clean his hands? Minutes later she discovered that her concern was unnecessary; the man used his finger to dig out his nostrils, later he took out a corn pancake and started eating. LuDongChun turned her face toward the window. The bedbugs disappeared with first light; the train was averaging 85 miles per hour and the sound of the wheels on the rails, and carriage swaying lightly, made her dream of other places.

Chapter 56

ARRIVING IN BEIJING, SHE was repeatedly making inquiries, until finally she was standing outside of ZhongNanHai (the place where the national leader's lived). As she expected lots of people could give her directions. ZhongNanHai was familiar because it was the government centre, it is where the CCP and State Council of China offices were located, the political heart of China, so almost anyone could provide directions. It had been built during the dynasty of Liao Song, more than 700 years earlier. History of the palace buildings attested to the longevity of the country of the People's Republic of China. The brave army march had ended here, the national anthem, and the Five-Starred Red Flag had come into being here. Since that moment in time the words issued from ZhongNanHai, had been heeded by all of China.

To the worldview... it looked strange surrounded by a red wall from XiDan of Beijing to the Tianaman gate tower. Hundreds of metres long and 6 meters high, the red wall had concealed the emperor's home and gardens in the Forbidden City since 1406. The Forbidden City entered through the Tianaman Gate; the "Gate of Heavenly Peace" contained over a hundred acres of ancient gardens and the Emperor's Palace complex. The Forbidden City is believed to be the oldest such site still in use in the world and is renowned for its mysterious beauty. The treasury of China through five dynasties had spared no expense in the development of the Forbidden City. The story going around was that the scenic gardens developed through Liao, Jin, Yuan, Ming, and Qing dynasties, collected Mountain, Sea, Island, Bridge, Pavilion, corridor, veranda, pavilion, and Imperial Palace into one garden, making it a human fairyland on earth. But common Chinese had only seen the strong red wall, green trees and birds that flitted from the tree branches above the wall.

The main gate of ZhongNanHai is called the: 'YingHua gate', and faces ChangAn Street; beside the gate a guard stands duty and a red flag with five starts floats in the sky above. Here the attitude of the people is affable, their words serve like sweet lipstick making their mouths glossy and smooth; they gave LuDongChun directions and a rolled map too. An arrow on the map showed the few turns she would need to make; LuDongChun carried the map most of the day before she found the office of appeal.

The office of appeal looked like a Mountain confronted with a sea of people. LuDongChun was the last in a long line of people that appeared to be at least several hundred and wondered how long she would have to wait. She tried to ask the man in front of her: "Hello sir, are you here to appeal too?"

"Who would come here for nothing?" The man sounded angry and very vulgar, he was wearing a cotton-padded jacket that was dirty and the cotton was hanging out in places. He looked like he was seventy years old, and his face was the colour of the earth, covered with wrinkles resembling a peeling stick of hickory. The only bright spot on his body was the Badge of a national leader, the size of an apple, sparkling golden on his chest.

"Can I ask what kind case you have?" LuDongChun asked kindly.

"Me? my son was a school teacher who was beaten to death." The old man spoke in an unfamiliar dialect.

LuDongChun soliloquized. "If he is dead already that is not a rush case."

The old man replied angrily: "What did you say?"

LuDongChun waved her hand to signify that she was just talking to herself. Then she moved up the line asking other people. When she started to ask a man she was surprised: "Are you?"

The man was surprised too, he held her hand for a long time shaking it like he would never let go, and then he said: "Oh, sister Lu, is it really you? How are you?"

They had been comrades during the Anti-Japanese War. After the National liberation, they had gone their separate ways and not seen each other in all these years.

He asked: "You didn't get durance?"

LuDongChun smiled bitterly and said: "Yes, I was in and out. What about you?"

"Me? So they didn't put me in; I stayed outside while they checked me but they made me suffer too."

The man had a bitter smile, then he asked: "What are you here for?"

"A case for my son in law. What about you? There are many people here, when we will see an officer?"

"You just have to be patient."

"Patient?" LuDongChun felt like cold air had entered her chest, she couldn't be patient. Lin's life was under the knife now; she must do something as soon as possible. She asked: "Do you have any good ideas of how I can present my case immediately? I don't have much time."

"Everyone here is in a rush to resolve a pressing problem." he said.

LuDongChun didn't believe him, and wanted to go to the front of the line to ask; he took hold of her sleeve and said: "Trust me, I'm an appeal professional."

LuDongChun turned her head thinking to herself, do appeals really have professionals too?

"Didn't you hear me?" he faced her and said: "Today I'm so lucky to meet you, you must speak for me so that I can receive justice. They say I joined the army of the KMT. I was with you in the peoples army since I was fifteen years old, fighting the Japanese until the national liberation. When did I have time to join the army of KMT?

Their fucking story is ridiculous, they made the story up to punish me; I was so depressed I tried to commit suicide."

LuDongChun had been his leader from the time he joined the revolutionary army, he was from the countryside, without education, but was a bold fighter bearing hardships and suffering, he was a good soldier. She asked: "Who said you joined the KMT army?"

"Those fucking sons of bitches...the Red guards." He was going on like a radio, the words spilled out without stopping.

Several times LuDongChun asked: "Can I say something first?"

He said: "You need to listen first."

She really tried hard to listen patiently to him, then stopped him and said: "You can believe me, I will try my best to help you, but right now I have something one thousand times more important. How about let's do this, I will give you my home address, and you can contact me later. Oh, what is you name?"

"My name is TianGen. Ha, ha, we slept together, have you forgotten?"

That was thirty years ago, she was man then and she had many companions; she just remembered their faces and personalities, those didn't change. She gave him her information then asked some other questions. "Can't we do anything except stand in line?" she asked.

"There is no other choice." he said.

"With so many people in front of me, how many years will I be waiting?." she asked.

"In here they work 24/7," he said, and then his eyes became excited. "Look, look, they are coming to pick up appeal letters again, this truck comes every day and loads up"

LuDongChun was concerned, my god, with so many letters the officers reading them will take years. She looked at TianGen and said: "Please tell me, do you have any idea how to go in directly?"

"No, who is not in a rush? Who wants to stay here? Mother fucker, we have the sun burning us, then rain comes making us feel like a chicken in soup, and at night it is cold..." LuDongChun interrupted his words.

"Night time too?"

"I just told you, have you forgotten, here they work 24/7, of course we are in line all night."

LuDongChun fixed her gaze on the truck, and an idea came to her. She said: "I will go and have a look."

TianGen's voice followed her: "Hold on, you need a number."

She didn't hear him, and she didn't know that the people in the line needed a number. The number was to protect the people who came early and schedule them first. When she got back again, there were ten more people in front of her.

She went to the side of the truck, to get a clear view. Lots of documents, the bags inside the truck were all numbered 1, 2, 3... she tried to get closer but a guard came to stop her. Then she focused her vision toward the window of appeal, there was a narrow passage way with an iron gate. She moved closer wanting to get some information, but, an angry voice from behind her said: "Get in the line up, line up, don't try sneaking in."

She explained: "I'm not trying to sneak in; I just want to ask a question."

"You need to line up for that too." The voice soon became many voices, and no one could afford to incur public wrath. She turned back from the passage way and seeing a guard she asked: "Sir, can I ask you a question?"

"Yes, go ahead" the guard very replied kindly.

"Do appeals all have to go in this line up?"

"Yes."

"No special cases?"

"No."

"But, the case is very special, it is very important and an emergency."

"Sorry, I can't help you." he answered firmly.

"Can you ask for me? My case is very rushed."

"My job is only to maintain order." he said shaking his head.

"Can't you just go to the window and ask for me?"

"No, I'm sorry, I can't do that."

LuDongChun went back in the line where she had been before. TianGen had held a space for her when she got back she just stood there thinking it was not necessary go to the end of the line again.

She said thanks, but he did not need any thanks, he just wanted her to give proof of his history. Since he had trouble, he had tried to find many people including her, he had sent mail to her, but received no answer back. He knew that everyone was like a clay idol fording a river; they needed to protect themselves. He had never thought she might show up here, he thought probably she had become one of the common people.

Yes, he thought he was right; the appeal system of China was for the common people to prevent unnecessary bureaucracy, and to correct false and wrong cases for the stability of society. The appeal system was set up to encourage people to write letters to the government, and to make suggestions and express different views. This system was set up in 1949. Letters and visits from the masses were a very important function of the national system for legitimacy.

The officer who was a big man showed up again to give people a number. LuDongChun took the chance to ask: "Sir, can I ask…"

"Go ahead." the big man said.

"My case is very rushed. Can I…"

He stopped her and said: "Who isn't in a rush? Can you find anyone here not in a rush?"

"I am from another city."

"These people are all are from other cities."

"My case involves a person's life."

"That has to go through the line up too. Every one who comes here has to wait in line."

"Sir…"

The big man stood beside her looking down on her and asked: "Do you want a number or not?"

"Can I go in without a number?"

The big man laughed coldly, then he said: "You ask them." he pointed to the people waiting to appeal: "If they all say yes you can go in."

LuDongChun submitted to the humiliation in a soft voice: "My family has a person accused of anti-revolution, he will be killed at any time, can you help me to make a special appeal?"

"Do you want a number or not?"

LuDongChun had no choice; after she received the number she lowered her head in deep thought. TianGen said: "That idea doesn't work here everybody knows that; many people have had better stories than yours, they have heard them all."

She said quite disappointed: "It was not a tricky idea, it is true."

TianGen shrugged his shoulders and said: "No choice, just wait."

LuDongChun took a deep breath and said: "Just wait, yes, if I don't have any other choice, I will wait but if the procedure takes too long he could be dead." She had left home two days ago, at this speed, she will still be waiting for a few days to submit the letter to the appeals office; then for an officer to give her an answer would take a few more days...my god. If there is enough time it is fine. If waiting was the only way she could help Lin she would be patient and wait.

TianGen passed LuDongChun an old news paper for her to put on the floor to sit on. She remembered he said he had been here many times so she asked him: "Hey, how long did it take for your appeals?"

"Two years."

"I had to submit the document and then go back home and wait." She tried to recall the procedure that she knew from Long Shan city; they had the same office set up.

"Go back after awhile, and if there was no answer, then come back again..." He was interrupted by a woman's voice. Looking in the direction of the voice they saw a protesting woman being forced by two men into a car, then it left.

"What happened?" She was dumbfounded at what she had seen. And she saw the woman's face when she tried to get close, her eyes showed her concern as the woman was forced into the car.

TianGen smiled and said: "That is a persistent person; someone who just keeps coming back." He explained to LuDongChun: "To handle these kind of people the government has a solution; there is a factory not far from here, they put them to work and when their thinking gets better they let them go out again..."

"What is a persistent person?"

"People who do not agree with the verdict for their case; when there is no appeal left and that are still not satisfied and keep returning again and again..."

The sky was starting to get dark rather quickly. LuDongChun felt hungry, and asked TianGen where she could get something to eat. He surprised her when he said:

"We don't need to concern ourselves about eating, there is a little pavilion nearby; just past it, there is a bungalow where we can eat for free."

"Free?"

"Yes. It is not great food, just corn pancakes and a bowl of soup, but it is better than nothing."

LuDongChun didn't go there, instead she went to a little restaurant and had soft tofu and deep-fried twisted dough sticks; with garlic juice and tofu that left her breath smelling like a ruminating cow.

Autumn in Beijing was hot days and cold nights, and the little heat energy from the food in the restaurant was soon lost in the cold wind. She saw other people like her stand up and shake their body to relieve the cold, while other people lay or sat on the floor and slept. She thought to herself that the people who slept must be professional appealers like TianGen.

Listening to TianGen, LuDongChun knew she would be in line just to submit her letter, and then she would need to stand in line again to get an answer. There were different answers possible with each individual case; if it was a small case the national office might give power to a local office for solution, or maybe require a consultation for a second opinion. ...the best answer to look for was "matter reported." That meant that the matter was important and serious, and would need the national leader to make a judgment. .

For her the line up for ten hours more to submit the documents and waiting another seven days to get an answer was reasonable. She finally got the reply she hoped for. "Matter reported."

Then she sent her daughter a telegraph saying: "Everything is fine." the same night she got on the train to return home.

Chapter 57

WENJUN'S WIFE MING HAD sensed that something was wrong ever since her marriage to army cadre WenJun. She was a clever woman, and knew very well the differences between men's, and women's relationships.

It was perfectly clear to her that WenJun did not love her because her girlfriends all complained about their husbands wanting sex every day. One girlfriend said that on her wedding night, her husband had made love to her five times. My god! ... had sex five times in one night? The night they were married, WenJun spread her legs and was finished very quickly. The first time, she thought maybe it was because he had no experience, but later he was still like that.

In reality she knew that he really didn't like her.

His sex with her was not hot and not cold either. They made love twice a week, always on Wednesday and Saturday. If this Wednesday or Saturday her period were coming, he would delay until the next scheduled time...

She had guessed that WenJun loved another woman, because he made love with her with his eyes closed and sometimes called another name almost inaudibly in his throat. When she asked who he was calling he suddenly stopped, but even in this situation Ming still continued to show love, and she always took the initiative.

Ming knew that she was not a good match for him; and that if she was not the daughter of the chief of staff of provincial military region, he would not have married her.

Ming was a woman of foresight and sagacity; never ever in the anger of a moment would she lose her good man. In the meantime, she has known man needs what kind demanding. When it was time to make love, she always washed her body clean, and made sure the smell of soap was fragrant in the bedroom; then she would change into bright coloured underwear and lie down on the bed like a pet waiting for its master. When he came to bed, she would jump up to help him take off his clothes, massage his back and legs, and then wait like a vagabond hoping he would make love to her. She used her soft small hand moving to his under belly, in the between his legs to touch, and feel the male organ to get it excited so it would stand up to say hello to her; when her body like land in a drought received a few drops of rain, it made her happy but also thirsty for more.

Ming knew men had sex and romance outside the home and that had been common knowledge from ancient times to the present: Chinese men, who held high positions, almost all had several wives. After the liberation, women had received equal rights and their positions in all areas were much improved; polygamy had been abolished and women had gained the right to marry who they chose.

Remnants of the feudal ways were unavoidable and lingered in the minds of men. For the woman or first wife, it was very important to be able to discern her husband's heart. How a woman dealt with a husband who had extramarital relations could end in divorce that would save a little only to lose a lot. Ming knew if she got a divorce she would not be able to find such a handsome husband again. Ming was well prepared to deal with his disinterest. She acted like an innocent young wife with him and flirted in bed; she believed that even if one person was cold but the other one was hot they still could have sex. From the first day she was married she knew what it meant to be a woman, and she tried to use women's seductive powers to lure him, as Eve had lured Adam.

Even though she hated him for going too fast every time, she never showed it; she still flirted, still talked to him, and let him know much she enjoyed having sex with him. When WenJun entered her body, she always groaned on time, and some times made sounds like a cat or dog with a soft voice. She tried very hard to be a dutiful wife, and with WenJun they looked like a good couple on the surface; they had never had a fight, an argument, or an angry face.

But, recently she had been thinking about their relationship a lot, he doesn't even touch her anymore; what does that mean? Hundreds of women would have the same answer; he must have another woman. If a man had another lover then later one of two things would happen; one is divorce the other is to live with it for the benefits of the marriage. She analysed the situation very carefully, and believed that there was a strong possibility that WenJun would divorce her because she has still not become pregnant.

She went to the hospital to check, and both of her oviducts were blocked, and she had been treated by a doctor but without success. Any woman, who is unable to give birth, loses control of her man. For the time being her father can handle WenJun for a while, but later on when her father retired WenJun would divorce her for this reason.

The extremely intermittent sex had been bothering her for a long time already; now with no sex she was even more nervous and concerned. Ming knew that she would have to become an even more magnanimous woman if she hoped to keep her husband. How magnanimous, and how could she gain control over her husband? She needed some good ideas, and a plan.

Chapter 58

ON THE LAST DAY of his life, LinLin was recalling the most important people in his life.

His father's name was Rong who had been born into a family of Traditional Chinese Medical practitioners. His ancestors had been doctors of the king until Rong. Because of the chaos and war, Rong left Beijing and moved the northern city of FengTian, where he met a person who helped him to find a place to stay. There, he lived for a few years, following in the footsteps of his family practicing medicine, his reputation grew greatly; he was praised by the people for his supernatural medicine. Rong married the daughter of a local peddler, planning to spend the rest of his life in FengTian.

But at that time a warlord- a regimental commander of the Northeastern army had a second wife who was very sick; he only trusted western doctors but they had been unable to help her. He had ordered her a coffin and it was ready just waiting for her to finish her last breath. Someone recommended Rong to him. The army officer loved his second wife very much, and was willing to do anything he just wanted her to live. Rong went there, and checked her belly and vagina. The warlord saw Rong touch his wife's lover belly, then from her belly go into her vagina...then he turned his face to the side. Rong used a needle to puncture her belly three times and black blood flowed out. After three days the woman was recovering slowly; the warlord was so delighted he kept Rong there to continue treating her, and he treated Rong like a distinguished guest. When the woman had recovered and Rong was leaving, the warlord gave him 600 RMB. At that time 600 RMB was a small fortune, and Rong was making plans as he travelled how he would use the money to develop a business, and make his family rich.

Half way home, two soldiers sent by the warlord caught up to Rong, and cut off his right hand; they told him that it was the warlord's order, because he had touched his lover, and that he must disappear forever.

Rong took his wife and left that night with his bleeding wrist. He decided to go to a forestry centre close to the Soviet border. Rong knew a man there named Wei who had come from Shandong province to live in the Forestry town; he was a logging labour contractor with a bold and unconstrained disposition. Wei gave aid to Rong, to help him open a small doctor's office; though the business was small, it provided a living. The following year, both Rong's wife and Wei's wife became pregnant. Following an old custom, they pointed to their belly and pledged an engagement for their children to marry, if they give birth to a boy and a girl.

Life does not always treat people fair. Rong's wife died soon after her son LinLin was born.

At almost the same time Wei's wife gave birth to a girl, that they named Lian. Lian and LinLin were both nursed by the same woman's milk and grew up like twins.

Between Rong and Wei many things happened that LinLin did not know about because he was in another city studying; and because his father Rong had tried to hide things from him and let his heart stay pure.

Rong's secret was like this:

Wei had become impotent, and was concerned that his wife who he had purchased from a brothel would leave him when he could no longer satisfy her sexually. Wei had begged Rong to share his wife with him, to keep her satisfied. In the past it had been a common practice with poor people who couldn't afford to support a wife themselves. Rong didn't like the idea and refused many times, but Wei persisted and applied pressure that finally forced him to accept. At night, Rong drank medicine to prevent pregnancy, and then through the heavy snow made his way to Wei's house. In the quiet mountain forest, one woman and two men's love story began.

Wei never had to give up his wife with Rong helping him out. They had a schedule, Wei slept with her on odd numbered days and Rong slept with her on even numbered days. Two men with one woman in the same room, one slept on the south Kang, the other slept on the north Kang.

Rong wanted to leave, but his duty made him unable to make up his mind; he talked to Wei's wife about taking her and the children and leaving. She knew Wei very well, and that he had another side that was fierce and malicious. She knew that if they made him angry, they could both die...so the relationship of the threesome continued until after the liberation; when the new government cadre told them one had to leave, and that the other two could stay together.

That evening they sat around the table drinking, Wei's wife now with government support had showed clearly she wanted to go with Rong.

Wei had agreed and said: "Very good, I will help you guys." They decided that tomorrow, they would separate.

That night, they both drank a lot.

Wei was crying and laughing, he knew very well that if they separated, he would not have another woman in this life. Later that night, when Rong went out doors to pee he walked into a bear trap. Wei's wife and daughter both heard Rong's voice calling from outside, and wanted to go out and check, but found the door was locked.

Afterwards, Wei told his wife: "You are my woman; you can't be another man's woman ever again."

LinLin only knew that his father had died, and that Wei had given his father an elaborate funeral with great ceremony. Wei had given LinLin a ceremonious wedding too.

Therefore, Lian had been the second most important person in his life.

Lian loved LinLin very much, and she knew her family owed LinLin his father's life. Wei's wife and Lian both wanted Lian's love life to be dedicated to LinLin in compensation. Lian loved LinLin like a mother with her own baby, and wanted him to have a healthy body and mind. Lian was a member of CCP, and hoped that LinLin would become political like her, when she discovered that LinLin thought differently about the CCP her big wish was to get him help. She reported his words to the Party; the year was 1957 and China had launched an anti-rightist campaign. LinLin lost his job and was in jail three years.

Afterwards, LinLin divorced her.

YingLi had entered his life twelve years later, and they had fallen in love without even trying. When he first met her she was pregnant; when he found out that she had used her body for an exchange he had no respect for her; but because she was the daughter of LuDongChun he wanted to help her. Later when he learned the whole story he realised that he had jumped to a conclusion prematurely. Her special innermost feelings of loyalty and filial piety caused him to have insomnia. He was very happy to give his blood to her for a transfusion when she was suffering badly from an induced abortion that was drying out her blood vessels.

This act by a mature man to a little woman showed his admiration. In a world with a lack of kindness and friendship and full of common customs and prejudice, that a little girl, a weak little woman, would fight for justice, to stand up and struggle... that surprised him. Even more important later when he had an accident and was stuck in the hospital, she had used her hand like a Bodhisattva to bring him back from death's door to life. But, he still did not understand her really until after they were married. On their marriage night he was kissing her, and touching her lovingly and she started shaking suddenly. He asked: "Are you Ok?"

She said: "I'm fine." Then she took off her underwear by herself, and opened her legs to him in, but he couldn't enter, she was too nervous and rigid. She cried and said: "I love you, I love you."

He said: "I love you too, I love you too." He lay down beside her, and caressed her soft body, inch by inch, her skin was young, smooth and shining, the burning fire of love made her tremble in anticipation. However he was unable to enter her because she was so tense. After several attempts he asked her if she felt sore. "No." she said, but her face showed that she must be hurting. She lied because she loved him, and wanted to give him her all. They failed in their first and second attempts, and later many times. His medical knowledge led him to know they would find the solution to her problem was in her mind. He was patient with her and treated her lovingly. But never asked her about her experience with LiuJiahuai, and in time they enjoyed a healthy and rewarding sex life.

"Oh! YingLi! My dear, my heart, my lover...where are you? Where are you? During the last day of my life how much, how much, I want to see you! One more time; one last time...

Chapter 59

WHEN CROWS FLY LOW and disorderly, screaming like they have microphones, circling their prey, their enemy is near by. People's heads were straining, and their hair was blowing in the autumn wind like it wanted to fly to the sky. The sun was hiding in the clouds; was it afraid to show its face, or just angry? Who knew?

YingLi saw the crimes trucks slowly coming; each truck had three criminals on it, and LinLin was on the first one with his hands tied behind his back, and a sign on his chest with his name with a red big x on it.

The street was overcrowded.

This was an exceptionally grand occasion. Beside and following behind the trucks, were many straining necks and faces. They were very excited about their victory, and the shouted slogans came and went.

YingLi could not catch LinLin's attention. People blocking the way sometimes stopped the young Pedicab driver. YingLi's eyes were riveted on LinLin. How badly she wanted LinLin to see her, to be able to communicate her feelings, deeply and warmly. She wanted him to see her, to know that she was with him; it was their last chance to communicate in this life and she wanted to make a date to go hand in hand shoulder to shoulder to the new world with him.

The road to the execution ground was becoming narrower. YingLi had escaped from her home only after scheming and drugging aunt-Yu; she just wanted to finish her incantation of love: "We can't be born on the same day in the same month and the same year, but we can seek to die on the same day in the same month and the same year." During this life their love had lasted only a very short period; he had been her only lover, teacher and helpful friend, she had no regrets. For now she just wants him to know that she came and that she will go with him, she wants him to wait for her at the bridge of NaiHe: (the bridge to hell.)

She had been following him, and becoming very worried.

LinLin was thinking about her too; in the final minutes of this life, LinLin was concerned about her and that she would give birth to their child. When he received notice that he would die, he wanted to make out a last will to them, but he had torn up many papers and still couldn't write one word. Yes, he had lots to say, but didn't know how to say it, and finally he just drew a picture of a big tree that had been cut down and a little tree growing from it's roots, a woman standing beside it was watering it...posterity would continue, that was the sole extent of life.

On the way to the execution ground, he sighed a great deal with deep emotional feelings, and suddenly wanted to express endless love to his wife and child. Now how he wished he had a pen to write a letter to YingLi, he would write using his blood for ink until the last drop was gone.

YingLi sitting in the Pedicab raised her head and face to gaze at LinLin. The mood of the masses surrounding the truck was filled with indignation, the shouts of the announcer and the masses' slogans were rising one after another, deafening. LinLin's face was very quiet, like a baby sleeping during a lullaby. YingLi called out to him in her heart and mind, LinLin! You will see me. I'm coming. Your wife and child are coming...

She wanted him to know she was there. How could she let him know? The time was passing by: 30 minutes... 31, 32, 33...She was almost hopeless.

Beside her, the slogans were beginning again; time was moving so fast, and then she had an idea.

"Long live the proletariat dictatorships." During the announcer's intermission, YingLi spent all her bodily strength to hooray, and had the masses following her. "Long live the proletariat dictatorships."

She continued to hooray. "Overthrow the anti-revolution person LinLin!"

YingLi was the top soprano in her school, and understood how to use abdominal breathing to achieve the result of sympathetic response. Her voice was special to LinLin already; it would make a strong magnetic field, to draw him to her.

Her voice jolted him like he had been shocked with electricity; his eyes that had looked dead came back to life again. In the mass of people there were so many faces around the truck, moving through his sight, he felt his vision had flashed, he closed his eyes. He knew today that she would not be allowed to come and suspected that his sense of hearing had gone out of order.

YingLi saw the life radiate from LinLin's eyes, then fade as his facial expression showed disappointment.

She cheered again and held her arm high a long time. But, her wish still didn't come to pass. Why? Why doesn't he see me? She was crying; tears dropped from her nose onto her face and mouth, and clouded her sight. She used her hand to clear the tears, and then found that her hand was dirty, and then she realized the truth suddenly.

In his mind she was quite beautiful, she is an angel; with such dishevelled hair and a dirty face, of course he can't recognize her. She used her fingers to comb her hair and used saliva to clean her face;; when she felt clean she asked the Pedicab driver: "Is my face clean now?"

The young guy looked at her clean face and was surprised that she was so beautiful, and said: "Yes, it is clean and beautiful now."

YingLi tried again with a clean face and used another key to open LinLin's memory.

"LinYing!" She hurrahed again.

LinYing was to be their child's' name. When YingLi got pregnant, LinLin could not wait to name the child and he thought of a name for the baby, he chose a part of both of their name's resulting in: LinYing.

The familiar voice and the chosen names inspired, and became the key to opening LinLin's locked memory. His heart started beating stronger, his nerves started convulsing, his larynx warmed, his eyes became wet...his vision took wing to find the voice. His eyes found hers. Ah! It seemed like a spring wind blowing on his heart, and he followed the wind to fly from death in the barren land. He stared at her; in her eyes he saw only a drizzle with spring breeze, no lightning and thunder.

That drizzle, showered into his heart, he seemed to drink a cup of delicious wine, and was drunk. Oh, my little lover, my life, my heart, my honey, my...all. You came. Wonderful! Wonderful!! How much I wanted to see you?! In this life's last minutes, seeing you I will die with my eyes closed. My little lover, you look emaciated... you must not sink into depression for me! You must continue your life...Carry our child...child? Oh, your belly is getting bigger. Let me see, our child will be born the end of this year that is just three months away. Oh, God! Why did you allow such a cruel disaster? Why couldn't you let me see my child before I go? Oh! Destiny, it is destiny? Ah, my life has been plagued by politics, rightist...anti-revolution...such a big joke. If my politics were known I don't give a damn, I have never been interested; then I found you, my little lover, do you understand me? I didn't want to cause trouble; I just wanted to be with you and have a peaceful life...it looks like you understand me, you came. In this world only you understood me. Ah, my love, my heart, and my life...how did you get out? I know would have a guard watching you; you must have done some thing wrong again, what did you do? Did you kill some one or start a fire? I know in your heart it was very important to come, but you need to be concerned about yourself and our child. For the sake of our child, you can't be doing bad things. Please, please...his throat was numb; he could only move his eyes.

YingLi opened her eyes as large as she could and winked very slowly. This golden time is their last, she doesn't want it to pass meaninglessly, but she couldn't talk, and she didn't want to break contact and be separated forever.

Her eyes said: my dear, I came, I came. We had a life, we lived together, and we will die together. How can I tell you without speaking that I want to be together with you in life, and in death. Our love was only for a very short time, but it was ours and no one can substitute for you. I know you love me and our child. You must be praying in your heart to let your wife and child live, and have a good life. But...but...how can I live without you? You were my sky. The sky is falling, there is no sun, no moon, and no stars... what would I live for? I will go with you. I will carry our child and go with you. We will leave together forever. Oh, my dear you have got skinny. The expression in your eyes is melancholy, the corners of your mouth are sagging, your cheeks are hollow...why didn't you shave your moustache before you went? Your moustache, I hated that so much. Do you remember? You always liked to use your moustache to scratch me and make me itchy...joy I struggled against your chest and begged for mercy, saying: I love you; I love you, until you stopped. Oh, you won't hear me say that again, for ever... You can't scratch me again, for ever...Oh, are you leaving to go to hell to scratch and itch me? You are bad, you are bad...

YingLi sitting in the Pedicab used a sign language she created herself to pour out her heart to LinLin.

He had to use his wisdom to guess what she was saying.

He was thinking to himself, are you with me today to say good bye?

She is saying: on this long trip I will be going with you.

Ah! He said in thanksgiving, you were once a wisp of spring breeze in my life that was enough.

He said: you were my life spring season, even too short, but that was enough.

She said firmly, I want you to have every spring season, and summer too.

He said euphemistically. You were a wave in my sea of life.

She said in unreasoning passion. I will become your sea.

He said in happiness. You are a maple leaf in the book of my heart, and will be forever.

They stayed in this special reverie using telepathic thought to communicate and feel, using the electrical waves of the soul, they launched the secret code of their love. The words of hearts beating in unison linked as one. They looked like happy pigeons, flying free in the sky of their hearts.

LinLin saw the smiling face of YingLi, and it dispelled his worries of the last few days; he believed that she would live, and carry their child to birth.

YingLi had her chin raised and her face resting on her shoulder, they had not moved their lips in some time, but hot feelings flowed from one heart to the other. At this moment, human language was redundant, a look, a flying kiss, or a smile served to let them yearn or remember.

Along the way they remained locked in each others sight, and communicated in ways that others were unable to understand. When YingLi lifted her arm to hooray: "LinLin needs to die ten thousand deaths", it was only so she could call her lover's name. When she shouted, her pronunciation was very heavy on 'LinLin' and very light on the other words.

A few times, the crowd had blocked the Pedicab; but the young man had strong hands and feet, he was handling the Pedicab aggressively. Violently like a shark on the sea he had been moving ahead hurting people who were in the way, and screaming at people to get out of the way. This was a time when heaven and earth were turning upside down; it was a revolution and no body thought that his actions were excessive.

The terrain of the execution ground was like a natural stadium with a depression in the middle, surrounding it there was hillock with a few scrubby little trees; and a very high stone mountain, ferocious in appearance, like a strange beast. The convicts had been pushed into the centre of the depression, kneeling on the ground side by side, facing the crowd. Marksman stood ten feet behind the convicts. These soldiers had been chosen carefully by the army for their high political consciousness.

A wall of soldiers and People's militias held the masses back. By convention, when the execution was finished the army and people's militias would withdraw at once; then the revolutionary masses could move in close to view and admire. The masses could

use stones to continue their dictatorship, and smash the dogs'
heads of the convicts.

YingLi stayed in the crowd where she could see LinLin, but
at the time LinLin was not able to see her even though she had
pushed her way through the people to try and get as close to him
as she could.

When the guns roared it would be unnecessary to check the
time, it would be exactly 5 pm Sep, 26, 1969 as posted on the notice.
The roar of the guns exhilarated the crowd, for a moment.

YingLi's heart was as peaceful as water on a calm lake. She
looked like she had been riding on a red carpet to a far off land
where happier times would begin. YingLi looked like she had been
on a long trek and finally reached her destination; or like a little
bird, that had found a branch in a tree, she just wanted to rest, and
didn't care where the nest was.

YingLi had fainted before the guns roared.

When she woke up she discovered that she was in the emergency
room of a hospital, and saw a dirty piece of paper with a message
that said: take care your self.

She guessed that is a young guy had left it.

But now her mind was not thinking about herself.

She unplugged the IV needle from her hand, and asked a nurse
for directions to the execution ground.

Chapter 60

THE APARTMENT BUILDING HAD seven floors and WenJun had rented a room here on the 7th floor for his dates with YongHong. They had just finished writing her letter, turned off the light, and were starting to make love.

YongHong's moods, since had lost her virginity to WenJun were extremely complicated. First of all, as a party member and cadre, she felt that she must not continue the relationship, and from traditional moral standards she was concerned that ZhangYong would lose face if she was found out. A Chinese man who had an unfaithful wife was labelled "green hat", causing him great humiliation, jealousy and shame. She had decided to break off with WenJun but when he phoned begging she was compromised. In this life she had experienced few things that made her compromise even a little; she really was surprised that he had been a special exception. Was it really love, she was not sure.

Since she discovered that she couldn't get a divorce, she had put her heart in a far corner of her emotions, and became a Buddhist nun in her soul. But, WenJun was pulling her into the sewer; ever since her heart had been lured it refused to go back to being peaceful again. She felt special in the time she spent with

WenJun, and inevitably her woman's nature to be jealous some times bothered her.

"How does she make love?' YongHong asked.

WenJun was dripping sweat on her body, and asked: "What, who?" knowing very well her question.

"I know that you are just playing stupid." YongHong said unhappily.

"Really I don't know who are you talking about?"

"How many women have you had?" YongHong yelled at him.

"Oh---," WenJun seem to suddenly understand and said: "You are lot better than her; you are far better than her."

YongHong's face looked like a peach flower blossoming, red lips, red chin, and beautiful eyes. WenJun was kissing her again like she was something delicious and juicy.

"Really?" The answer made her happy again, she felt it was unnecessary to ask, if she was uglier than Ming, WenJun would have left her. This was men.

"But..." WenJun wanted to talk but stopped half way. YongHong has a beautiful face, tall body and soft skin, like a goddess; but there was one thing she did not do well, when he made love to her, she responds like she was made of wood. If she could learn Ming's style and learn to play as a woman, on his chest, pose as spoiled child, make him excited that would be wonderful.

"But...what?" YongHong's voice was getting louder. "What?"

"Will you promise not to get mad if I tell you?" WenJun knew her temper, but he really wanted her to become a better lover too, but he worried that she would get angry.

"Don't mumble, talk."

"Do you swear you will not get mad?"

"I swear, tell me!"

"You...in one way...are a little bit...less than her..."

"Which part is less than her?" YongHong pushed him down.

Then he said: "See? You said you wouldn't get mad, but you did."

"How is she better than me?" YongHong asked sitting up.

YongHong raised her hand slightly toward WenJun's face and said: "You said, when you make love with her you close your eyes, when you open your eyes your desire melts away.

"That is true; if I close my eyes, I can imagine I am feeling you and pretend her voice is your voice it will make me drunk. I feel like I am king of the world. I don't do anything, just have sex."

"What does she do?" YongHong asked sounding disinterested.

"Let me teach you. You say WenJun--, like this." WenJun pinched his nose and sounded like a cat purring, slowly dragged out his name accenting it.

A moment passed in silence and then.

"WenJun," YongHong was irritated, and her voice sounded cold and hard.

"No, not like that; you say it gently and romantically, repeat it again WenJun..." he said in a childish voice.

YongHong said impatiently: "You tell me, do you like me or her?"

"Of course I like you, I love you."

'Really?"

"Yes, really."

"Come here"

"For what?"

"I want you to come here." YongHong said pulling him by the ear drawing him close to her, he had tears from the pain.

He said: "Oh! Oh...take your hand off. You are like a tigress."

"WenJun, tell me the truth; you just want to have two women; am I right? You want be a king, and you lied to me telling me you don't like her and married her because you had no choice. That is just a story, right? If one day, I want you to divorce her and marry me, you will have a reason you can't leave her, right? You are playing with me; you are just playing with my emotions..."

"Stop it, stop it, I just wanted you to be more like a woman." WenJun said.

"Oh! You feel I'm not like a woman?"

"You are like a woman. Oh, no, you are really a woman. I just wanted to teach you to be a more perfect woman, lovelier woman... like a movie star...sexier."

YongHong always prided herself on being better than anyone else, and she couldn't be less than Ming for any reason. After awhile she said: "Teach me how to pose like a lovely woman."

"Forget it, forget it." WenJun touched his ear that was still red and numb.

"I will die soon if I try to teach you."

"I want to practice."

"You want to practice? But, you must promise not to get mad again, don't hurt me again"

"Ok." YongHong said laughing.

"We still start with saying my name, WenJun..."He said.

"WenJun..." She repeated.

"With emotion, sound and emotion mixed together WenJun said. You sound like a judge talking, you need to speak like this... in a soft, seductive voice, like a horny cat. You need to sound like a cat in heat...me...ow...me...ow..."

YongHong was a woman who had joined the revolution and was used to saying I am not afraid of anyone. Words of love didn't come easily to a revolutionary woman and couldn't flow through her mouth with out great effort. She had lost patience with him and said:

"WenJun, go see your ghost; let me tell you something, you wear an army uniform, but in your mind you have a lot of Capitalist class thoughts, you need to be careful, you need to re-mould your ideology."

"Ok, ok, don't get mad, let's go back to bed and make love again."

Just then, someone knocked on the door.

WenJun said: "Who could that be?."

YongHong was surprised to see him rush to put on his uniform, and started making her self ready. She said:

"Maybe it's someone to check the HuKou(ID)."

WenJun said: "You go and open the door, let me hide some where." YongHong turned to look but couldn't see a hiding place, and said: "where?" Looking around she saw a closet in the corner, she pointed and said in a hushed voice: "Hurry up, and get in there."

WenJun had just got in the closet, when he heard a woman's voice; it was his wife Ming.

My god! He wanted to jump out of the window, but this room was on the seventh floor...he would die either way.

Chapter 61

LINLIN'S EX-WIFE LIAN FIRST heard the news of his execution on the radio. She borrowed a newspaper from her team leader to read, and it convinced her that it was her LinLin; the same age, birthday and background all fitted his description.

. His name had been in her thoughts almost every day for twelve years. Oh! My god! She did not know if she felt grief or was glad, her heart was light in a moment; even without me, you still have trouble. She thought she would be free from the past, but she was not. She was crying from her heart, for what? That man had broken her heart, and left her feeling guilty for twelve years. For him, she had given up her political life, her position, and was hiding out here, just so that her son could grow up.

Lian's thoughts often wandered back in time; her mom had been a very beautiful woman who had been freed from a brothel. She was not only beautiful, and had a soft temper, but was also ingenious. Life in the brothel, had left her with a bad habit, she could not, or did not want to spend a night without a man. Lian's father was tall and strong, and no matter how hard he worked all day in the mill, at night he would still make her yell once or twice. His splendid love making was almost all a result of her training, techniques that she had acquired from her patrons in the brothel.

Lian from the time she was very little had known that her father always hit her mom in the night and that her mom liked being hit. If a night passed without yelling and hitting, mom's face would get long. Mom's yelling was like music, it woke her up and sent her back to dreaming again; she grew up with that music. She vaguely remembered when she was five or six years old, her mom had not been laughing for a while. She started laughing again when LinLin's father had moved in with them to live. Then she learned about the things between a man and woman, she knew her mom had a relationship with two men; from her mom she learned that her father had pushed LinLin's father Rong to help keep the family together, and fulfil the duty of husband to her mom.

Mom was wonderful during the daytime, she never hollered, and was industrious and thrifty in running the home. She remembered that she always drew attention from other people to herself because her clothes were always different than the other girls. A piece of ordinary cotton print, in her mom's hands could become new clothes for a baby doll; a roll of coarse wool yarn, in her hand would become a beautiful hat or sweater or...what a woman.

The year after Rong died, her mom had left her father.

LinLin had never suspected that his father had been murdered. Later when Wei was sick, he treated him like his own father. Lian felt that was not fair and tried to tell LinLin the truth. But LinLin stopped her. He had said: "A person who has died can not come back to life again; just try to understand and make an excuse for the person who still lives." If he could be so tolerant why couldn't she? If he had forgiven her, she would have worked like a horse to do everything for him. After twelve years tormented between love and hate Lian had become too consumed to close the book. When this book had seen sunshine it should have delivered her from oppression or persecution. Was it retribution? Was it karma? Would she suffer more? How long; the rest of her life?

NianLin was the son of Lian and LinLin. Lin came from LinLin's name and Nian from his mother's; in Chinese it meant remember.

For as long as NianLin could remember, his mother had never had good clothes to wear, or good food to eat. They would feed a pig to be killed for Chinese New Year, and only keep half or maybe only one kilogram for her self, and her son to eat. Her face was the colour of a vegetable, and her body was very weak, even though she was just over forty, she looked like sixty. No one in this village knew anything about her past life, they just knew that she was the CCP party branch leader's cousin, who brought one son and moved here twelve years ago. She did not like to talk to anyone, and when she walked, she always lowered her head like some thing was wrong.

When NianLin became an adult he thought if his mom had a spouse to live with, it would help.

Their village had a lot of single men, but who could be a match for his mom?

His plan was to ask Crippled Sun, the village leader to help.

Because there were so many single men, and he was the team leader for production, he was also the village matchmaker. The village single men, counting those 25 years of age and up, was over 50 percent of the population.

There were many single men because the village was very poor and isolated; and the people still relied on primitive farming methods so it was very difficult to improve their lives. Most women from the outside didn't want to move in, and the village girls wanted to leave.

Crippled Sun had been in the Korean War, and injured his right leg leaving him disabled for life. He didn't know about politics; he just knew the people needed food to eat, and clothes to wear and the men needed to have a woman.

One day when he was driving the village's tractor out on business, he had met a woman who he brought back unexpectedly. He matched the woman up with the man who was the best farm worker.

After that Crippled Sun often went out looking for women for the village farmer's, the women he brought back were all running away from problems, either floods, droughts, natural disasters, or their husbands. Women who had been brought back, and married a village guy looked happy too. A few single men got married in this way, and only once the woman had left. Crippled Sun had made a rule for those women; if they wanted to leave after giving birth for the farmer, they were free to go.

NianLin's uncle, his mother's cousin, who helped them move here, was the CCP Party branch secretary. His position was higher than Crippled Sun's and he kept an eye on his activities. As the senior CCP leader and unsure of the legality of bringing these women to the village, he kept one eye open and the other one closed. There was no buying and selling involved, just a little cheating. As simple countryside farmers, the national laws seemed very remote.

Every morning before the men went out to work, Crippled Sun always said. "Hey! Hurry up let's go! Get to work; and work hard to earn a wife!"

In the village some men desired Lian, but she had not been interested in any man since she had been divorced and moved to the village.

Chapter 62

THE NIGHT THAT YINGLI woke up and left the hospital a nurse told her the execution ground was nearly and gave her directions. She was walking in the dark and it had just rained and the road was muddy. She walked for almost two hours, and was almost exhausted. As she entered the execution ground she heard the crying, and wailing, and some men who were talking loudly; she knew that it was people removing a corpse, and wanted to avoid them. She went to the far side of the execution ground and stood quietly under a tree waiting for them to leave; then she would find LinLin's body, lie down beside him, take all of her drugs, and snuggle with him forever.

Suddenly, the crying stopped, the black shadows stopped moving and everything was silent for a few moments, a man said nervously.

"Elder sister has fainted. What can we do?"

A man in the dark who seemed to be their leader said: "Hurry up, we will take her to the hospital, we must help the living first."

YingLi thought fast, then she rushed to the side of the woman, and kneeling on the ground, she picked up the woman's right hand, to check her pulse, at the time, a man was at the woman's head lifting her up and ordered the other people to help saying: "Come on, give a hand, and don't delay."

YingLi speaking in a stern voice said: "Put her down!"

There was silence for a few seconds, then the man put the woman back down, and the other people crowded nervously around YingLi. YingLi was not nervous, she had learned from LinLin a good knowledge of medicine and she knew first aid very well.

"Let her lie still." she ordered. "Let her lay flat on her back with her legs up a little bit, not too high, just a little bit. Yes, like that..." YingLi pushed on the woman's philtrum, then she realised her strength did not match her ambitions. She ordered and showed the men how to do it. The men gathered around, one pushed on her philtrum, others applied pressure to points on the hands and feet... YingLi took a deep breath and said:

"Don't worry, she will come around soon."

"What is wrong with her?" A man asked.

YingLi did not answer. She was thinking about her own plan, and hoping that they would leave as soon as possible, but she could not be unconcerned about the woman's life. The woman had come to, and people were supporting her to sit up.

YingLi stood up, and divided the wall of people to get out. But soon the sound of crying followed her and then stopped suddenly, and she heard voices calling: "Ms, Ms, she needs your help again."

She went back and coached the men to repeat the procedure.

"What is this disease?" The same man repeated the same question who asked before.

"She has lost consciousness it is called syncope, it is caused by strong stress, because of frightened sharp pain when a relative dies...it causes the blood vessels to expand, and the heart adjusts blood circulation to reduce the blood pressure; the sudden decrease in blood pressure caused her to faint."

"How can she get relief if that happens again?"

"She needs to remain calm."

A concerned voice asked: "Doctor, do you have any idea how we can make her calm?"

"Let her sleep." YingLi said.

"How?"

"Give her some pills"

"What kind of pills?"

YingLi went back beside the woman; took two little bottles from her pocket, checked the labels, then put one pill in the palm of her hand.

YingLi held the woman's chin up, opened her lips, and put the pill in her mouth, then she stood up and told the people: "She will get well, just don't disturb her, let her sleep as long as possible. When she wakes up again, she will be better."

A low and hoarse voice asked YingLi: "Are you here to pick up a corpse too?"

YingLi did not answer she just wanted to leave; but the voice continued to ask questions. "Are you here by your self?"

YingLi was walking away when the man called out loudly behind her: "Do you have a car? We can help you."

"No! Thank you." she answered and kept moving; she heard the same voice telling the people. "We must help her."

"Ok! Let's do it." Several people said at the same time.

"I said it is not necessary." YingLi said as she stopped walking. Behind her back the shadows stopped moving too.

Another young voice explained to her: "You helped us; we want to help you to return the favour."

"My family is coming. You can go." YingLi lied to them. She really wanted them to leave; a lot of time had been wasted already."

The low hoarse voice said: "Doctor, can we have more pills to give her after we go home?"

YingLi thought they were right. The woman should continue two or three days on sedatives, she pulled out both the bottles of pills to check which one contained the sleeping pills; but someone snatched the bottles from her hand. It happened so fast in the dark that YingLi was shocked at this sudden action. In front of her there were several big men, she didn't know which one had snatched the pills.

"Go point to the one you want. Let's go. Which one is it?"

YingLi had no choice but to go with them. She bent over and looked at the six corpses but did not find LinLin.

"No hurry, just look at them one by one." The low and hoarse voice said.

YingLi called out with grief: "Lin, Lin, I came to pick you up to take you with me." After she looked the first time she asked: "Where are you?" and after she had checked three times she screamed.

"My husband has disappeared!"

Chapter 63

AT THE MOMENT NINE black rifle muzzles had belched fire, LinLin's soul left him briefly not knowing the bullet had not sent him to hell.

When the soldiers lifted their guns to take aim at the head of their enemy who was only unarmed flesh and blood, some got very excited. The soldier who was supposed to kill LinLin, didn't know he had been unsuccessful, his bullet had not pierced through the head, it had just cut off part of his right ear, and torn some skin off the side of his face.

LinLin woke up in pain and wet from the cold rain, around him there was an eerie silence. He discovered dead bodies laying on him; his mind suddenly cleared, and he realized that he was still on the execution ground. He had just been shot, and was wondering where he was. Was this hell? He lifted his eye lids and saw a cloud on the peak of the mountain. The air was blood-stained, and reeked of blood. He turned his head and saw bodies, and he was sure he was still alive. He could not move under the weight of the bodies that lay on him, and his forehead was bleeding. He wanted to stop the bleeding, but his right arm had no feeling; and his left arm was pinned under a body; he thought he would slowly bleed to death. He recalled how YingLi had looked and wondered why she had left, and where she was? How nice it would be if she were here now! How nice if he could die on her breast with his eyes closed in happiness!

Then he heard people coming to pick up corpses, and closed his eyes, feigning death. His mind never stopped thinking, he continued recalling that YingLi had followed him the whole trip, they had talked in sight of each other, and had wonderful communication. How he wished to talk with her once more before he died, have one last cuddle and kiss, to see her to say good bye. The people left, and he opened his eyes again wondering where YingLi was? Didn't she want to take my body back...no, impossible. Maybe...she went to get people to help, she couldn't move his body alone. Yes...he must wait for her to come, just wait.

As the curtain of night descended three corpses had been removed already, and the wind was getting stronger, and colder. He tried to move his right arm but was unsuccessful, the left was the same. He thought about his legs and discovered that they were both working very well. He was extremely happy with this discovery and moved his left leg forward slowly from under a corpse, and then started pushing the corpse off. It was working, as the corpse was pushed away his arm was freed. He sat up, his right arm felt heavy and numb, and warm and wet when he touched it. With his doctors sense of touch, he could tell that it was sticky like blood. His forehead and ear were also covered in blood but it was dry. He wondered how his arm had been injured; it needed immediate attention to stop the bleeding and he had to think of something he could use. Eventually he took off his socks, tied them together, and bound up the cut.

He felt tired, and laid back down again, he felt time passing very slowly, it seemed like hours had passed, and YingLi still hadn't showed up. Night in the north in autumn is cold, he sat up again, tried to stand up, and he finally did; very shaky to begin with, but excited that he could actually stand up and walk. His mind began racing, thinking my legs work, I can walk; maybe I can escape. Now he had a very strong will to live, for YingLi and their child. Thinking about her and their child gave him the strength to carry on and made him feel positive, even later when he would live in another county, no matter how hard his life was, his faith in her would carry him through. He would never forget this day with her, or the other things that he had lived through with her. In his later life, these memories would follow him forever: even if he was sad or happy, success or failure, positive or negative, near or far, night or day.

But after a while he changed his mind reminding himself; "I am a criminal now; I cannot go back to a peaceful life. Why should I want to take her with me I do not know where? It is better for her to think that I am dead so that she can have a new life.

LinLin found the big dipper in the sky, blinked his eyes to find his direction and headed north.

LinLin had been born and raised in a was a forest district and was no stranger to mountains, but the condition of his health was very bad now, due to the gash on his forehead. He had not eaten anything all day, and his prison uniform needed to be replaced soon. Those things were simple for most people, but for him, any single one could be life threatening. The prison uniform was just a summer one, except for long pants; he was only wearing a thin summer jacket, underwear and a shirt. He could not go far in these clothes because the autumn nights were too cold. He couldn't be seen wearing the uniform in public because that would get him arrested. The only safe way he could travel was to continue on the mountain trail going north, and hope to cross the border into Russia. He thought Russia would be his best chance for survival.

He loved his home, and his wife, but he couldn't go home; he had to go on because he had no other choice. He passed one mountain, and then another, how he wished to see a chimney or a tent, but he knew that was just wishful thinking; he was struggling against death; in the next second he might fall down with never get up again. The leaves on the forest floor felt very soft under his shoes, and gave off a pleasing fragrance as he walked on them. Trees and bushes growing wild on the path made progress difficult as if they were jumping out just to stop him. He tried to conserve his energy; he was concerned that walking with out direction would exhaust his strength. He felt no pain from his cut and knew from his medical knowledge that since it had become numb, it indicated that it was either infected, or the nerves were damaged.

It was necessary to bandage the cut and he chose a flat area to sit down but discovered it was very wet so he got up and found a big stone to sit on. He took off his jacket and shirt, and didn't know which one he should use; they both had the name of the jail on them so he tried to tear out a piece with the name on it but wasn't successful. He gave up trying to tear out the name and concentrated just on how he might be able to tear the material so he could use it. He decided to use a sleeve off the shirt, it should have been easy to tear but, not for him; his right hand and arm had lost their strength. He used his left hand and teeth to rip the sleeves off. He used one sleeve for his forehead, and put the other one on the right arm. His shirt had now become a vest, and he turned the jacket inside out, and put it on. The next thing he needed was to find something to eat and drink.

In movies that he had seen of China or other countries, all criminals were given good food for their last meal before they were executed. He hadn't been offered anything to eat, since he was rousted from his sleep early in the morning; he had been on the truck all day to receive criticism, and be exhibited on the streets, to advertise his execution, without even a drink of water. His body was healthy and strong, his stomach was good but nervous; one day without eating wasn't a serious problem, but who knew how many days it would take to starve to death he didn't know.

LinLin was gratified that he had not taken YingLi with him. He still had to escape the big net of the law; to break free of this net determination and courage was required, and might not be enough.

He sensed that hell and life were just steps away; maybe in the next second he would fall into death forever. YingLi's vision supported him and he forced himself to follow the dipper and press on going north. Who had said heaven never seals off all the exits? He was determined to survive this calamity; as the first night ended, and day broke his nerves broke too; from his position on the top of a mountain he could see nothing but mountains as far as his eyes could see. It looked like a road without end and he wondered if he could make it across all those mountains.

His legs felt heavy and numb; he knew if he continued like this he could die of starvation or exhaustion. In the course of all people's lives, water is the fountainhead of the life force, finding water was a necessity. He planned to rest little a bit and think about where to begin to look for water; he sat on the ground, and then laid down to rest. He was dreaming that YingLi had come carrying a big soft bedcover to warm him, and used her tongue to lick his face and neck. It made him very itchy and he woke up to discover that it was not YingLi. A bear was busily burying him and it had licked his face and neck, as if savouring him for a meal when he got ripe. At this time, all tiredness was gone; he wanted to jump up and run, but he knew that the bear could easily kill him, and it was much wiser to play dead and wait until the bear left.

Chapter 64

YONGHONG HEARD SOMEONE CALLING from the hall; she went calmly to the door, unlocked it, and opened it; a woman was standing there and she asked her:

"Who are you looking for?"

Ming with her chin raised said: "You."

YongHong felt a little strange and asked: "What for?"

"For you." Was all that Ming replied.

WenJun was in the closet, and since he had heard Ming's voice, he had become very nervous, and prayed silently. Oh my god, let her leave! Let her leave...Then he prayed to YongHong, you talk nice. Ming is a real bitch, she will reject force, be nice, be nice.

"For me...? I'm sorry, I don't know you." YongHong said.

"That doesn't matter, I know you; you are the Director of the Women's Federation for the province."

YongHong said with a smile: "You can see me tomorrow at my office to talk, I do not work outside of the office." She had forgotten that it was WenJun who rented the room; this was not her home.

Ming was laughing and said: "You are wrong, I did not come to appeal for help; I came to look for my husband."

WenJun's heart was jumping in his throat.

YongHong's heart was racing too, but she tried to look calm, and said: "Then you were knocking on the wrong door, I am the only one here. Please leave."

Ming laughed a terrifying laugh.

YongHong was being careful and asked: "Who are you?" She had guessed who it was but did not want to believe it; she wanted proof.

Ming stopped laughing and said: "Who I am is not important; I will give you a name you know. His name is WenJun."

WenJun got mad and thought to himself: Ming, you are bitch! When I get home I will kill you!

YongHong hesitated for a moment in shock, and Ming ducked under YongHong's arm entering the room hollering:

"Dear, you can come out now. WenJun, come out here!"

She smelled the air like a dog, and looked like she had found something. She sat on the bed with her legs swinging as if she was in her own home.

YongHong quickly started thinking to how handle this woman; she closed the door then confronted Ming pointing at her nose and said sternly: "I can not let you be mischievous here, you must leave."

"What will you do if I do not leave?"

YongHong made an angry face and said: "I will call the police." She had been thinking about what she should do and decided that either Ming goes or she would leave. She would just leave WenJun in the room to settle his own problem; that would be best for her. She had already underestimated the intelligence of Ming. Ming heard her but continued to swing her legs, just watching YongHong with without blinking, appreciating her indignation. Ming was overjoyed at YongHong's discomfort; her face showed the happiness of a Spanish bullfighter about to finish off a moribund crazy ox.

Ming had many complaints since she married and in this moment revenge was sweet; she had her husband where she wanted him now and could end his career. Ming knew that they would both be very concerned about their political futures and aware now that she had the power to end them. She was very happy and very smart too; she knew their end would also be her end. To injure one of them would be very unwise for her own future; she wanted an intact family as an officer's wife and to live to a ripe old age. For her vanity, she intended to use this situation to further her own goals.

Having a guilty conscience and seeing that intimidation wasn't working YongHong threw down the gantlet and commanded: "Are you crazy? You listen! If you do not leave I will call the police."

WenJun was becoming very concerned about YongHong talking like that. He knew that would make Ming become worse. Ming was a woman who had grown up in a powerful family, and was used to being spoiled by most people; he forgot YongHong had come from a powerful family too.

Ming said mockingly: "How about we settle this privately?"

YongHong said: "I have nothing to settle privately with you; it will be best if you just leave; I will give you one minute to get out, otherwise I will call the police."

Ming jumped down from bed, yanked open the closet door, and WenJun came out sheepishly.

YongHong stood by stiffly.

Ming was laughing again.

WenJun had a red face, and was sweating.

Ming was the first to break the silence, she asked: "How would you like to proceed?"

YongHong and WenJun looked at each other, and YongHong said: "He came to help me write a report."

WenJun was quick to add: "Yes, yes, I came to help her; we were classmates Dear Ming, you have made a mistake."

Ming saw her husband's face was nervous and panic stricken and she felt both pity and hate, as she glared at him for the first time in her life; she continued and said: "You rented this apartment, that woman is the director of the Women's Federation of the province, she is from Long Shan city..."

WenJun was sweating, his body was like a balloon that had been punctured; he waved his hand like a dead pig that was not afraid of boiling water, and said: "Shut up, what do you want? Just say it."

YongHong jumped up in front of WenJun, and said: "What does she want? We were just working together writing." Then, she gave

WenJun a glare that said you must be strong; don't lose this one yourself.

Ming lifted up the bed sheet and said: "Write on here?"

YongHong wanted to take the bed sheet, but Ming grabbed one corner and held on to the sheet like a bulldog. YongHong had the advantage being taller, and had most of it in her hands. Breathing deeply she said: "If you don't go I'll go! I don't want to be involved in your family problems." She was holding on tightly to the bed sheet and wanted to take it and leave.

Ming was just a little woman but holding on to a corner of the sheet; she jumped to the door and opened it, saying. "Leaving is not easy." She stuck her head out the door, and whistled; heads came popping out to look. She turned her head and saw that YongHong and WenJun's faces had both turned pale.

Ming whistled again, the heads disappeared right away. Ming turned back to WenJun and YongHong, cackling and said: "Write an agreement. I need you both to swear to me..." She could barely finish speaking for laughing, and then looked at YongHong. "This agreement will be very easy for you."

Swear? YongHong's whole body was sweating and she was thinking even without swearing I don't want to be with him ever again.

Ming said: "You can still be together."

WenJun and YongHong were both taken aback; it was not clear to them what she wanted. They heard Ming say very slowly and clearly: "I want you to guarantee to give birth to a child for me. I only want to have my husband's child; is that too much to ask she said to YongHong?"

Chapter 65

AFTER THE BEAR MOVED on beyond his hearing LinLin slowly got up shaking nervously, his legs felt weak and unsteady. He did not dare to be careless now and wanted to make the best use of his time to find water. The mountain path was already beginning to disappear, if he walked without direction he would get lost quickly, and surely die of exhaustion.

LinLin was a half son of the forest; he had been on school vacations with his father in the mountains, in the summer picking traditional Chinese herbs for medicine, and hunting in the winter. His father had taught him how to find his bearings and where to look for water by the kind of trees and plants that grew there. The mountains were almost all covered with red leaves, from the top of the mountain LinLin looked into the distance searching for the milk yellow colours of willows which grow close by water. Tears came to his eyes as he strained to see in the distance, only the red fire colour was within sight. He knew he would have to find water soon; he might go on without eating for a time but not without water.

How many mountains he had passed during the night he didn't know, he had taken his bearings from the big dipper and travelled north. From memory, LinLin believed that he was not far from the border with the Soviet Union and a river that separated the countries. He knew that the border office was set up on a bridge; and that people from both sides could cross the border freely on the river; the year he was 16 his father had taken him across to the Soviet Union. In his present condition, the best solution would be to go to the Soviet Union to hide for awhile, this idea had been in the back of his mind all along and that is why he had been walking north. LinLin wanted to find water first of all to fill his stomach, and then he could continue hurrying north. He was scaring up pheasants and startling rabbits as he pushed on, but they were not wild fruit that he could pick.

If only he could find water he knew he could survive for a few days. He decided to go down from the mountain ridges into the valley where there should be water, and he walked very carefully not wanting to meet up with a bear again.

LinLin was concentrating only on what was ahead of him and one of his feet failed to find ground beneath it and he lost his balance and plunged into a pit. He soon realised that he had fallen into a bear trap; the hole was very deep; when he stood up he was just able to reach the surface with his finger tips. He raised his head, and estimated that it was at least two feet below ground.

Standing on his tiptoes he could reach the remaining camouflage and take it off, he believed that there would be less chance of an animal falling in on him and perhaps the hunter who had built this trap would find him sooner. It was warmer in the hole than above ground and Lin was going to take off his jail uniform to hide his identity, but he was very tired. He fell asleep thinking about it, and was still wearing the prison uniform later when he was woke up by hunters.

"Are you a criminal?" One of the hunters asked him. He couldn't say no, but didn't want to say yes, so he remained silent.

The leader of the hunters was checking him over and said: "Tie him well and lift carefully"

LinLin was thinking, tie and lift? They must be planning to take me to the government to take credit for my capture. Things develop beyond one's control, just as a dead pig is not scared of scalding hot water; he was helpless to stop them. His four limbs were tied to two strong poles like a bear, and lifted by four men. In order to prevent his body from falling, they tied a rope around his waist. But his injured arm was very sensitive and the pain when they lifted his body made him yell. He didn't need to hide any more and the sound of his yelling rang out high and wretched echoing through the mountain forest.

"Let's stun him." LinLin heard someone say before he lost consciousness.

When he woke up again he discovered that he was lying in a little shack. His prison clothes had disappeared, his upper body was naked, and below he was wearing pants made of animal skins. The injured arm had a new bandage, and the wound had been treated. He felt very hot and started to take off his pants, but just half way he discovered he didn't have any underwear on. He pulled his pants back up and feeling very thirsty he began looking around. He found a jar of water close by his pillow and drank half of it and then realised that he has hungry but there was no food to be seen. He took a deep breath, and tried to recall how he got here; he didn't wait for an answer, he fell asleep again. The next time he woke up someone was talking to him; when he opened his eyes he saw five or six people gathered around him. He thought that he was going to be arrested and closed his eyes, feeling like dead meat on a board.

"Hello, hello, wake up." The words were coming from several men's mouths.

LinLin closed his eyes and did not answer.

"Should we fill him now?" One man asked.

LinLin had wondered to himself fill what?

Another voice said: "No he could easily choke, we have to wake him up first."

"Hello, wake up please, your medication is waiting." the same voice said.

LinLin opened his eyes, and saw a face covered with beard stubble, and two bright eyes examining him. When the man saw him open his eyes he said very happily: "You have woken up finally, now you need to take some medicine."

After he was sat up and supported, he was fed a pack of white powdery medicines dissolved on a spoon. He swallowed it down, but the bitter taste made him choke, and cough; the man spooned water into his mouth, but he still couldn't stop coughing. Then the man placed a coarse white porcelain bowl of water to his lips, and let him drink, and then the coughing stopped.

The man asked: "What is your name?"

He wondered what to tell him and decided it was best not to say anything; so he just shook his head.

"We know that you are a runaway convict from the government. You needn't be afraid; we are all the same here brother. The man with the beard said: "Here you can feel like you're at home." LinLin could not believe his good fortune and his spirits soared.

Chapter 66

LIAN BEEN HAD BEEN in a good mood since she heard about the death of LinLin, that information had let her heart feel like the sun was shining again. The black clouds had disappeared that had been haunting her mind all those years. The sunshine lightened her conscience so that she no longer felt guilty. Without her, he had the same trouble as before; she thought that LinLin had been a reactionary all his life. She thought she had been silly to think that she had caused him to get into trouble. She had no reason to repent, he had always thought differently than the government. Her reporting his words as a reactionary were meant to be helpful, she had not meant to hurt him. Now at last, he had proved that even without her he could get himself into trouble. The spiritual shackles for 12 years had been opened and she had been liberated. His death made her a little sad; after all they had been a couple, loved each other, and had a child. Thinking about their child, she suddenly was thankful and felt lucky that he had abandoned them mercilessly in the past, and she had taken their son and left the forest.

If they were still together, her NianLin would have been involved now too. This sentence prevailed through out society; if the father is heroic the son would be a brave man, if the father was a reactionary the child would be a wretch. She felt that it was a good thing that she had saved her son from receiving that label.

The busy time of the autumn harvest was over; the grain had been thrashed. The people of the mountain village had their food put away for the year; their main menu would only change a little from cooked rice to porridge. How many years it had been like that they did not know; it just seemed to be their traditional life style.

In Lian's kitchen there were several big jars that stood about four feet tall and two feet wide. Every family in the Village had jars like that made from baked clay, acid proof, and alkali-resistant; they were able to bear high temperatures and were antiseptic, used to store grain, and salted vegetables.

Lian brought in the crushed grain and covered it in the jars in the fall. When she cooked she would get some crushed grain from a jar; this was customary in all families rich or poor. Some people by early autumn didn't have anything to eat, because they failed to measure how much they took from their supply every day, and would often take more than they needed. Lian was not like them, she always measured when she took food from the jars...how much for the day, and when to make cooked rice or porridge. The life of the family under Lian's frugal management even though it was simple was never short of some thing to eat. She did anything that she thought would be good for her son; she always reserved enough grain for them for the future so that the next summer and autumn they would still have food to eat.

That evening gongs sounded signalling that the people were called to a meeting.

NianLin was busy cleaning out the pigsty and he had not had dinner yet.

Lian called him from the house: "We have to go to the meeting, come and eat."

NianLin followed his mama into the kitchen and used the wash basin to wash his hands and face, splashing water on his pants and the floor. Lian held a towel for him, and when he finished washing she passed it to him. He dried his face, went out and dumped the wash water; then he grabbed a corn cake from table, and some salt Vegetables in his other hand, and walked out eating as he went.

Lian's words followed him: "Wait a minute, and we can go together!"

The meeting place of the group was a square yard with a cowshed, a stable, and a grain mill. The live stock hand lived here, and the yard was about half an acre, enclosed by adobe walls, and a two piece wooden gate. The ground was littered with cow and horse dung. When she entered the yard, she couldn't stand the smell in the air, even though she had been living here twelve years she still was not used to it. The house had the two standard rooms, the inner one had a desk and a chair that were very old, and the outer room had a Kang for the livestock hand. When Lian got there, both rooms were full; there were more than a hundred people, and the two rooms were not big enough for so many.

When Lian arrived the meeting had already started, and there were many people standing in front of her. She heard Crippled Sun speaking; he was talking with a hero's voice, loud, sonorous, and forceful saying.

"Our national situation today is very good..." That was Crippled Sun's usual introductory commentary. Our leader Chairmen Mao said: "Class struggle is capable of bringing about the desired results of the revolution."

Outside, the people started whispering.

Lian heard Crippled Sun say: "Today, we have caught XingYun in the class struggle..."

XingYun was an old single man who lived in the village. Many years ago he had been introduced to Lian, but because Lin was still her love she was not interested. He was a carpenter, honest, and quiet most of the time. Lian wondered why there would be a class struggle against him.

Crippled Sun continued: "XingYun you are a bastard, you are a bastard who has lost face. Even if our village is short of women, you can't sleep with your daughter in law."

These words made everyone open their eyes wide.

Crippled Sun said: "You mother ### if you want a woman, you will have to find another one...or get a dog a goose!"

Everyone started laughing. Someone interrupted asking: "Would you like to make out with your goose or dog?"

236

The leader intentionally coughed and cleared his throat to settle the laughter down, and then he said: "Don't interrupt, and stick to the subject."

XingYun's son had died from lung cancer, leaving no children and the daughter in law had infantile paralysis. His daughter in law wanted to live with him, and their relationship had started a year ago; they were still living together; and the daughter in law was pregnant. Because she was pregnant she wanted to get married so the child would have a HuKou. Marriage was very important for the child so it would have benefits in the future such as food, fabric stamps etc. When they went to the local government office to register, the old HuKou showed their relationship causing problems for them. The officer said he could not make the decision, and he asked his leader who told him to ask at the next level of government officers to try to find the rule about these special cases. But the national rules for married people didn't have it either. Therefore, the local officer's answer was. "No."

XingYun said to Crippled Sun: "You tell me to sleep with a goose or a dog; if geese and dogs are like a wife, why do you always go out and bring women back for single men? Why don't you give all single men a goose or a dog?"

Crippled Sun said: "Mother ###! We are trying to help you; we just want you to stay on the revolutionary road. Now anybody can talk; speak up and tell us your idea."

XingYun said: "Before the liberation it was acceptable; at that time we still had brothels, any man who wanted a woman, only needed money and he could have one. Now we do not have brothels, money, or women. Although my son died and I am now living with my daughter in law you say this is no longer acceptable; how can we solve this problem?"

Lian heard Crippled Sun say: "That we let XingYun's daughter in law go to another man, and then when the village gets a new woman we give her to him."

Lian heard a woman yell: "No, I disagree!"

The meeting was at its peak, the people were all excited about the subject. In the past they only struggled when there was not enough food, or material was in short supply; the only people they talked about were the single pock marked man and the widows. Now they had a new person to talk about and it looked like the class struggle was going in a new direction; prospects of getting a new match made them very excited.

Crippled Sun seeing that the woman objected said: "If you don't want to marry some one else that is fine, we will send you to the people's commune, and let them find a solution. XingYun what do you think?"

XingYun realised now that it was not so simple; the fact that a meeting had been called means that it is very serious. He and his daughter in law now had different views. He lowered his head and murmured. "It is better to have a deal here...make a deal here..."

Finally, XingYun's daughter in law reluctantly agreed to marry another man, and Crippled Sun promised XingYun he would find him another woman.

Chapter 67

TWO MONTHS LATER IT was winter and the mountain village was freezing cold. But, XingYun was very hot because now he had a woman. The woman had been brought to the village by Crippled Sun from outside; and her hands had been tied together on her chest. XingYun was busy working between her legs, and had totally neglected her breasts. The woman's face was scratched, and there was blood and tooth marks on her lips; she had closed her eyes and stopped struggling, and yelling. The silence and her yielding let him relax from being so nervous; he even showed a smile of victory; the woman would accept her fate.

The woman was YingLi.

The evening when she couldn't find LinLin's body YingLi was driven home by the people with the car; but her suicidal thoughts still remained even after she was back in Long Shan city. LuDongChun was watching her daughter closely and talking with her and it seemed to be helping.

LinLin's corpse had gone missing; YingLi thought a long time, and the only reason she could think of was that she had signed in the wrong space. She recalled having the paper in her hand and the officer saying: sign here. She recalled that "want corpse" or "do not want" were on the same paper, the officer showed her which side said want corpse, and she had signed there.

YingLi was still very sad, and depressed when a new problem arose. The community cadre Aunt-Yu passed word to LuDongChun that the government was going to deport YingLi to the countryside.

Deport? That meant that she would carry the black mark against LinLin anywhere she went, and it would be the same for her child too as an anti revolution relative. This label was so bad that it made her afraid for their future; the child was innocent and she didn't want the child to be discriminated against.

YingLi planned go into hiding, but where could she hide?

LuDongChun closed her eyes and thought about it all night; she had a older sister in the countryside; but they were all from a landlord's family and that had caused problems already. She had been unable to protect herself, and she was not able to protect YingLi. Among her friends there was only one she felt she could trust. LuDongChun planned to take her daughter but YingLi didn't want her mama to go; because anywhere her mama went, people would recognise her, and she would be unable to hide

YingLi left home alone the next morning carrying a letter from her mama, a small bag, and got on the train. Three and half hours later, she got off at a little station following the directions that her mama gave her.

She was remembering that her mama said she would have to walk another ten miles; the winter sun was already starting to go down, and her feet were swollen, it would be better stay in hotel tonight, and start walking in the morning. She went looking for a hotel but, the village didn't have one. With no hotel she was wondering if she should try to go on or not. If she went on she would have to hurry to get there before dark or she could stay and spend the night in the waiting room in the train station. In her hesitation she saw a lame person repairing a tractor, and she went over to ask directions. Talking to him, she was pleasantly surprised to learn that this driver and tractor were going the same direction as she was; she had decided to get a ride on the tractor and had been brought back here as spoils.

The lame person was Crippled Sun.

That night, YingLi had been locked in small room without a window, and the door was locked. She knew that it was already too late, but she had shouted loudly beat on the door and screamed: "Let me out." She attacked the door kicking and pushing with all her might and said: "You're a big liar and cheat. You have the audacity to kidnap me in daylight...and swindle a woman. What you are doing is illegal; I will make an accusation against you!"

YingLi was full of indignation and threatened him with everything she could think of. Seeing that he was not responding she tried another route and said: "Call your leader to come here! I want see your leader!" She thought to herself this place is remote but it is part of China, even though it is backward the leader of the unit would know the new national law.

"Hah, hah, I'm the leader."

"You are a liar, you are just a driver."

"I'm the production team leader too. My last name is Sun, people call me Crippled Sun."

If he was a criminal abductor of women he could not be so frank and strong willed when speaking; she thought his words must be true. After listening to him, YingLi half believed and half doubted him. "You are abducting a woman, you are committing a criminal act"

"You needn't try to frighten me. I'm not making money. I am just doing a good thing for a farmer. If you don't trust me you can ask the other farmers. Miss, it looks like you don't want to stay. That is not a problem, you can stay here one year or two years, let a single man have a wife, or birth a child for him...and you can leave. We won't try to stop you."

YingLi was thinking rapidly and asking herself if this is good or bad? Is this a good idea to hide and is it safe or not? Whatever, she doesn't have any other choice for now. She heard the lame man continue saying: "My village is very poor, we have a lot of single men in the village. I work as cadre for these people and must do some things for the people."

XingYun was vigorous, and he had vented his pent up desires on her all night. YingLi's belly was nervous and very sore; then she discovered she was passing bloody water, a sign of miscarrying. She changed her mind; she had to protect her child.

Chapter 68

LINLIN STAYED IN THE pit house that he had watched the hunters build for him. After two months of treatment and rest he was healing very well. The hunters had been a big help.

He went out when the weather was good, wearing wolf skin clothes, and shoes made from grass. The pit house was hidden in a dense pine forest, located on the south side of a hill, it was excavated to form a cave about five feet high, three feet wide, and six feet long. The entrance was concealed with bark and grass. Inside there was a Kang and with a fire in it the little cave was snug and warm. Staying here was very lonely, but every day, Hu or his wife would come by once bringing him water and food.

When he woke up and discovered that was wearing animal skins and they were too hot, but he did not want to get back into his jail uniform. Then he realised that Hu and his wife also wore animal leather clothes.

Hu's wife explained to LinLin: "We have no HuKou, so we get no tickets for fabric or cotton, we just depend on what we find on the mountain to eat and wear."

Hunter-Hu talked to LinLin and told him: He was a right winger, he escaped from a jail farm; was there ten years. Hunter Hu told LinLin his life experience and his love story; how his girlfriend was from a powerful family, and she had quit her job to marry him, and moved here to live with him.

Then LinLin told him that he was anti-revolutionary, and Hu said:

"We are all similar here we have other friends with political problems too. It doesn't matter about your past, just relax, you can live here forever."

LinLin had thought about living here for a few months, but he really didn't have any plans about forever.

LinLin was deep in thought one day when he heard someone coming up behind him, he turned his head and saw Hu coming, and he wasn't carrying anything. From a distance Hu called out: "Hi, I see you are up, let's go. Our friends heard you were better, and they want to get together and have a drink. They are all good friends, and you don't need to worry, they will not betray you."

Hu's pit house was over half a mile away; it was the same style as LinLin's, just a lot bigger.

"Is dinner ready?" Hu called from outside; his wife answered: "Yes, everything is ready."

"Ok, I will call them."

From a side door he took out a shotgun, aimed at the sky and fired, after a few minutes he fired again, a total of three shots. When he was finished, put the shotgun by the door and welcomed LinLin in to his pit house. Then he said: "This is our signalling system, three shots close together is urgent, three shots spaced out is get-together."

After around half an hour, five men started arriving from different directions. They called LinLin young brother or old brother according to how they viewed their relative ages.

Hu said: "These men have all helped you."

LinLin said sincerely: "Thank you all very much."

"Thanks are not necessary we are all the same here, just outcasts." A handsome young guy said.

An old man spoke up and said: "Sun, you were degenerate, don't confuse our new friend."

Laughter rose in the pit house.

The young guy named Sun had a red face, and he opened his mouth to reply but Hu stopped him saying: "That's enough, today we have new friend, and everybody will act like a gentleman. We are going to sit down and eat; let's annihilate some food and wine, we can talk while we eat and drink. Everybody, cheers, bottoms up with your wine, and dig in to the dinner."

"Cheers" Everyone said as they raised their cups and drained them.

An old man said to Sun, "Before you get drunk make sure your belt is tight, don't take off your pants later and scare our guest."

Sun made a face and said: "My belt only comes lose in front of a woman. I just like women, what is wrong with that? Everyone has one, except me..." Sun had been a worker in a factory, he had a girlfriend and wanted to have sex with her before they got married, he never expected she would go to the police station and reports him. He was convicted of rape, spent three years in jail, and lost a good job. That experience bothered him and made it difficult for him to find a new girl friend. Depressed, he had moved to the forest to get a part time job.

"I am not in a good mood today, I want to fight." Sun said.

"Son of a bitch, you are always like that...cheers." The people said together.

Hu's wife brought the last courses of the meal in, and said: "That is all your dishes, I hope you guys enjoy it. I will go to the other place and take care of the children."

Sun in a loud voice asked. "Sister in law, do you want to have a drink with me?"

A guy said: "She doesn't want you mining even in drinking."

"Why did you say that? Can't a friend kid some one's wife? I'm an honest man."

His voice was drowned in a chorus of jeers.

The next day when Hu saw LinLin again he said uneasily. "I am sorry about yesterday. When that bastard has wine he just wants to drink until he passes out. We are always like that here; whoever gets drunk first and passes out is the best friend.

"Yes I knew that, I grew up in the forest." LinLin said. Looking at the sky he saw that the wind was coming from the north-west, blowing his hair.

"This winter is coming late." Hu said: "This time of year usually the mountains are capped with snow." Then he changed the subject saying: "Can I ask how many children you have?"

"I..." LinLin thought and said: "my child will be born the end of November or early December. What is the date today?"

"Today is...may be..." Hunter-Hu using his fingers to count said: "It must be the end of November. What day I'm not sure, but I am sure it is the end of November."

"It could be born any day now." LinLin said.

Suddenly Hu hollered. "Stop, it is dangerous here."

LinLin stopped in his tracks.

Hunter-Hu was breathing deeply, and said: "I was just too busy talking; I have a trap just ahead. You need to be very careful here, it is easy to step on... When your wife gives birth, do you want to bring them here?"

Hunter-Hu waited for LinLin to answer. After awhile when he didn't say anything, hunter-Hu continued. "I know that life here is not very human, but it is better to be together than separated. By the way, the people here are very nice, and they don't care if you are a rightist or leftist."

LinLin said: "Who says life here is not very human? Life here is like a different world, a peaceful world where no one is trying to control you. Have you read the Record of The Peach Garden?" LinLin asked. "That 'Peach Garden' sounded like it was just about the same as here."

"You sound like an educated person." Hunter-Hu said.

"No big difference, we are the same." LinLin said modestly.

"We are not the same. If I had not become a rightist, I would have gone to university; can you guess what I wanted to study?"

"No what?"

"Archaeology."

"Oh, why are you interested in that?"

"Actually I don't know why. I just have an interest in it."

While talking they quickly arrived at Hu's pit house; he called out cheerfully. "Hi everyone, come out and see who has come for a visit."

The pit house door opened with a thud and out bounded four children. The children were all about half a head shorter than their next older brother. Some wore wolf leather, and some wore rabbit leather clothes. They all had dishevelled hair and a dirty faces. The youngest still had food from his last meal on his face, and his mama was standing behind him holding one hand up in greeting and cleaning the baby's face with her other hand.

LinLin remembered that yesterday when they were drinking, hunter Hu's wife said she would go to the other place to feed the children; they had two pit houses.

Hu had his hand on the tallest child's head and said: "This one's name is Tiger." Moving his hand to the next one he said: "This one's name is Wolf; the third one's name is Bear, the youngest one's name is Leopard."

LinLin was laughing and asked: "Why do they all have animal names?"

"Because they came uncalled for; we have suffered hardships and that is our karma. They have come to follow me and have to suffer; it would have been better if they were not born. Hah! Hah!

"Did you not practice contraception?"

Hu's wife Yajie said: "We tried different things but they didn't work; the babies just came anyway."

Hu said: "She finally had her uterus taken out."

"Is it easy to see a doctor near here?"

"The forest workers help, they pretend Yajie is their wife. There are lots of people here who are very friendly. Oh, yes. You didn't answer me yet. Do you want your wife to come?"

"That would just be more work and trouble for you people."

"Who are we now? We are brothers! Your problem is my problem. Let me tell you, you needn't hesitate. The conditions of life in the forest are not great but with your wife here you all will be better off. I will arrange things to bring her here if that is ok with you."

LinLin couldn't say anything; he just nodded his head in gratitude.

Chapter 69

IN THE MORNING, XINGYUN got up naked and told YingLi:
"Today I will make breakfast; starting tomorrow you will make breakfast. Man does the outside work, the woman does the inside work...in the home, the wife should do everything for the husband."

XingYun was wearing a greasy cotton jacket. He started to go out to the yard to get some wood when he saw YingLi looking out the door and said: "Better forget your plan to leave. I will tell you clearly: this is a mountainous area, without knowledge of the area it is not easy to leave here. If you want to try; I will let you try!" He said with a cunning smile, showing a few big yellow teeth that looked like soy beans.

The breakfast was maize paste. YingLi took a thick dirty old porcelain bowl; half filled it and sat at the table to try and eat. The maize paste was dense with alkali. XingYun was already finished half a bowl, his lips on the bowl edge, sucking sounds like a pig smacking and loud slurping. YingLi glanced at him and saw wide thick lips, a nose like a garlic head, and unusually small pig eyes, with a dark complexion. Maize dribbled from his mouth running down his chin and his beard was turning yellow. Suddenly his nose started running, and he started sniffling. YingLi lowered her head and looked away feeling nauseous.

What had Crippled Sun said last night? If you want to leave give a single man a child. According to what law do I have to give birth to a child for him? I do not believe these are the manners and morals of the time now. That is robbing a woman, I will inform on them; but how can I inform without exposing my identity?

After breakfast XingYun was horny again, he pushed YingLi back down on the Kang and started riding her again. This time he didn't tie YingLi's hands. He said: "If you still resist like last night, I will tie you up again."

He was happy, in the daylight, he could see her very clearly, and she was a very beautiful woman. She was much more beautiful than his daughter in law! Her skin was smooth as silk, her face like a flower; her breath like perfume; having sex with her was like being in a dream. I'm so lucky he thought to himself.

He was being rough and soon she started having pains in her belly. She hollered at him: "You have to stop that! My belly is starting to have pains."

"Why does your belly have pains?"

"I'm pregnant, and that is very bad for the baby."

He had made his daughter in law pregnant, but never heard her say that.

"All women give birth to children, are you saying you can't touch them when they are pregnant? I never heard of that." He said.

"You can ask someone else if you don't believe me." YingLi said in a pleading tone of voice.

"This is my home, my woman is not delicate!" he was holding YingLi's hands, and said: "Besides, this is a bastard child; if you lose it that is a good thing; I want you to have my baby, to give birth to my child."

His words made YingLi mad and nervous. She didn't care if he was joking or not, his actions from last night to this morning could make her lose her child very easily. She looked at his penis, hands, and face, and the idea of living with him that she had briefly considered was now gone. She had to make him lose his sexual desire and a bold idea came to her, she said: "Let me show you a different position..."

Soon after, XingYun ran naked into the street screaming: "Help me! Someone help me!"

His screaming brought everyone in the village out into the street. He had both his hands stuck in his crotch and they were covered with blood. "Help me, she has cut my penis. Help me, I am bleeding..."

Crippled Sun heard the commotion and came running. He moved XingYun's hands so that he could see what was wrong and he touched the injured penis making him scream again. "The pain, I will die..."

Crippled-Sun said: "That is ...get some clothes on! Hurry and we will get you to the hospital as soon as possible." Then he ordered a man who was a tractor driver to start the motor, and someone else to bring clothes to cover him. As they put him on the truck, XingYun said: "This woman I give up! Mother ###, she is too dangerous. I will kill her..."

The tractor and XingYun's curses left in a cloud of black smoke.

In the village Crippled Sun said: "He doesn't want this woman anymore, who wants her?" Crippled Sun was really unwilling to just send her out and he stood in the street talking loudly to the people who were watching. "Does any body want her? If no body wants her I will send her back."

YingLi was dressed and ready to leave; her face still wore a murderous look.

None of the single men spoke.

Chapter 70

YONGHONG WAS IN A dilemma and having a hard time, complying with Ming's demand. If she didn't get pregnant, the proof Ming held in her hands could be used anytime, and she would fall into disrepute, and lose her position; if she got pregnant, what would she tell ZhangYong? They had never had sex together, and to tell him she had a lover would be a big insult. For several weeks she had given it a lot of thought. She had dozens of different ideas and had given them up one by one and thought some more. She cursed WenJun every day, and cursed the day he was born. She also was wrestling with the question of who posed the greatest problem for her; was it Ming or ZhangYong. Since she had agreed with WenJun had they had to comply with Ming's demand, they now had to come up with a plan to deal with her husband. ZhangYong's temper was well known to YongHong, and she knew if she made him mad he could ruin her political life too. What plan would work to satisfy Ming and also restrain ZhangYong too? These questions gave her a very big headache. When her head ached, she became impatient and was tempted to just tell him straight that her being in this condition was his responsibility too.

ZhangYong had been transferred by the Party to follow YongHong to the provincial capital so that they could remain together. On the surface, they still appeared to be a very happily married couple. No one knew they were not living together. The provincial government provided her apartment, he had a key but he had never used it. He rented and lived in a single room near the factory where he worked. He was the leader of the factory now, and it was staffed entirely with people with disabilities. Since he had gone to work in the factory, his mood had been much better than before. Being employed had greatly improved his self-esteem. But his present good mood was not enough to guarantee that he could accept such an insult. If he could accept her having someone else's baby, how could she tell him? If he wanted to know who the child's father was, what would she tell him?

One day, she remembered a case that had happened in Long Shan city; a man beat his wife for having a baby that he knew was not his, she had complained about the beating and when he was charged he demanded a DNA test. When his wife was ordered to take the DNA test she changed her story and claimed that she had been raped.

Maybe if she told ZhangYong that she had been raped she might obtain some sympathy from him, and he wouldn't feel quite so mad about the pregnancy.

Making the decision she reached for the phone to call WenJun, she thought while dialling the numbers, about having a child and wondering how to go about it.

WenJun knew that YongHong did not want to meet him, and was not crazy about him like before. It had been two months since his wife had gotten proof of his extra-marital affair and they hadn't been together once. Ming saw that the relationship had cooled and kept pushing him. YongHong had been cursing him on the telephone every day, and he was feeling like a mouse between two cats. Both women were bullying him. Some times he thought that YongHong was lovely, but except for her smiling face, tall body and soft skin, she was a shrew. She had a temper that no man could live with. Comparing them, Ming had been much better than YongHong. Even though Ming held proof of his infidelity in her hands, she still treated him like a loving wife making him feel even guiltier. In his mind he sometimes thought: that an ugly wife was the safest, and it would be a good idea to give up YongHong and go back to Ming. He had told Ming his thoughts, but she had disagreed. He was confused, why in the world would a woman like Ming push ahead and be happy to share her husband with another woman? WenJun had no choice, he just had to be patient and listen to YongHong on the phone cursing him and hoping one day to be back with her again.

WenJun was beginning to suspect that big men who had a lot of wives in ancient times, might really have not been lucky after all.

For this occasion they both needed a lot of courage for their meeting. WenJun had allowed Ming to write the agreement, but it had been her idea, and now he carried a bottle of wine.

It was the same room they had used before but now it had lost its old romantic feeling. They drank the wine but after the bottle was empty they still were not in the mood to have sex.

WenJun remembering that YongHong had sent a report acknowledging an omission in her duty regarding the LinLin's case asked: "Have you resolved your problem?"

"The case is resolved."

"What was the verdict?"

"Perform self criticism and get educated."

"Why did you do something so stupid? Did you have to help an anti-revolution person?"

"That material I prepared, if it is true, could prove the person was not anti-revolutionary."

"Yes, but the problem is that you don't know if it is true or not."

"My mama wrote it, she would not lie, and there is a witness too. It must have been a wrongful accusation as far as I can tell. This is a case the provincial leader wants resolved too; it was difficult to extricate myself from a most embarrassing and dangerous situation. Proof that the government is wrong involves a lot of people, supporting the original judgement against LinLin is an insult to many others as well. This is a political game."

"Anyway, in the future you will learn from this lesson; you are a leader too; you must do every thing with your brain, from the political situation, not from your emotions."

"WenJun, you are concerned about my position, aren't you?"

"Y...Yes. You did not get your position easy, did you?"

"Ha-ha! Who told you it was not easy? It was very easy, I just wrote a big-character poster against my mama, and married a disabled guy; then toot, toot, up and away."

"Are you drunk?"

"You were the same; how many days did it take after you joined the army to become an officer? Did you finish high school? What qualifications do you have to be an officer" She laughed contemptuously, then said:

"I will tell you something WenJun, I actually had no ambition. I wrote a big character poster about my mama, because they were wouldn't let me join the revolution ...mother ###. Why could you join, but I couldn't? You were only a revolutionary with your mouth. I took action, I did something; I wrote a big character poster against my mama, and they said: 'YongHong, you are an excellent true revolutionary denouncing your mama.' I thought in my heart, why not? Why should I wait for you to do it? If I don't do it, someone else will. Mother ###! I took the initiative; I'm not like you think. The truth is, on this road, you become a donkey in a mill, with people holding a whip behind you..."

WenJun thought her words were departing from the orbit of the revolution, and stopped her saying. "You shut up!"

"You do not need to worry! I'm not drunk! They wanted me to marry a disabled guy. You asked how I could do that. Yes, I married, and became a model of the revolution; they wrote me a talk show and made me have a red face saying how many times I struggled in my heart, how many times I used Chairman Mao's words to solve my struggles...fuck. From the beginning I felt guilty and couldn't sleep. After I got used to it I could go on the stage, and talk big and lie easy. Now, I realise that my mama is really a good person..."

"You are really drunk"

"WenJun, if I lose my position, will you still love me?"

"What did you say?"

"I said love, love. You said you would love me forever. In this life I have only been with one man and that is you. You are a bastard. If...If..."

253

WenJun replied. "We are both officers and we can't be free. In the future our talk and behaviour must be in the best interests of the Party and country."

"Is that what you really believe, or only an excuse to break your promise? Or were you only kidding me so that you could use me? Kidding me, ha, ha, ha."

Chapter 71

CRIPPLED SUN TOLD YINGLI: "You go back in the room and wait; when the tractor gets back I will drive you to the train station."

Just then, YingLi's water broke and she started screaming, she was holding her belly and squatting on the ground, then she kneeled on the ground. This development terribly frightened Crippled Sun. He had been driving women back to the village for several years; those women had stayed here even if they were not willing, because they needed a place to stay and food to eat. This pregnant woman was the first to cause such problems; she had cut a man's penis, and who was at fault no one knew. Why was she like that? It was winter, her forehead was sweating, and her face was pale, it did not seem like she was lying. Anyway, it was not necessary for her to lie; he had promised her already when the tractor got back he would drive her to the train. What was wrong with her? What problem did she have? God bless me, if you want her to die, don't let her die here.

A woman checked YingLi and said: "Her pants are wet."

Cripple-Sun became more nervous, what kind of disease can make her pee in her pants? He started yelling for help.

"What can I do?"

The woman spoke again: "It looks like amniotic fluid, not pee. You see, the water is still running, no body can pee that long. How do you feel?" she asked YingLi.

"Pain…"YingLi murmured.

"She said she is in pain, she will give birth soon" The woman told Crippled Sun.

Crippled Sun wiped his forehead to dry the sweat, and said: "Go call the barefoot doctor quickly."

"What does the barefoot doctor know? She has not even had a baby herself, it would be better to call the midwife."

"Who can go?" Crippled-Sun pointed at a man and said: "You go, hurry up!" After the man left he said: "It is such cold weather we can't leave her out here to give birth." He raised his head and asked: "Who wants to help her and let her stay? After she gives birth I will appoint teams to help and supply food for her to eat."

Lian was watching and hearing Crippled Sun's words she answered: "I will help her." She had been thinking about her son when Crippled Sun asked if any of the single men wanted her; she thought if the woman might eventually like NianLin, that would wonderful; if not, she would not lose anything by trying.

Chapter 72

SUN HAD BEEN ENTRUSTED by hunter Hu to go to Long Shan city to pick up YingLi.

Two weeks later, he came back alone.

He entered hunter Hu's pit house, took off his leather jacket and threw it on the floor; and said: "I have no success to report; only hard work, and disappointment. I really need a good meal and some wine; I am almost starved"

When hunter-Hu and his wife saw that Sun had returned alone, they asked: "What happened?"

Sun looked at the jar on the floor, and said: "I need a drink first, it is a long story."

Hunter-Hu put the wine jar on the table of the Kang (bed), opened the cover, and the alcohol fragrance assailed their nostrils. Sun was breathing deeply, enjoying the aroma. Hunter-Hu poured a big cup of the sweet potato wine for him. Sun tilted his head back and drank deeply. The wine trickled from the corners of his mouth, and he used his hand to wipe it off and continued drinking.

Hu's wife Yajie, went to invite LinLin to join them. When Sun saw LinLin, he got up from the Kang and holding LinLin's hand said: "Brother Lin, my trip was unsuccessful; however I have done the best I could."

"Please sit down, talk slowly, and tell me everything." LinLin said kindly; however Sun felt LinLin's hand tremble as he spoke.

LinLin sat down with Hu and Sun around the table, and listened as Sun described his experiences in detail.

"The reason I am so late in coming back is because I went to Long Shan city twice; the first time I went there, I couldn't find your mother in law at the address you gave me. The gate was locked, so I asked the neighbours, they all shook their heads said they did not know!"

Finally I went to the Long Shan city police office, I told them that I was a businessman and came to research your wife and family background. They asked if I had a letter of introduction; I said yes, and showed them my letter for hotel one, then they found some information for me, your wife's HuKou is still there; they have been looking for her for weeks and haven't found her. They said she is an anti- revolutionary's wife and the police want to send her to the countryside."

"The greatest possibility is that your mother in law has hidden your wife some where. That will be good for her, and it is not necessary for you to worry about her. Anyway, if you want me to go back again, I would go anytime."

Three meals were put on the table; the hot steamer was giving off a delicious odour. Sun with his big wide eyes said: "My sister in law, I love to eat your cooking so much, you always cook a wonderful meal. I could never get tired of your cooking" then he turned to LinLin, and said: "You should come to the U.S. with me; you could send for your wife after you get there; she would be safer there than here

Hu said: "You are a son of a bitch! You have always had your heart set on joining your cousin in the US. How is the situation better there, do you really dare to go?"

"There the women are open, not traditional and so serious as here, so I think that is the best place for me."

Hu and Yajie laughed at Sun and told him he was crazy. LinLin who had been quiet for a long a time, asked:

"How did your cousin get to go there?"

"His mother and father died early; my mama adopted him. You could say we are like brothers. It is a long story; to make it short he has an uncle there who is very rich who picked him up in Hong Kong and took him to the US. His uncle would have taken me too but my mama said no. I was very young and didn't have any choice; later when I got into trouble my mama said: oh! If I knew you were going to be like this, I would have let you go, but then it was too late.

Hu asked: "How did he get there, by train?"

"Brother Hu, the US is in the western world, no trains go there."

"Where is the western world?" Yajie asked.

"I don't know how to explain it. "Sun said shaking his head.

LinLin described it for them this way: "Just think of your head as the world, and the right side is the eastern half and the left side is western half. Between east and west there is a lot of water, the names are the Pacific Ocean and the Atlantic Ocean."

Hu pointed to his own head and asked: "Where is China?"

LinLin pointed to his left ear and said: "Here, on the eastern side." Then he pointed at his right ear and said: "The US is there."

"Oh my god!, you had better forget your dream! You can't go! How big is the ocean?" Hu asked.

"Have you seen the sea?" LinLin asked Hunter-Hu.

"No, I have just seen a river."

"Then it will be hard to explain to you." Sun said.

"You have not seen it either. Why do you act like you know so much?" Yajie said, and both she and her husband laughed at Sun.

LinLin said: "The position of China is in the Eastern Hemisphere of the earth, from WuSu town in China to the US state of Alaska is probably close to 4356 kilometres."

Sun not waiting for him to finish patted LinLin's shoulder and said: "Lin brother, let's go together."

"What do the women look like?" Yajie asked.

"My cousin didn't say; I guess they will look like Russian women, with yellow hair, green eyes, big ass, big breasts, and a very thin waist."

"You are just dreaming about a big ass and big breasts aren't you?" Yajie said.

"I don't have any other bad habits; I just like women." Sun said.

LinLin asked: "How would we get there?"

"My cousin said there are two ways, one is from Russia, the other is from Hong Kong."

"Either one is not easy, you better forget it." Hu said.

"Hong Kong is very far from here, but Russia is very close." LinLin said.

"That is a problem too, because we don't speak Russian."

"I can speak Russian." LinLin said.

"Oh, wonderful! hah, hah! Brother Lin, let's go!"

Hu said: "Brother Lin, don't believe him. We are Chinese, and even staying in our own country is not easy, there it could be much worse."

Chapter 73

IN THE MOUNTAIN VILLAGE the team leader talked to Lian quietly: "This woman has a strong temper, she will yield to a soft approach but rejects force; if you are kind to her, she might stay."

Lian nodded happily.

Crippled Sun said: "If you are able to keep her in your home, she will be for your son."

Lian had the same idea before she offered to take YingLi into her home, and she was encouraged by these words from the leader; her heart was filled with enthusiasm.

The midwife came and ordered her to boil water.

"How much water?" Lian asked.

"As much as possible" said the midwife, she was checking YingLi's condition and said: "don't hurry, she is just open one finger" and then she told YingLi: "don't push or use force, save your strength, just do deep breathing. You can yell and scream if you want. When a woman gives birth, the first one comes slowly, after that it is like a chicken laying eggs." she told YingLi.

Lian had only had one child, NianLin so she had no experience like the midwife described.

Time passed by slowly, and the boiled water got cold and was heated again several times. YingLi was having contractions and hollering louder than before; however, the babies head was still not in position yet.

Crippled Sun and his wife both came to find out what was happening. Other farmers, both men and women were standing out in the cold with their hands shoved up into their sleeves and stretching their necks trying to see.

Several hours later, YingLi was still suffering, and screaming regularly.

NianLin had orders to keep the fire stoked and he was squatting beside the stove with a lot of dry wood, holding his head low, watching the fire, and sweating.

Lian talked to Crippled Sun and said: "We better send her to the hospital so we don't make any mistakes."

Crippled Sun had been thinking the same the same; his wife had given birth to five children, and never had an experience like this. When he discovered that the driver who had taken XingYun to the hospital was not back yet he said: "I will drive, NianLin, you come with me."

Neighbours helped lift YingLi on to the truck, the engine was started, and the Crippled Sun saw NianLin had a red face, his body didn't move. He said loudly: "Your wife is giving birth, if you don't go who goes?"

People were grinning, even though nothing had happened yet between them, those words from the leader's mouth made it become true. Under the team leader and mama's orders, many hands pushed NianLin on the tractor with them to go to the hospital.

The doctor said he would have to do a caesarean delivery. Before the surgery a family member had to sign. Crippled Sun pushed NianLin and he wrote his name on the agreement.

YingLi gave birth to a boy, and stayed in the hospital for seven days; during her stay Lian sent NianLin to nurse her.

NianLin was a dutiful son, and even though he did not want to do it, he obeyed his mom.

In the hospital, both NianLin and YingLi felt very awkward because they were strangers to each other. He was supposed to bathe her; and he moved her body from side to side, and used a hot towel to wash her, but he did not wash her ass because she held her legs tightly together.

When Lian came and saw that YingLi's ass was very dirty and starting to stink, she washed it saying:: "My god. My god."

After YingLi left the hospital another problem arose; she did not have enough milk for the baby. The little boy was crying because he was hungry, and when the baby cried, YingLi cried too.

Lian killed a hen to help YingLi start producing more milk. and she sent NianLin to town to buy milk. NianLin came back carrying one little box of powdered milk, and two pork feet.

Lian asked: "Where did you get the money for these pork feet?"

"I borrowed it from Crippled Sun."

"You are lying, the team leader has gone out, and everyone knows that. Where did you get the money? You can't be doing bad things." "Mama, I did not do anything wrong like you think. I...I followed another guy and sold some blood."

NianLin spoke in a very low voice, but YingLi heard him very clearly and thought: what a good mother and son; she knew what they were up to, and she was determined not to give in to them. Instead, to thank them, she wrote a letter to LuDongChun and asked her to send some money to them.

She mailed the letter but did not receive a reply. Chinese traditional custom was to stay in a house for a full month after a woman had given birth. At the end of a month she would ask directions to the address of her mom's friend and go there.

Lian knew that YingLi had the address where she had planned to go before Sun kidnapped her, and that it was a long ways away. She told YingLi: "If you don't like my son and don't want to stay, I will not push you. But, it is a long way to travel. How about waiting until after seeding and I will send my son to guide you? The weather will be warmer then too." Lian said. She was calculating that it would be five months, and she might change her mind during that time.

Chapter 74

NIANLIN'S ONLY EXPERIENCE WITH the opposite sex had happened during the past spring. In his memory, that night had been cold as winter, but his body had been as hot as summer. It was late in the evening, and he and his classmate Yan were standing by a tree in the graveyard on the other side of the village. The graves were silent, the only sounds were from their own weeping. NianLin tried to use his body temperature to warm her cold shaking body. They were combined into one murky shape in the gathering dusk. Cold breezes from the mountains came and went causing the tree branches to sound like they were crying in the wind. Some dead twigs and branches were falling to the ground. They looked like they were the only ones in the world just holding each other.

NianLin said: "Yan, tomorrow you are getting married you need to go home and get some rest."

"No" she said.

Suddenly, something passed in front of them, the girl yelled in fear afraid of the unknown. He loosened an arm free to take a look around, and then said. "It may have been a wild rabbit."

"I'm afraid." She said sweetly.

NianLin said: "We should go home now."

Her cold hand covered his mouth, and she said: "Don't talk about that!." She was sobbing, and snuggling against NianLin's chest. Her parents were forcing her to marry a man who had a city HuKou and worked in a factory He was more than ten years older than her, and had a very bad case of psoriasis that made his face look like a half boiled lobster. When she thought about his face she wanted to vomit. She loved NianLin; they had been classmates since they started school. But, her parent's arrangement for her could not be disobeyed.

Hot steam was rising up from the cold soil; the wind had stopped, and the mountain was silent. The stars in the sky had closed their eyes...Yan was waiting for him, waiting for him to enter her and join her body to his. She wanted to be with him forever, in this life and the next one. There was just one problem, her parents liked money too much, and wanted her to marry some one else. She could not spend this life with NianLin but they could be together now and that would have to be enough.

That one night he would remember forever; as perhaps most people do. How many times he had recalled it since, and how he wished his Yan would come back to him, and that they could be together, and never separated again. But, this was only a dream, since she got married, he had never seen her again; someone had seen her in the city, and said she had a good life, but someone else had said she was not very well.

YingLi in NianLin's eyes maybe was not a good woman, she had come to the countryside to have her baby and then she planned to leave. She had never said where she came from but anyone could tell by her skin that she was a city person. Her face had soft skin, her hands had no calluses, and she screamed when she got chicken shit on her feet...she was like the young students from the city. Since students had been coming to the village, the farmers all had eyes for them. One rich farmer in another mountain village who married a city girl said he felt like he had the life of a Buddha. These city girls were not good workers inside or outside but their dispositions were much better than village women; they had gentle manners, smiled when they were happy, not just grinned, and remained silent when they were angry instead of screaming. NianLin looked like he didn't care if YingLi went or stayed; however, he was always ready to help her.

Sometimes his mother did things to impress YingLi that needed his co-operation, and that made him feel embarrassed. One time, he had bought pork feet again, and when Lian saw them she purposely berated him: "My god, did you sell your blood again? You need take care of your health too."

He answered smiling: "Mama, what is happening to your memory? You gave me the money this morning,, have you forgotten so quickly?"

NianLin saw his mom wink her eye at him to quit, but he continued: "Mama, what it is wrong with your memory?"

Lian had a red face, but she still held own and continued to talk. "Oh, you think your mama is foolish? The money I gave you was very little and couldn't buy all this. You have not even married yet and you are starting to stand on your wife's side to speak. Ok listen: if we need to sell blood l will go. I'm old, and it doesn't matter if I die early or late; you are young, and you need to care for the family."

Finally NianLin understood what his mama was saying. He said: "Mama, it is not necessary to impress her; if she wants to stay she will stay, if she wants to go just let her go, you can keep her body but you can't keep her heart. Mama, I'm only eighteen, why do you worry so much?"

"Who isn't eighteen, all the single men were eighteen once."

Five months was really a long time for YingLi to wait. Though she stayed in Lian's home and was treated like a first class guest, it just made her feel more nervous. She constantly kept to her plan to go to go to her mama's friend's home uppermost in her mind. When the planting was finished, NianLin took YingLi go to find her mom's friend, but they could not find him.

On the way back, YingLi did a lot of thinking. Her main concern was about getting a HuKou for herself and her son. It was much easier to register for a HuKou in the countryside than the city, she would not need to show where she was from, or need a letter from the police. Her biggest problem was her son; the village people viewed YingLi's son as a bastard, if she wanted benefits for her son, she would have to get married. With a HuKou as an adult her son would be able to join a work team and get food; a child was only a group's burden if he was the product of a legal marriage. She cried during the whole trip back.

NianLin seemed to read her mind, and before they got home, he said: "We could have a false marriage, that would solve your problem."

YingLi felt very grateful but she didn't want to cause him more trouble and said: "That would be a problem for if you wanted to marry another woman later."

"I don't have any body to wait for he said." He just wanted her to be happy. "You can trust me, I swear I just want to help you get your son get a HuKou then we can divorce."

She could see in his eyes that he was being honest and she was touched.

Chapter 75

YINGLI FINALLY DECIDED TO go ahead with the false marriage; seeing no other solution.

When they told her they planned to get married Lian was so happy she couldn't stop talking, and got busy making plans for the wedding beginning with a lucky date for the occasion.

The old style of wedding had been done away with during the Cultural Revolution in the city. In the countryside it was a little bit better, perhaps half and half; for example usually in an old style wedding there would be a big meal and fish on the table to treat the guests, the guests would bring a bed sheet or cash as practical gifts for bride and groom. Half and half now was a big dish meal and the fish was gone, tea, candy, wine, and cigars replaced the fish, and the gifts changed to works of Chairman Mao...for the joyous occasion.

The newlyweds would be hazed on the wedding night, gangs of men would appear to create obstacles to the bride. They would have a hundred different ways to make a great noise and the louder and happier were best for proving that in the future the bridegroom and bride would have a wonderful life. At the newlyweds hazing there were no words of respect for who was younger or older. The bride was expected to be very nice and receive everybody and not get mad at anyone no matter how they acted. Usually, a wedding day was a holiday for the men. The mountain village had many single men who would never have a woman; and it was a chance for them to joke, and it also got them excited. Lian was worried about the problem that YingLi had with the other man when she first arrived. If the men were afraid of her and didn't open their mouths to haze her, she would lose face so Lian went around the villages to invite anyone who was even distantly related to her.

The wedding day coincided with the off-season: the people were finished seeding, and had not started hoeing or cultivating yet. A lot of people showed up. Becoming a mother in law made Lian look radiant, her yellow skinny face, was transformed so that she seemed to be glowing with health. She bought seven feet of blue fabric, and made a jacket for herself. Her hair was usually in disorder, but today it had been cut and brightened with hair wax.

She was a little nervous looking around YingLi, and advising her about how to cope with the hazing: "Today is a very special day! Just let them talk and joke, and don't take offence." She added. "Today there will be no customary signs of respect for who is older or younger; they will haze you, and if their words are offensive, you should not get mad. If they talk with dirty language, just pretend that you did not hear them. If some one touches you, just let them touch, we do not suffer anything from being touched."

YingLi nodded and smiled; she had not expected a false wedding to become such a big affair and she felt awkward. When she saw NianLin, he was busy giving people candy, cigarettes, or sunflower seeds...he didn't have time to be concerned about her feelings.

Almost everyone was wearing clothes that had been patched many times. Women were nursing their babies, with their breasts exposed to other women and men and they were not the least bit shy or modest about it.

YingLi didn't wear a heavy cotton jacket; inside she wore a cotton-padded vest with terylene lines on the collar; her outer garment was a grass green coloured woman's type military uniform, with a little open wide winged collar, and a narrow waist that made her look very attractive.

When the wedding started, NianLin and YingLi led in a salute to Chairman Mao, followed by Lian, and finally all the guests. The next step was that the bridegroom holding his bride's hand would go off as newlyweds that were the high point of the wedding. The time was everyone looked forward to the most. NianLin took YingLi's hand, and they were to going to their room when a traditional prank before entering the bridal chamber, caused a fight.

A man with a pockmarked face said loudly: "I just heard the bride has four nipples on her breasts; how about letting us see them?"

That was clearly bullshit; however, many people, particularly the men were intrigued with the idea of seeing her breasts. Country women after they had a child were not shy about exposing their breasts to nurse their children. But it was highly unusual at a wedding to demand to the see a bride's breasts. All men would naturally like to see this beautiful woman's breasts, and the possibility that she had four nipples was even more enticing. The single men had itching palms wanting to touch, and some of their trousers crotches had already become wet.

NianLin's brain was buzzing with this turn of events in the wedding. He had joined in wedding parties before and had hazed too, however the people had never wanted the bride to take off her clothes and let them touch her breasts before, and he took it as insult to him and his family. He found his sickle and raised it high, letting everyone know that if they dared to expose her breasts he would use it.

Lian had been busy treating people outside the house and inside, and when she heard the lewd request she was not mad just worried about YingLi's temper.

The village people were very excited about seeing her breasts and they were shouting loudly. "Go ahead, go ahead." They were just all talk and not really ready for action, when one man saw NianLin had a sickle in hand, his voice got weak and he changed his tune asking: "Who dares to look?"

"I'm not afraid of that." The Pockmarked faced man said; he had seen the sickle too; but he thought NianLin was just trying to scare people. His face was rough and deeply pocked marked; and his last name Qian, people called him Pock Qian. In the mountain village, he had been single the entire fifty years of his life. But he had actually been married once, for one night. A match making woman had introduced him hiding his pocks and said how nice he was; she tricked the girls' parents and they agreed to let their daughter marry him. After the wedding when the bride took off her head cover and saw his pockmarked face she repented and wanted out, but he tied her hands and raped her. She was very upset and when he played himself out having sex and went to sleep she hung herself from the roof beams...since that episode Pock-Qian had a nasty reputation, and no woman wanted anything to do with him. Pock-Qian missed having a woman, and now he lusted to even just see a woman's breasts. This desire made him forgot everything else, and he grabbed a hold of YingLi's jacket with two hands and tore it open. There was the sound of cloth tearing, and the cloth buttons dropped to the ground.

Almost at the same time, NianLin's sickle was descending towards the pock-faced man's head but the first swing missed. That seemed to prove to Qian that NianLin was just trying to scare him. NianLin heard his mouth like woodpecker. "NianLin, are you trying to kill me? You mother ###! I will kill you, and fuck your mama."

NianLin hated anyone who cursed his mother. Even when he had been going to school, he was fighting with his classmates about slurs against his mother. The kids could joke with him about fucking his grandmother, but not about fucking his mama. He had always respected his mama and never allowed anyone to insult her.

The excitement of the hazing was gone, the farmers were scared now and their faces had turned pale. NianLin made a second swing with the sickle that connected, and Pock-Qian's head started bleeding. As he raised the sickle again Lian rushed in and intercepted the blow yelling at NianLin: "He is a perverted bastard but you need to stop right now!"

She reached up and blocked the descent of the sickle, and held it tight; blood started streaming down her arm.

271

At the same time, YingLi was holding NianLin from behind, and when she saw blood coming from Lian's hand, she screamed: "Hurry up, get cold water; we need cold water to stop the bleeding."

Some people went to take care of Qian, and discovered his head had two inch cut on it.

NianLin said: "Use a cigar quick!" He let go of the sickle and removed his mama's hand from the blade, and with both hands he held his mama's wrist tight trying to stop the blood flow.

"Cigar." someone said. YingLi let go of NianLin, took the cigar and applied it to the cut on Lian's hand, and soon had the bleeding stopped.

Lian's little body was bent over, and her face was as yellow as the soil.

Pock-Qian was cursing, and he left pushing people aside.

The health worker from the main group was carrying the first aid box. He knew only simple first aid, and was accustomed to handing out aspirins; he had never been in a situation like this and he had never had to deal with blood. He was shaking and didn't know what to do.

YingLi opened the first aid box, and took out a rubber band to make a tourniquet for Lian's wrist, then she took out tweezers, and used them dip a cotton ball in alcohol and clean the cut. The centre of Lian's palm had a deep cut that had gone to the bone.

YingLi stood up and said: "The cut needs stitching, she should go to the hospital right away."

"No! No! No!" Lian flatly refused, saying: "If I went I would not be able to relax, NianLin is a foolish boy; and he might do something stupid."

"Mama, you go to the hospital. I will not do anything stupid" NianLin said.

"No, no. "Lian repeated, in a firm voice.

"The cut needs to be stitched up." Ying Li said.

The health worker told YingLi: "I have sheep intestine line, can you sew with it?"

YingLi did not have experience with that either, but when she saw that Lian was very determined, she said: "Yes, I can" Sewing muscles was a basic surgical skill that just required good eyesight and a hand that is steady. LinLin had taught her many times how to stitch on the bodies of animals. It should not be a problem, but she remembered another thing, and said: "I can sew it up for her, but she needs a tetanus injection."

"If I order someone to bring it back to you, can you inject it?" Crippled Sun asked.

"Yes." YingLi said.

Crippled Sun sent a man along to bring back the vaccine. YingLi, with all the people watching knelt on the ground; flushed the cut with water, then alcohol, and put tincture of iodine on the cut area. She injected Lian in the palm of her hand with an aesthetic, and then she started sewing with a needle and thread.

Later that evening, Pock-Qian returned with two police men who arrested NianLin.

YingLi went to talk to Crippled Sun about NianLin. He said: "Pock Qian's family reported him to the community police, NianLin will probably go to jail for awhile."

Chapter 76

WHEN YONGHONG WAS CERTAIN that she was pregnant, she planned to tell ZhangYong that she had been raped.

She and WenJun had researched other women who had been raped and what their condition and appearance looked like afterwards.

She made her hair look dishevelled in a mirror, and tore some buttons off her jacket.

WenJun said: "You will need some blood on your forehead that will prove you struggled."

YongHong laughed at him and said: "Fuck you! If I make my head bleed that will hurt and I will have a scar. Would you like to have a scar on your face?"

WenJun nodded and said: "Oh, forget! it"

The next thing was that her pants would need to be torn or taken off. They argued a long time, and finally YongHong accepted WenJun's suggestion: that from not far from ZhangYong's apartment, she would take off her pants and give them to him; then she would use her cotton jacket to cover her lower body before she knocked on his door.

She decided after all that she did need some blood on her face, and told WenJun to cut his finger and smear some blood on her forehead.

Anyway, their carefully planned show failed.

In the beginning ZhangYong believed her, and hurried to get her on the Kang to get warm, and got a bedcover to cover her. He knew her feet would be very cold and need caring for so he started to massage them but they were warm.

ZhangYong had experience in the world of ice and snow, in this kind of weather if Hong had been raped her feet would have been very cold.

ZhangYong asked her: "Why do you need to make a show and lie to me?"

YongHong was greatly surprised, but said: "What kind of person are you? What did you say? Why don't you have any Sympathy? I have been raped and hurt and you don't show any concern."

"Do you think I'm a three year old boy?" he asked.

YongHong did not answer.

"You can have another man, and you don't need to tell me the truth. Do you understand? I'm not angry, because our marriage was unfair to you."

"It is not necessary for you to be hypocritical. You knew you were unfair to me; it is not enough to owe me, you have ruined my life."

"Oh hold on, you know I have not ruined your life. I gave you the political life that you wanted in your dreams. You were successful and used me to get a high position, have you forgotten? You had a national talk show, and were the woman's model taking care of a disabled man..."

"What is wrong with that?"

"Did you ever really take care of me? Even once?"

"Hold on, I didn't write the manuscript; someone else wrote it. It was the top leader who directed everything. If you have a complaint you can go to talk to my leader, it didn't involve me."

"I do not have a complaint; I have helped you and am very happy to let you be outstanding. I am just a stepping-stone to let you get on the horse. I like to serve one faithfully."

"Hypocritically." she replied.

"However, I want to know the truth."

YongHong felt cold inside, and afraid that she couldn't get free by her self. But, she was unwilling to lose face and let him win. She insisted. "I really was raped. Really. Anyway, if I got pregnant today, I will keep it. I want to have kids. I don't care whose kids. I don't care if the kid's father is a rapist or a criminal. Anyway I will keep it. If you think you will lose face you can file a complaint. Let's talk about you now. You are a man, but you never acted like a husband. You knew I wanted to improve and go to the top; but I'm also a woman too. I'm a woman with normal female feelings; I have been without a lover, and without a love life.

She saw ZhangYong's face turn pale and then he stood up and dropped his pants. She panicked but when he didn't make a move towards her she looked and saw that between his legs was a little penis with a scar the size that a two-year-old boy would have. He was disabled from inside to outside; she suddenly understood why he had never made love to her.

The sound of ZhangYong's voice rang in her ears. "I'm just your stepping stone to get on the horse."

Her knees went weak and she knelt on the floor in front of him, the first time she had kneeled to anyone in her life.

Chapter 77

THE EARLY MORNING SUN was radiating off of Dragon Mountain beside the mountain village intermittently like a little boy; playing a game of hide and seek as clouds passed far overhead between the sun and the mountain. Mist rose like steam from the river and the land where moisture was to be found.

The duck is a water loving animal, farmers who had ducks would drive them to water in the morning, and drive them back in the evening to keep them safe at night. Every farmer had his mark on his ducks to prevent making mistakes.

Lian's duck was marked too.

While NianLin was in Jail Lian was sick and laid on the Kang. YingLi took the initiative and did the household chores

One day by mistake YingLi drove a neighbours duck back, and pushed it in into their nest.

The owner of the other duck was famous as a bitch in the village. When she discovered her duck was missing she stood in the Village Street cursing and then went door to door looking for her duck. When she went into NianLin's yard she found her duck; she lifted her ducks wings, and yelled from the yard: "If anyone is home come out here."

Hearing her holler, YingLi went out and found the bitch woman holding a duck; she was confused and asked: "I just drove them back a few minutes ago, what it is wrong?"

"Shit, this is my duck." the bitch woman said.

YingLi went to the duck house to check and there were two ducks in there. To her, ducks all looked the same; she remembered Lian telling her they had two, and she drove two back. Then the bitch woman said:

"Give me back my duck's egg."

YingLi went into the duck house to check, and came back and said: "There are no eggs yet."

Then she said the ducks just came back, and have not have laid any eggs yet, how am I supposed to find an egg for you?"

"Are you saying I am lying? Let me tell you, my duck always lays an egg right away when it gets back. If you want my ducks egg that is ok, just give me a chicken egg, but I would need two of those for one."

"Two for one?" YingLi felt this bitch woman was trying to bully her too much, she said: "Hey, be nice. Are your duck's eggs as big as two chicken eggs?"

"Ha-ha. You don't know that? Your chicken's eggs are small like your husband's testicles! Of course I need two for one."

YingLi couldn't hold her tongue any longer and, said: "Even if you saw my husband's testicles that doesn't mean, I have to give you anything."

The woman had another agenda and wanted to show the other people how formidable a person she was. Since YingLi had cut the farmer's penis, all the village farmers had shifted their dread from her to YingLi. Some women used her to scare their children saying. "Don't cry or YingLi will come." The woman had heard that her rating had come down, and today she wanted to compare herself with YingLi and find out who was the highest.

"Don't feed me shit; everyone knows you are a loose woman from the city."

YingLi was really getting very angry at her, she felt like she had been given a hard slap on the face. But she bit her tongue and resisted the urge to retaliate. She didn't want to make the whole village upset, or cause problems for NianLin and Lian. She was human, and needed some dignity, but she conceded that she had already given Lian's family trouble and didn't want to cause another problem.

The woman saw YingLi was giving in, and she was very proud of herself. She lifted her loud voice hoping all the village people would come to see her victory. The commotion soon drew a crowd who were curious to learn what was going on. Most of these people didn't like the woman. Women suspected she enticed their husbands, men complained that she was too greedy for money; if they had sex with her it, it looked like they owed her their life.

Hearing the commotion Lian came out of the house; she had been sick, her face was pale, and her body was trembling when she walked. She said feebly: "YingLi! My god! Can't you bear it? You don't want our family to have more trouble do you?"

YingLi's tears began to fall, she cried and said to Lian: "She shit on our heads and I did bear it. What can we do?"

Lian said. " Just give her two eggs. Is two enough?" Lian asked the bitch woman. Finally, the bitch woman took two chicken eggs and left with her booty, pleased with her victory.

Later after having been so angry, Lian's condition was even more serious. YingLi wanted Lian to go and see a doctor, but Lian was concerned about saving money and didn't want to go. She said: "I saw that you know medicine, it would be much better for you to treat me."

YingLi said: "I'm not a doctor; maybe I would make your problem worse."

"Who said you are not a good doctor? You can see my cut is healing very quickly. I say you are able to treat me as well as any doctor. Anyway, I trust you. You just use your experience to do it, if I get better it is good; if I get worse that is Ok too. I'm old, I don't care if I live or die."

YingLi put her hand on Lian, and checked her pulse, it was deep and weak; she found that Lian had been depressed for a long time, then asked: "What has made you so depressed?"

"Who told you I'm depressed? I'm not."

"Your pulse is weak and deep, the pulse of your liver shows that. The cause is depression, your Qi to the liver has been blocked, that bothers your stomach, and then you detest food and get insomnia."

Lian said in wonder: "See! I knew you were able to take care of me; your diagnosis is the same as the doctor I saw before. Who is the doctor in your family?"

"My...my friend..." YingLi wanted to say, "My husband" this was on her tongue when she remembered that she had told Lian that she had never married.

Lian was not paying attention and didn't notice YingLi stammering when she replied. She continued and asked: "Is my condition because I am waiting to get my son back?"

"Yes, of course." Ying Li said: "Your body health is not a big problem; it is just your emotions, you need try to relax and not think about it so much."

"Only you can help me relax."

"Why?"

"When NianLin comes back you can give birth to a child for him..." She saw YingLi lower her head then she said: "NianLin has treated you a hundred percent."

"Yes, I know that." YingLi replied.

"It is good that you realise that; and you should have a conscience and conduct yourself accordingly.

Lian's health began getting better day-by-day with YingLi giving her such good care. NianLin had been sentenced to re-education through labour for six months; and it was said if he made good progress, he could come out in three or four months, and they went to visit him every mouth. Re-education through labour was the same there as for people from the city. When she went there again, she sighed with emotion at the changeability of life's fortunes; gratified that she had been favoured by the good luck to meet Lian and her son.

Lian soon broadcast YingLi's skill at treating disease throughout the whole village. Some of the people knew they had a disease but did not have the money to go to a doctor so they went to see YingLi; from her they got herbal prescriptions, and went to the drug store saving 60 or 70 percent of the cost. The farmers and their families began to highly respect her for her great skill in treating them.

Chapter 78

NIANLIN CAME BACK FROM his re-education through labour in late summer. Going home his first problem was how to sleep in the same room with YingLi. The day of their marriage, he had been arrested before bedtime. NianLin went in the bedroom and said in a low voice. "I will sleep on the floor."

"The floor is cold you will get sick."

"That is no matter. I'm young, I have a hot body."

YingLi said: "That is not good idea, if your mama comes in, what you will tell her?"

NianLin agreed, and slept with YingLi on same Kang; with the child in the middle.

Since NianLin returned he had found his mother a few times with her ear to the wall listening. She soon discovered their sleeping arrangement, and asked her son why he slept like that.

NianLin lied to her. "That is so that the child will not get cold because the baby likes to kick off the covers."

Winter passed and Lian was always looking at YingLi's belly. After six months with no sign of pregnancy she said to NianLin and YingLi. "You both need to hurry up, I'm not getting any younger, and you need to have a baby soon to let me take care of. Ying Li and NianLin both had red faces.

NianLin had learned a new skill in prison he learned how grow tobacco from another criminal in the re-education through labour facility. It was not just the rubbish of society being re-educated, there were some very talented people there too. The tobacco grower was very good at teaching and had taught NianLin how to grow better quality tobacco. In the spring after he returned home he convinced his mama to agree to let him try to grow some. The seeds were planted and grew quickly; by the time they were at the three-leaf stage other farmers noticed that his tobacco plants had leaves twice the size of theirs. The beautiful leaves rustling in a warm wind gave off a distinctively different aroma than their traditional plants. Other farmers speculated that this tobacco on the market would bring a higher price and be easier to sell. They wanted to learn but were afraid that NianLin would not teach them so when ever they had time they would stop by to joke with him and watch what he was doing.

"NianLin, what are you always researching for? If you are really smart, research how to plant and grow bread or a delicious dish menu like a restaurant. When we get hungry, we can just go to the field to eat." While talking, the speaker would be stealing a glance at the tobacco, trying to learn his secrets.

NianLin knew very clearly what they wanted, he just acted confused, and went along with the joke and said: "If I was able to do that, I would planting woman for you to help you end your single life. That you would not have to look like the flagpole at the UN, always standing and looking so pitiful."

"You are a son of a bitch! I will kick your ass..." The farmer said as he left laughing.

Chapter 79

YongHong's face was covered with sweat and it looked like she had a sweat gland disorder. In this weather, other people were still wearing cotton-padded clothes and pants; she was wearing a summer short-sleeved shirt, but was still dripping with sweat. Her growing abdomen made walking difficult, even when she didn't wear her favourite clothes and changed to wearing loose fitting men's clothes. What angered her the most, in her fifth month of being pregnant was that she could no longer highlight her beautiful body in tight fitting clothes.

After awhile, her face started to show butterfly spots: like she had dark clouds on her cheeks that she couldn't cover up or take off. She thought that being pregnant made her look ugly. She could not bear seeing herself in a mirror any more, and when she did she couldn't believe it was her. She wondered with regret why anyone would ever want to be pregnant. And why she had given in to the manipulating of that ugly woman.

There had been no way out since she signed the agreement. Shit! This was the first she had been subjected to the will of another person. She knew that Ming didn't want to break up with WenJun and ruin her future; she just wanted to keep her family together. YongHong also knew that when she handed over the baby that her relationship with WenJun would end too. She wanted it to end early and wondered why it ever started. It was just that bastard WenJun had been...so pushy and begging...and raped her when she was drunk. Why hadn't she charged him with rape? Here she had to laugh. Women in China did not dare to do that; YingLi was crazy, and foolish. Anyone else would be afraid to lose face or chance to get a husband, and have a normal life.

ZhangYong was a good man, when he learned that his own wife had been raped, he didn't say he would divorce her. Yes like ZhangYong had said, he was her stepping-stone to climb on the horse. Now, she doesn't need a stepping-stone; she is satisfied with her present position, and doesn't want to rise higher up. Compared to her mama who had been in the revolution her whole life, in a real life and death situation, and only rose to a city position; she had risen higher.

ZhangYong really knew how to keep calm; even when his wife said she had been raped, and he didn't believe her he let it pass.

She had thought about ZhangYong, raising a little child, she even considered giving her child to him; but she realised the idea was impossible.

Ming was watching YongHong very closely looking forward to getting the baby. The expected date for delivery was the middle October. Ming, saw YongHong's belly getting bigger day by day, and showed her self-satisfaction; she was flying two kites now, the lines were long for now, later she would shorten them. WenJun if you want two women that is just your dream; you will just be a docile husband, and another thing, when you have your next life think again.

Ming thought this was a great idea; the other woman wouldn't have him either. She had got this idea from a neighbour who was a cadre's wife whose husband wanted to divorce her; that woman was successful and kept her husband and family together. Afterwards when the other woman saw when the man had compared his position to staying with her and chose to keep his position, she was very sad and alone. All men are like cats, and women are like fish, where could you find a cat that doesn't like fish? No where. Cat's liked to have their own fish and other fish too, but they were not stupid enough to lose their home and position and their own fish because of their prowling. Men were not foolish, and WenJun was not foolish either.

Zhang's mama had wished for a grandson for many years. Since YongHong got pregnant, she had starting making things for the baby, a little bed cover, a little pillow, a little blanket and little shoes. She had been so busy that her fingers had been pricked so much with her needle that they were bleeding.

"Hey, old guy," she said to her husband: "Did you notice since Yong Hong got pregnant her temper has been a lot better than before?! A child is bridge between a husband and wife, and that is true very good," She was smiling as she sewed baby clothes and sucked blood from her finger.

"A child is just a big expense." ZhangXianmin said not looking up from reading the daily news; his glasses were on the end of his nose, he sniffled and said: "I really don't care." He hadn't forgotten that his son ZhangYong had given him a very hard time.

His wife didn't want to hear that, before the birth of ZhangYong she had argued with him too.

"Hey old man, what did you say? For our life to continue we need a child, without a child what are you living for?"

WenJun was constantly blamed, and cursed by Hong on the phone: "It is your fault' you bastard. You will not have a good death. You have lived eight wicked lives already. You will need to be a cow and horse for me in your next life..." Since early in her pregnancy YongHong had been suffering morning sickness.

WenJun said: "Hey, it is only for a few weeks. You aren't the only woman to get sick, all women are like that, aren't they?"

"If it is so easy, you get sick and try it

"I'm trying...Oh...Oh...it feels...not bad." WenJun said jokingly.

"WenJun, when I see you I will peel your skin off."

"What would you like to eat? Let me buy something for you. Do you want something acid?"

People say, if you want acid it is a boy, if you want spicy food it is a girl.

Later when she got a butterfly spot on her face YongHong became very nervous, and she pinched WenJun black and blue.

WenJun wore a big smile and attempted to comfort her: "Your belly is big, and your waist is thick now, but it has elasticity; after you give birth it will go back like before."

"If I was a woman, I would have lots of babies. How hard can it be, it's like a chicken having eggs, pop have one, pop have other one..."

"WenJun, you strap twenty lbs of rice on your stomach and carry it every day and see how you feel..."

National day is a major holiday in China, and YongHong was ten times busier than usual. ZhangYong's parents had come from Long Shan city to visit. To conceal that they were not living together, ZhangYong had moved into YongHong's apartment the day before.

In the evening of the national holiday, when YongHong had finished her work she got home very late. YongHong was satisfied, some very important work had been done for the year. She could relax awhile now, then after a holiday she would go back to work, she gave her assistant some work that needed doing during her maternity leave. Now she could rest and just wait for the day to give birth and she wished that day to be over so that ugly woman would quit pestering her. She had heard that giving birth was very painful, and she was scared; but she didn't want to ask Zhang's mama for help.

Zhang's family and YongHong had dinner together and afterwards they sat in the living room listening to the radio broadcast the events of the grand occasion from Beijing. Stirring patriotic music made the people very happy, and excited; they were sharing their happiness with those who were in Tianaman Square with Chairman Mao viewing the parade. YongHong wanted to listen, but, she didn't like being with Zhang's family so she left them and went to her bedroom, carrying a book so it would look like she was reading, but she was listening to the radio.

After awhile she felt pains in her belly like the aching of a period only longer, and more serious, afterwards they became frequent short and very painful. She started groaning that soon became yelling on the bed and Zhang's mama came rushing in and asked worriedly.

"How painful is it, is it serious?"

"So-so." YongHong said gritting her teeth.

"So-so is what kind of pain?"

"It feels like...like ...period coming..." She lied. The words passed through clenched teeth. She was praying to herself, wait until tomorrow. Let me wait until tomorrow."

"Let's go, we should go to the hospital right now." Zhang's parents said at the same time.

"No...I...to...mor...row..."

As she spoke her water broke. Zhang's mama reached in to check and the head was down in the cavity of vagina already; she was experienced at delivering babies and she used her hands to check on the baby's progress.

Zhang's father went to the kitchen to boil a cauldron of hot water. Usually it was very difficult delivering the first baby, and would take several hours at least, but for YongHong it took only forty minutes. It was a girl, and because she was born on the national holiday, she was named GuoGing, meaning celebration.

Chapter 80

IN THE MOUNTAIN VILLAGE it was the high point of Lian's life to be having her own grandchild.

Since NianLin had been back home, she was always behind the door eavesdropping on NianLin and YingLi. One day, she overheard them talking about divorce, she started crying right away, and rushed in angrily and said:

"Oh! YingLi! Are you without a conscience? Do you just plan to have your baby and then leave? Have you thought about how my son and I have treated you? We did everything except take our hearts out to help you! I have not treated you unfairly! My son was in jail because of you! I have not complained to you. Now you want to take off and leave... my son with no wife for the rest of his life... He is the person that went to jail for you, and has a big black spot on his face, so that no woman will like him, or want to be with him. You have seen the villages all have many single men, and they will have no children to carry on their family. If you leave we would have no family tree! What a bitter life my son will have? He hasn't had a father since he was very young; I used my tears to help him grow up... I wished he would a have happy life. Even if I gave my life to change his that was reasonable for me.

"Mama, don't complain to her, it is me who wants a divorce." NianLin said.

"It is you? Who wants a divorce, you?" Lian suddenly stopped crying, and pointing at her son said very angrily: "You want a divorce? You were away almost half a year; YingLi took care of everything. Do you know how hard it was for her to do everything? Her life was not easy either. You are being a son of bitch. You will see how I will fix you..." Lian reached into the closet, grabbed a broom. NianLin ran out into the yard with her chasing him. YingLi followed them and felt troubled. She and NianLin had an agreement before they got married; and the marriage was only to get her son a HuKou.

Lian said: "YingLi has a child, where do you want her go? Where can they go? How is she to continue her life? I know very well how a woman with a child suffers. The year your dad...die, Oh...no...it was your dad who went...Oh, when your dad died." Lian used her hands to demonstrate and said: "I'm was hugging you, crying, sobbing...I felt it would be better to die. If I didn't have you to look after, I would have died. You have seen my eyes that are sick from crying; you just knew your mama cried a lot. That is why I cried? I'm not stupid. I knew it was better to be happy than crying but when life offers only a lot of hard times who can smile? You have an excellent wife why do you want her to go? Maybe it is you who wants to go, I will see. Even if it ends my old life I wouldn't let her leave half a step. You will see!"

YingLi and NianLin began to have a sex life later on when YingLi became willing.

It was one evening in early summer. NianLin as usual when he finished work came home and had dinner, and that night when he went into their room the first thing he noticed was that his pillow had been moved to the other side of the bed beside YingLi's. His heart started racing, he wanted to ask YingLi who was still in the kitchen, but he was shy, and just stayed in the bedroom pacing from one side of the bed to the other. He felt like he had been waiting for a year.

When YingLi finally came in, she asked very quietly. "Why aren't you sleeping?"

"How...like...like that?" NianLin said stammering.

"It is OK?" YingLi's said softly.

"You are the boss." He said and he grabbed a cloth to run out and wash.

"Where are you going?" YingLi asked..

"I'm going to get washed." He said, and then ran down to the river.

After Lian had made the big commotion about mention of a divorce, YingLi had done a lot of thinking and began to see things differently. She was beginning to regard Lian and NianLin as her helpers for life; they had treated her very well and she had no reason to complain about anything they had done. For these reasons alone she should repay them for their help. But, NianLin was also a good man, he just had a temper that was irritable, but that was a common problem for young people. Compared to the other young men in the village he was the best of the lot. She thought about the city girls living in the countryside, and wondered how many of them married farmers; it was a hard life. But why should she suffer by herself as Lian had done?

Sleeping in the same Kang with NianLin even with the baby between them had aroused her sexual desires causing her to struggle with herself. The man by her side reminded her of LinLin; they were like copies of each other in walking, talking, eating and snoring... many times in her dreams she though it was Lin come back to life again. The sound of his snoring aroused a strong sexual desire within her. Yes, they were husband and wife in the sight of everyone, and they slept on a Kang together with Lian checking on them every day. NianLin was gentle and had never pushed her. She always woke up with his snoring, and in the moon light, she saw he was wearing his pants even sleeping in the hot weather; when there was no wind and it was so humid it made him sweat a lot. She had shed tears of thanks for his consideration of her; even if she had a heart of stone this scene would have melted it.

Eventually Lian's dream came true, and she had her very own grandson. She really felt proud and elated, now she had a family tree from her own blood. This was the event that she had worked for through all those years that she had struggled.

Nothing could have excited her more. Perhaps it was natural for her to compare this baby with YingLi's first one, and think her grandson was much more beautiful. However it was the custom to name children with the same last name and the first born was DaShan, meaning big mountain, and YingLi thought she would name the new one XiaoShan, meaning little hill. Lian was very unhappy at the prospect of her grandson being called little hill. Lian poked her son in the back and said.

"If you call this one XiaoShan, what will you call the next one? You would do better to call the little boy DaHai-big Sea."

Lian believed that she had given her grandson a great name; a sea was better than a mountain because a mountain couldn't move, but a sea was alive, and held boundless prospects. After the birth of the baby YingLi had a mammary gland infection and couldn't nurse the baby so he was fed cows milk. People were very superstitious about mama's milk, without it Lian and NianLin were feeling very sorry for the baby.

For a long time they didn't want to believe it was true and Lian pushed her son to massage YingLi's breasts, but it just made her chest red and sore and didn't work. YingLi was the health worker for the main group now. After a month of rest since giving birth YingLi went back to work again; she was a barefoot doctor (a legal doctor, but without qualifications) who worked in the big group. Since she was unable to nurse the baby and she was very busy she often did not get home all day.

NianLin loved YingLi, and often carried lunch to her, wind, rain or sunshine. Some people were jealous and laughed at him, calling him a "wife's fan" as a joke.

Chapter 81

Y ONGHONG CAME TO THE people's commune to hold her talk show, which at the time was very popular, and was designed to educate the revolutionary masses in new thinking and rebirth.

YongHong had been down and up again regarding getting involved in LinLin's case as the political scene changed. At this time, following the death of the number two national leader, who had reportedly fled in betrayal, crashed, and burned in Mongolia: all of his policies were wrong now, and anything against them was right. Therefore YongHong was a hero and welcomed as the latest news source, and authority on what was taking place, and what policies now governed China.

Ten people including her leader accompanied YongHong to the Commune for the show and broadcast. YingLi had learned from the Main group where she worked of her sister's coming tour, and was very excited because it had been several years since she had seen her. Since LinLin was executed and YingLi fled to the countryside, they had not talked to each other.

YingLi wanted to go to the people's commune to visit her sister, but usually only the leaders of the teams and the main group would attend these meetings because they were the only ones who would get credit on their day work records. YingLi decided she would just go without getting a credit on her work record, and the people couldn't say "No".

She had known about the event for several days, and as the big day approached, she could not sleep almost all night. She was thinking about many things, and wondering what she should do. How would her sister look now? There were so many questions running through her mind that she wanted to know the answers to; the main thing she wanted to ask about was how to go about getting LinLin's case redressed.

The team tractor left the mountain village early in the morning carrying the team; Crippled Sun, a woman leader who was Crippled Sun's wife, the team accountant, and YingLi.

Crippled-Sun's wife was like a radio, when her eyes were open her mouth never stopped talking. She was a very happy woman; anywhere she went there would be the sound of laughter.

As the tractor passed the main group a young girl raised her arm and stopped it and asked: "Are you going to the people's commune? Can I get a ride with you? I want to go there too."

When she got on the truck the tractor started moving again, then Cripple-Sun's wife asked: "Who are you are you going there to castrate?"

Everyone burst out in raucous laughing.

The young girl was not shy and replied: "Do you think I don't dare to do it? Ha, Ha, who do you want to castrate? I will help you."

The people laughed again.

This young girl was a city student who had been sent to the countryside several years before to receive farming education. At that time YingLi had been spared going to the countryside by a special policy of the government that one in each family could stay in the city. These students worked with farmers teams. The mountain village team where she lived did not have any students, because it was too far away.

The students lived like a big family: girls and boys shared a two-bedroom house with the boys in one bedroom, and the girls in the other. The students had a leader, and room leaders to help, and guide them. The students gave the teams and their leaders a lot of pressure teaching them how to live and work: how to plant vegetables, how to cook food, how to measure the year's food supply. The students all missed their homes and families, and often cried together, and felt sorry for each other.

This girl acted, and talked like a boy, with a loud voice and was very boorish. Her personality was rough too, a girl who worked at castrating animals, and she really enjoyed it. She was sitting beside YingLi. YingLi saw that she was smiling, and recalled some of the funny stories she had heard about her gelding animals.

Her name was Feng; she had a big body, but was very lazy, and especially didn't like doing teamwork. She liked to stay at home and cook, however this job was supposed to be rotated among the five girls in the collective family; they all liked to stay home and cook. Therefore a battle for the job of cooking started, and Feng brought two bottles of wine back from the city as a bribe to her team leader and she won the cooking job. But her cooking was really bad, her corn cakes either did not have enough banking power or too much; it was so bad her roommates wouldn't eat it.

When the team leader discovered that the main group's veterinary station needed an assistant, he had offered Feng the job. She said: "If I don't have to go on the land to work that will be fine." The team leader wondered since she was a girl, if she would be able to go this job, but he discovered later that she really enjoyed it.

Her job was looking after animals, feeding them, and giving them medication; some times the doctor would take her with him and teach her how to geld. At first, the farmers didn't trust her on her own, and the team leader had to show up to explain that it was just like surgery, and it was very common for women doctors in hospitals to do surgery. The team leader said she can do mine first, if you guys only trust the veterinarian you can wait. Don't say I didn't give you a chance. When they discovered that she did the job very well, they started to trust her. People said that when she handled testicles she never had a red face, and looked just as tough as a man.

The meeting room in the people's commune was very small, simple, and crude. YingLi went in and found the seats at the back were all full. When the countryside people had to attend a meeting they liked to sit at the back where they could sleep. Li chose a seat near the front because she really wanted to see and hear her sister talk; even if their talk was not private since she would be talking to the masses; it was her talk show, and YingLi wanted to hear every single word.

She met her sister before the meeting, but because Hong had to sit on the stage, they just had time to say. "Hello."

During a break in the meeting, they visited, and both of them had tears in their eyes. After the preliminaries YingLi said: "Older sister, I have something that I need your help with."

YongHong anticipated what her young sister would ask, and said: "I know you want to get LinLin's conviction overturned.

Since she had got her talk show she had been very busy running about in the city and country doing talk shows; now she was remembering her young sister again whom she had almost forgotten. Since giving birth, YongHong looked like she had put on a little weight and she still had a butterfly spot on her face.

YongHong nodded and said: "Yes, Mr. Lin really deserves a redress of his conviction."

"Having said that will you will help me?"

"Why not? I joined this group to do a talk show and Lin's case will make a good topic."

"How can I say thank you?"

"Don't say that we are sisters, twin sisters, we must share our luck and suffering."

"Oh..." YingLi suddenly had an idea, and asked: "If Lin's case is resolved can I change my son's last name? Would that be allowed?"

"You gave your son a different last name?"

"Yes, for his protection in the future, he was not involved in his father's case; he hadn't even been born. I didn't have any other choice."

"I understand, it will not be a problem. I will help you overturn the verdict in LinLin's case; just give me your address." YongHong said confidently.

YingLi said. "Older sister..." then the words stuck in her throat, without any words, she just cried silently and the tears streamed down her face.

YongHong returned to the stage to continue with her show.

YingLi watched her sister's face intently. The sound of her voice was musical as if she was singing; she had notes in front of her, but most of the time she did not look at them. She did an excellent talk show, and used her own discretion about what she presented; she talked about her own exciting actions and thoughts, since her marriage to Zhang; how she had struggled with the second national leader over Lin's case, it was all very impressive, and made some of people in front of the stage have tears in their eyes.

Chapter 82

LINLIN'S CASE WAS RESOLVED in just six months After YongHong went back to the provincial capital it was said that LinLin's death sentence had taken only six minutes; six months was considered exceptionally fast for overturning a conviction. Usually a case like this would drag on for years.

This case benefited from YongHong's high position and also the brothers LinHu and LinXiao coming forward as witnesses. After the case was resolved, a provincial officer went to the mountain village to apologise to YingLi and notify her of the decision.

That day, YingLi was working so she did not meet the officer. When she got home, she received the document that said LinLin was innocent of anti-revolutionary activity and 500 RMB. She cried until evening, and didn't eat dinner.

NianLin was out working, but Lian was at home and when she saw YingLi so upset, she made no attempt to console her. When she heard YingLi's ex-husband's name was the same as hers' it had made her heart race. China had such a big population, that people with the same names were very common. Seeing YingLi so sad she thought about other possibilities, she is a young woman, why would she have married a man so much older than her? LinLin really was much older than her, so it seemed impossible and although she tried to think positive doubt still lurked in her mind. She was afraid, and tried to stop it. She didn't want to think about it. For the past few days, Lian had been anxious, with thoughts she couldn't control, and serous insomnia.

Later when she saw that YingLi had settled down and appeared to be at peace, she asked. "Is your ex-husband DaShan's father?" The family was all at the table eating dinner, and she was feeding DaShan..

"Yes." YingLi replied while feeding the baby.

"How long were you together?"

"It was not very long...about two years."

"What kind of work did he do?"

"Waste recovery."

Lian began to relax right away; but she still wanted more information from YingLi, and said. "Oh, that was not a good match for you was it?"

"He was an excellent match; he had been a teacher in a university, and knew traditional Chinese medicine also. My knowledge was all learned from him."

Lian's whole body trembled. "Why did he give up teaching at the university?"

"Because he had a political problem, and he was accused of being a rightist."

Lian felt her head getting bigger, and inside many voices buzzed like flies in her ears; she tried to appear calm and asked: "Do you have a photo of him that we can see?"

YingLi went to the bedroom and brought back a small black and white photo: it was only a two inch image of her and LinLin.

Yes, it was him for sure! She could see him very clearly and there was no mistaking his eyes, nose, mouth, and the black mole on his forehead. "Oh, my god, it is evil." Lian thought to herself.

NianLin saw his mama's face change, and thought it was because she was sad for YingLi. To clear the air he said: "Let's hurry up and eat, I'm starving."

Lian shot a glance at him as her thoughts continued to race: "What is this, the father is not the father, the son is not the son... the whole family relationship is wrong. If the neighbours found out, they would laugh until their teeth fell out. How would I ever have the face to go out? How could I let my grandson live with this? No. They can't know, if I don't say anything, who can find out? No one else can possibly know unless I tell them." She remembered that women who had children with their father in law had ended up committing suicide under pressure from the people.

The tongue was like a knife; it could kill people. However, these thoughts just made Lian more depressed, and it continued for many days.

One night, NianLin asked YingLi: "Did you make mama angry this week?'

"No, I thought that you had."

"She cries a lot when she is alone."

YingLi said: "Since we had the baby, she was often smiling, that was a big change from before. What has changed to make her so unhappy again? I have wanted to ask, now that we are talking about it I must tell you that I always felt that she had something troubling her."

"Her life has not been good or easy, my dad died very early, and she has taken care of me all my life."

"Couldn't she find someone else, there are many single men in the village."

"Lots of men have tried, she didn't want them. You know the team leader's wife has a mouth like a woodpecker, but she couldn't change mama's mind. When I was in preschool, my classmates fought with me, when I got hurt, I would go home wanting my mama to find a dad to help me. She always cried for a few days. Even after I didn't need a father and wanted her to get married and have a life, she said: 'My son, except for this one thing I will promise you any thing; even to go and die. Your mama in this life lived only for your dad, no one else. While I live I belong to him, when I die I will be with his ghost. Don't mention it again. Ok?' Then she cried for many days; when people bring up this subject she gets sad for a long time."

YingLi thought to herself that all women fall in love like that. She remembered her self on the road to the execution ground.

"When I was young, I liked to fight. It didn't matter if they hurt me or I hurt them. The reason for most of the fights was that they were insulting my mama: they called me a son of a bastard. I couldn't allow people to insult my mama, so I fought; but at home I couldn't tell my mama the truth, so I was criticized by both my school teacher and my mama."

YingLi's mind had been in another world, and she answered: "Ok, let's sleep, I'm very tired."

NianLin was soon asleep and dreaming; but YingLi was thinking about LinLin again.

Chapter 83

ALMOST EVERY NIGHT, LIAN stared at the ceiling and repeated the words she had repeated ten thousand times before, however when the night came they kept running through her mind saying: "My god, look at what you have done, you have brought disaster to your family's blood. It is your fault, why did you lead like this? Who could have known that YingLi had a child with LinLin? If I had known, I would not have let them get together. If I had not made trouble for LinLin, they would never have had a chance to be together. Is it all my fault; but whose fault is not important now, it is a serous problem that needs a solution. How can I solve the problem, let them get divorced? That might be too much, they seem to be happy with each other; and love each other...divorce would make their little baby lose his mother. That's not good. DaShan is surplus to this family, without him, they would be a good family.

An idea suddenly came to her, but she said to herself: "No! No! I won't do anything like that." However, as much as she tried to shake off this idea, the stronger it played on her mind. She got up from the Kang and went outside and watched the stars for a long time, but she didn't find an answer there either.

Since that night, she looked like evil had taken over her body; whenever she looked at DaShan she remembered her idea.

Gradually, she began to think that was a good idea. Lian remained in this tormented evil state for three years. She watched DaShan grow from three to six years old, and her grandson was now three years old. She also listened to DaShan calling NianLin father all the time, and she felt her heart aching.

Chapter 84

YINGLI DID NOT LIKE the rural area educational system so she planned to send DaShan back to Long Shan city to go to school. She wrote a letter to her mama; and received a reply very quickly. Lu DongChun was not back in the mayor position yet, but had started working at city hall, doing some unimportant job.

LuDongChun was very happy to have her grandson stay with her; she also wanted YingLi's family to move to the outskirts of Long Shan city. Although it was still countryside HuKou, it had some benefits like city people, a lot better than the mountain village.

YingLi learned that there was a new national policy, that allowed city students to come back to the city to live, but there was one condition, that they could not be married. Some of the city students were divorcing their farmer husbands so they could go back to the city again; but YingLi didn't want to do that.

School would start Sep, first, and that gave Lian a sense of urgency but she still couldn't find a good solution. From spring to summer, she had been in a welter of inconsistency and pain. It looked like god knew, and sent a thunderstorm one summer morning, while DaShan was playing outside in the yard. He came running in, soaking wet, his body looked like a chicken in soup, covered in goose bumps and he was sneezing. Lian made him ginger soup, but as she carried it to his room she changed her mind, and carried it back to the kitchen and poured it in the pig food tub, then she sat down and cried.

DaShan caught a cold, and by afternoon he had a high fever. When YingLi got home from work, Lian almost did not want to have to face her. She felt like a criminal now because didn't give DaShan the ginger soup to relive his cold. She saw YingLi give DaShan some medication; and the next morning DaShan seemed to be much improved.

YingLi told Lian: "Ma don't forget to give him his medication, I'll be back at lunch time."

When the alarm clock on the desk rang to remind her that it was time to give the medication to DaShan, she took a cup, to the thermos and poured in some hot water, and added the little bag of medication that YingLi had left with her, and mixed it. While she was doing that, the little boy-DaHai had been trying to reach the alarm clock; the desk was too high for him, he tried to reach standing on his tiptoes too, but he fell on the floor. Lian put down the cup of medication to pick up DaHai who was screaming. After she picked the boy up he tried to reach the clock again, and spilled his brother's medication. DaShan's face was flushed with fever. Lian just consoled her young grandson, saying: "Don't cry my baby, I'm not biting you, and your brother is not mad at you. Going without medication one time is not a big problem. Ok don't cry that's a good baby."

Suddenly she strengthened her belief that god had given her another chance. God knew he made a mistake, and he wanted her to solve it. YingLi came home at lunchtime, and when she found DaShan had a fever again, she asked: "Ma, did you give him medication?"

"How could you ask that? Such a big thing I could never forget, you set the alarm clock, and even with my bad memory I couldn't forget."

"Ma, you don't have to get mad, I just asked and anyway he will have an injection tomorrow."

"Isn't having one drug to take not enough?"

"An injection will work much faster, I don't have any now, however some one is going to town to get it, and it will be here tonight or early tomorrow morning."

"When a child has a cold it is not necessary to worry like this. Who has had a child who didn't have a cold? Even without medication they recover, catching a cold is not like a disease."

"Ma, that is wrong, catching a cold can develop into many diseases, and can make people die too."

Lian's body shook involuntarily when YingLi said die. In the afternoon when it was time to give him his medication, she looked at the little face with a fever, it was red and his mouth was dry. DaHai woke up from his nap, crying and looking for milk. DaHai was three years old and still only drank milk. Because his mother had been unable to breast-feed him; he had been given cows milk and he still refused to eat other food. His parents wanted him to stop, but Lian always gave him milk when they were not at home. Lian warmed some milk for DaHai, and watched him suck it down, enjoying watching him.

Then she turned back to the older boy, the fire in his face changed in a moment to become LinLin's face, and said to her: "You don't go? I go!"

She kneeled on the floor, and said: "Please don't go, I love you, I really love you. Give me another chance please. Let me go to the Party office to explain everything"

"Too late, it's too late. I don't want to see you again. I am leaving, let me go." and he left.

Why was he like that and wouldn't forgive her? Why did he have such a hard heart? Was NianLin not his son? Her tears fell like rain, as she kneeled on the floor, watching him leave, and never looking back...Oh, my god!

Returning to the present she said to DaShan: "Baby, it is not only me that can't accept you; it is this world. our traditions won't accept you. You are surplus to our family, you should go to be with your father, and there you will find silence and happiness. Don't complain about grandma; I'm not your real grandma. Don't complain that I have a hard heart; I don't have any choice. While you are here, we are all messed up, only after you are gone, will we be able to make things right."

She went out and poured his medicine on the ground, and put the bowl on the desk, and then she went out in the yard and cried.

Chapter 85

Y ONGHONG WAS CRAZY ABOUT masturbating; she couldn't remember when she began to have this desire, she felt a man was unnecessary, that men just caused pain, trouble, and suffering. Masturbation relieved her urges; it was a loyal friend that provided her with relief and pleasure. Every night when she went to bed, before she slept, she would lie on the bed, take off her clothes, and admire her naked body. She would watch and enjoy moving her beautiful legs that were usually hidden in pants and never had a chance to be seen under light as they flashed like a ballerina's. Her long fingers reached out thin and long like spring unions that must have been made for a pianist; ten toes clean and standing on the point of her feet, like they were waiting for shoes from a king's son that would let her become a consort. The skin on her body was soft, smooth, and glowed like butter. YongHong experienced the exotic highs in her life just admiring her own body and thought that any man who did not feel the same must be crazy.

She didn't need a man in her life any longer; there had been two men already; the first one was only on paper, and the second one was married to someone else. When it started getting dark outside she would lie naked on her bed, it was her happiest time of the day. She would imagine a man making love to her, on her body her hands became that man's hands, fondling her, kissing her... then when they both had a thirst for love; they were consumed by each other. She didn't have an orgasm every night, but without a regular orgasm she would have insomnia for sure.

YongHong was very happy that Ming had cancer of the uterus and now was too busy with her own affairs, to be bothering her. She had heard that Ming was very skinny, and near death.

She had lost her passion for sex with WenJun since the delivery; she just saw him once or twice and then forgot about him. WenJun was still the same as before; his mouth was like honey, swearing that she would be his wife and that he would marry her soon, that without her he wouldn't have any body.

YongHong no longer had any illusions about men and married life.

ZhangYong had come to understand her and treated her child very well, making her feel even guiltier and she began becoming kinder to him. Recently she had given him a key to her house. The key made ZhangYong's heart feel warmth he had been missing for a long time. He was a male by birth, but since he lost his sexual function, he couldn't enjoy a man's happy duties and confidence. During the years that he wanted to end his life, he played a game involving YongHong, and his excuse was that YongHong had become a gorgeous flower in the political Party, and he was a green leaf to feed it.

The key gave him a feeling of peace. Since moving to the provincial capital, she had wanted to live separately, and he had no complaints. The provincial capital was not small like Long Shan city that was so small that anything that he or Hong did would soon be common knowledge; here few people knew he was a war hero, or that he was YongHong's husband. His situation allowed him to live freely; people were oblivious to the fact that Hong was his wife, they just remembered her position and act, a flower who became statuary, and didn't need green leaves any more.

Zhang held her key in his thoughts for a long time, and then he dropped it in a drawer at his office, locked it, and smiled. He continued to live in his rented room, until he died one day in 1976.

Chapter 86

L INLIN SENT A LETTER to YingLi in 1975.

He had gone with Sun to the U.S. in 1971; the day after China's number two leader had died in Mongolia in a plane crash. LinLin learned of the death from a Chinese newspaper and knew that following the death of such a high political leader things could change dramatically; perhaps his conviction could be changed too. However going back would not be easy in his situation, he had lost contact with his family, and been convicted of a crime in China; to apply for s Chinese passport would be impossible. He and Sun both carried temporary Russian visas and passports in the US.

Sun had dreamed of coming to the US for many years, but his wish for the ideal woman had not been fulfilled yet.

Sun's cousin was a doctor in a downtown New York hospital, and had a grand opening of his new office recently; but his house was half rented out so when Sun and LinLin arrived, he just let them stay until they could find work and get their own place.

Sun and LinLin soon found jobs in a restaurant, but the jobs didn't pay much so they needed to rent a cheap room to share. Chinese news papers with New York classifieds did not have many cheap rooms for two people to share but one add that had been running two or three days looked interesting. Sun and LinLin both went to the side door and knocked. A tall Russian girl with a beautiful face, apricot eyes, cherry lips, a high bridged nose, white teeth, big breasts and hips answered the door.

"Hello my name KaTia." she said in Chinese. Her accent was strong but Sun was delighted that she could speak even a little Chinese. "My name is Sun, and his name is LinLin, my best friend." Sun said in Chinese.

"Welcome, come on in." KaTia spoke in Chinese but her pronunciation sounded funny and her voice sounded like it was singing. Sun dragging LinLin followed her into the basement that was half under ground, damp and dark. A little window the size of A4 paper, with lots spider webs let in a little light. LinLin was pulling Sun close, hinting to him not to stay here.

The Russian girl was very smart and seeing LinLin's reluctance said to LinLin: "I can clean the place up for you guys." Her smile showed her beautiful teeth, and really influenced LinLin to quit objecting.

"What kind of landlord do you want, she looks very good." Sun lowered his voice and whispered to LinLin.

"We are looking for a place to live; not for a girlfriend." LinLin said.

"She might become a girlfriend later." Sun said.

LinLin remembered a common saying: "A toad wishing to eat swan meat." and laughed to himself.

"What did you say?" KaTia asked wide-eyed. She knew only a few words of Chinese and Sun and LinLin's conversation had confused her.

"He said, your, PiaoLiang (Chinese meaning beautiful), Clacevi (Russian meaning beautiful)." Sun used Chinese and Russian plus hand language to joke with her, and continued saying: "Is this a safe area to live?"

"Here it is very safe." she said: "Wo Xi Huan NiMen Zhu Zhe Li (I would like you both to live here)! Ni Men ZhongGuoRen (your Chinese) Bu (not) drunk, Bu (not) fighting, ShiHaoRen (only good people)!" KaTia said very seriously.

LinLin nodded and replied in Russian: "Ouqihalasor (wonderful)"

She said to LinLin. "You are nice, do you know you are very handsome?"

Sun said in Chinese: "You see, she starts to love you already. Be careful, if you live here don't take off your pants."

KaTia understood the words "Don take off pants", and asked: "Why not take off pants?"

"Ha-ha-ah." The men both laughed, and she began to laugh too; their laughter signified their decision and KaTia did a very good job of cleaning the room. It was a very cheap room typical of what most immigrants hoped for; the men would only sleep there, and eat free at the restaurant where they worked.

The enticement of U.S. dollars, made Sun very excited, he was unshakable in his determination to never go back to China again. He said to LinLin: "Buddy, we have to think about making money first; when we have money we can find foreign women to try out.

Every Monday Sun had the day off, and most of the time he would bring a woman to their room. On those days when LinLin got off work he couldn't go back to the room so he went walking to kill time. When he thought Sun should be finished he would go back and knock on the door.

Sometimes when he went back he could still hear them laughing inside, and he was so tired he would sit on the stone steps and wait.

Sun only needed money to pay his share of the rent, which was only thirty-five dollars a month so he had money to have girlfriends. When LinLin asked him about finding a woman he would like to marry he said he had not played enough.

Sun changed women almost every week. These women were mostly from the south part of china, and they liked the look of Sun's body and his personality: Sun was tall, healthy, strong, open-minded, forthright, and attractive to women. He claimed that in bed, he could make a woman forget her last name. While he played with the women he never forgot that LinLin had a problem with his passport and needed a green card.

One day when he got from work he said to LinLin: "I have a woman for you, do you want to hear about her?" LinLin saw Sun was smiling like a chicken about to lay an egg.

Sun knew what LinLin was thinking, because several times before he had said he would introduce him to a woman that he could have a false marriage with to get a green card, but he was never successful in finding a woman. This time he felt confident and said:

"Don't laugh, this time it is true."

"I didn't say anything, I was listening." LinLin said with a smile.

"You will get your passport very soon if you marry an American citizen."

"I know that."

"I have found one for you."

"You know, I don't have that kind of money." Though he did not believe what Sun said about how good life was in the U.S. he still held a wish; the image of YingLi on the road to the execution ground burned in his memory, she had been there with her big belly in a Pedicab, chanting so she could talk to him, and they could exchange looks to embrace each other..."

They had learned from a friend that the only way to get a green card soon was to marry an American citizen. But, that way also required a lot of money.

What Sun had said made him wonder: "You don't need any money for this one" Sun said: "This woman is not like the other ones she has lots of money, she just wants a well equipped strong man who can make love to her when she wants." As he spoke Sun's eyes moved to LinLin's crotch as if he was trying to see if he was well endowed. He suspected LinLin might have a dysfunctional problem because he was not interested in any women.

Sun continued, saying: "After you marry her you have to live with her for three years to get a resident card."

"Oh, I will have to serve three years as a sex slave?"

"Why not? You need a woman; she needs a man, it is mutually beneficial, go and enjoy it. Just remember we have to go this Wednesday."

Sun saw that LinLin looked undecided and said: "Brother, this may be your chance of a lifetime. It is not necessary for you to get seriously involved with this woman; and you do not to feel guilty because of your wife. Just think you are doing this for her, how else would you ever be able to go back to China or bring her here?

"OK, that's enough, I will go with you."

Wednesday afternoon, LinLin followed Sun to the woman's home. She was a white woman, and after Sun introduced LinLin to her, he left.

As Sun left he felt a little jealousy; this woman was really beautiful, she was old but still Ok. He waited close by the door hoping he might be able to hear something; and thinking that a woman this age could be very hot and able to satisfy any man even him. It hadn't taken him long to discover that the beautiful young women he used to dream about were often only lukewarm or dead in bed. Sun thought to himself, LinLin you are really one lucky son of a bitch, and he got an erection just thinking about having the woman.

Sun had his ear to the door, and was dying to know how LinLin was making out. It had been very quiet inside for quite awhile and then one of the woman's neighbours came by and wondering what he was up to stopped to ask what he was doing there. He was unable to communicate much with her because he knew almost no English, so he left the building in case the woman might call the police. He went out in the street and while he was wondering what to do LinLin came out. LinLin had a red face, angry eyes, his facial muscles were twitching, and he was scowling.

"What happened?" Sun asked as he looked for signs of a struggle; LinLin's clothes, and face showed no sign of being damaged. Sun had heard from a co-worker that this woman had a nasty temper; and he hadn't told LinLin because he was afraid he might not come. He also knew this woman liked younger men, however LinLin looked much younger than his age, and he had told his co-worker that LinLin was only thirty-five, and then made the date for him.

"What happened?" Sun asked again.

"Let's just go home" LinLin said very angrily.

"What went wrong my brother? You knew this was your golden opportunity, and that if you missed it you would not be able to bring your wife and child here. Let's go back and ask what is wrong."

Sun took LinLin by the hand to go; but LinLin resisted refusing to budge, and said:

"No, no. I don't want to go back. I never want to go back."

"You wait here." Sun said as he started to run back into the building. After about a hour, he came back, all smiles, and said: "When you get your resident card, don't forgot me.

"How did you make her happy?" LinLin recalled she was really a beautiful woman, even her skin had not lost its' glow. When LinLin was in bed with her he looked like he lost his mind, he don't know why she said to him: "get out." He saw her using a finger to point to the door and said: "Out. Get out."

Sun laughed and said: "When I went in she was still mad; when she saw me she said: "No Chinese. Chinese are no good." I said: "Who says Chinese are no good? Try me, then you tell me that. My brother what else can I say? "

"Did she say you were good?"

"It doesn't need to be said, I am a master of the art in pleasing a woman in bed. What woman could say I am no good"

"It is good… you need a resident card too."

"My brother, I'm only doing it for you. I will make love to her, but you are to marry her." Seeing that LinLin looked uneasy, he said: "Brother we are friends, if you are happy I'm happy. You have a wife and child to worry about; I only have myself. She is a little bit old but she is a beautiful looking woman, and much better in bed than the younger ones that I've sampled. Think about it this way, I won't need to go out and spend money on women, I can save my money, and in a few years I can buy a little restaurant. This benefits both of us, why not?"

At the time, Sun was very happy, and later when he died in the woman's bed from a heart attack his last request to her was that she would see that LinLin would get his residents card in the future.

LinLin soon got his resident's card and citizenship; and then he got his US passport in 1975. He stood in front of the cemetery where Sun was buried, remembering a young guy who dreamt of western life, wanted to have lots of women and died making love to a woman. He remembered an ancient people's verse: " He who died under flower (woman), and becomes a ghost still feels romantic."

To LinLin's way of thinking, Sun had died for him. In any event Sun died doing what he enjoyed most of all. Even with US citizenship and a passport LinLin could still not dare to go back to China.

He wanted to know how YingLi was and what her living condition was like now. He wrote to LuDongChun several times before receiving a reply.

When LuDongChun finally replied YingLi was having a problem with NianLin, and had gone back to Long Shan city with their son DaShan.

Chapter 87

WHEN OTHER STUDENTS WENT back to the city YingLi did not divorce NianLin; if that was the only way she had to return, she preferred to stay. It was not because she had started to like the countryside, but because Lian and NianLin had treated her so well.

The barefoot doctors worked on the farms as well as serving as doctors to the farmers; if they had a patient they took care of them, when they had no patients they were required to go to the fields to work. Bare-foot doctors received no salary, like a farmer when they worked it was recorded until the end of the year when accounts were settled. Supplies of grain and other expenses were deducted, and the balance if any was paid in cash.

YingLi from the beginning as a barefoot doctor had been busy doing medical work all the time. The farmers liked and trusted her so much that she seldom had dinner on time. Recently many people had caught bad colds; not only her son DaShan, every day, people with fevers and sniffles came to her for injections of medication. If she had patients who were too sick to come to her she had to go to their home to treat them.

YingLi lived in a group that consisted of three villages located within a radius of fifteen miles, sometimes she passed her home during her rounds treating patients and she would stop and check on DaShan to see if he was improving. She had continued the medication for several days with DaShan, his fever was going down, and his coughing was relieved. She knew very well that he would need time to recover, however she was anxious that he would get better soon. Her mother in law now appeared to be becoming more partial to her own grandson, something YingLi had not noticed before. She realised that Lian's tone of voice and looks were now different between the younger one and older one. She understood the little one was only two years of age, and really needed more attention than the older one. However, Lian had definitely been negligent about treating DaShan's illness, and YingLi was concerned.

One day she had no patients waiting for her, and she had no rounds to do so she decided to run home, expecting to return right away. Her office was just three miles from home; she could make a return trip in forty minutes. She had just locked the door when a young girl approached with her head lowered, she saw that YingLi was just leaving and had stopped in her tracks. YingLi knew that she was a city student, and her name was Feng.

Feng was now a veterinary assistant, who spoke loudly and did not fear sharing dirty jokes with the farmers; but today she was completely changed and looked like a different person.

YingLi unlocked the door, took her in, sat her on a chair, and told her to put her hand on the little pillow on the table; she sat down on the opposite side taking her hand, and asked: "What is the problem?"

"I am uncomfortable." She said, with her face turning red; and lowering her eyes.

YingLi checked her pulse, and asked: "Has your period been normal?"

She lifted her head and looked at YingLi awhile, then shaking head she said: "No."

"How long since you had a period?"

"I don't know, two or three months?"

"Do you feel like you want to vomit?"

"Yes, I have stomach trouble..."

"Stomach trouble? You look like you're pregnant."

Feng had already expected to hear that, she started weeping, and with both hands took hold of YingLi's hand, and said: "YingLi sister, can you help me? I am afraid to do it by myself, will you help me please?"

This request forced YingLi to do some quick thinking; there were serious things to consider: first, she would have to take time off without pay; second, her son had still not recovered a hundred percent. She thought about it, and looking at Feng weeping, remembered being in the same situation, and suddenly her heart softened. She promised to go with her the next day to Long Shan city hospital, and afterwards take her to her home and ask her mama LuDongChun to give her a birth vacation, that would keep this as secret as possible.

Before leaving, YingLi gave Lian very detailed very instructions on how to take care that DaShan recovered. Lian responded positively and seemed to appear to understand her instructions.

Chapter 88

Y INGLI WENT TO LONG Shan city, and was gone for three days, two days travelling, and one day with Feng at the hospital, doing the abortion. She had no time to spend with her mom, even though her mother asked her again and again to stay one more day. Concerns about DaShan and her job compelled her to return home as soon as possible.

She never expected she would find that DaShan was in the community hospital when she got home. DaShan was lying on a bed in the emergency room with an IV in his hand. NianLin said this was the second IV and that they had done a blood test, and took a urine sample, and waiting for the diagnosis. He said DaShan had a fever again since last night, and he couldn't find any medication at home; Lian had told him she didn't have any either so he had brought him in to the hospital last night.

The doctor came in, and seeing YingLi asked: "Are you the boy's mother?"

YingLi rose from her chair and said yes. The doctor said: "When you are a mother you have a duty to your children; when a child has the flu you need to get him treatment as quick as possible, delay can be very dangerous."

YingLi was confused and, said: "I started treating him on time; I gave him both pills and injections."

NianLin added: "My wife is a barefoot doctor."

"Barefoot doctor? You said you gave him medication? What kind of medication?"

"Aspirin orally, and muscle injections ..."her words were interrupted by the doctor asking: "What treatment yesterday?"

NianLin and YingLi exchanged looks with each other, and NianLin answered: "Just oral medication."

The doctor shook his head and left. That afternoon he called YingLi into his office, and waved a paper saying:

"This is the report of the medication level in your son's blood. I wonder how you, a barefoot doctor have treated your own child! Why did you lie to me? Your lie caused our department to meet for hours researching your son's illness..."

YingLi interrupted him saying: "Really we did have medication for him."

The doctor pushed a paper in front of YingLi and said: "This report is science it does not lie; you can see for yourself if he had medication or not, the medicine density in the blood is very clear; if you understand the report you can see for your self."

YingLi didn't know what to say; she remembered this morning when she got home and asked her mother in law about the medication, Lian had said firmly: "it was always on time."

In the evening the doctor finished his shift, and another doctor who YingLi knew came on for the night shift. He was very careful checking DaShan's lungs; temperature and pulse, the fever was coming down...the next morning before he finished work, he checked him thoroughly again, and afterwards he told YingLi: "He should have no problem now. You know how to treat him so it will be best if you take him home, there is a lot of disease here and a high risk of infection."

They took him home and YingLi stayed at home to care for him herself.

Lian complained to NianLin saying: "She doesn't trust me and when he gets well she will take him everywhere with her and not let me look after him again."

NianLin told YingLi: "Mama is mad at you; it will be best if you go back to work and let her carry on looking after the children."

YingLi still continued to look after DaShan and when he opened his eyes, YingLi looked into his eyes and asked: "Baby, Oh, my baby, are you better? Do you have a headache now?"

He shook his head.

"Oh, no more headache, that is very good, how is your throat, is it still sore?"

He shook his head again.

"Oh, if your throat is not sore, and you have no headache, you are well now."

He nodded.

"Why don't you talk? Talk to me: Say mama."

DaShan opened his mouth, and moved his lips, but no sound came out.

YingLi became nervous; she used her hand to move his chin, leading him: "Say-mama, ma-ma..."

"A-a-,"

She took him back to the hospital, and had him checked all over, there were no problems with his organs; he was diagnosed to be suffering from temporary aphasia.

Aphasia?

YingLi could not believe it. DaShan was a very smart boy, when he was two years old he knew some words and could count to a hundred. How happy she was with him; she had talked to herself and LinLin's soul: See how smart your son is. He is like you. When he was three years old, one day, he asked her: "Mama, is a train wheel really square?"

"Who told you a train wheel is square?"

"Grandma did."

"What do you think?"

"I tried it, the square one could not move, but the round one could go. I said it is round."

How pitiful he is. In this world, he lost his blood father, he can't have his own original last name, he has to call another man dad... was that still not enough for him? Why? God, can you tell me: why?

YingLi was very unhappy every day, she could not stop asking Lian: "Ma, are you sure you did not forget to give him the medication?"

"Why do you ask that?" Lian had become more evil in her thinking, and spoke harshly. She had not given DaShan medication after YingLi left; she thought that if his life were short she would have a solution to her dilemma. But, the doctor had said that he didn't have a problem with his organs, which meant in the future one day, he would continue to call NianLin father, and call her grandma. When he called out like that, her heart would ache like she had been beaten.

YingLi went to work again, but she did not believe her mother in law and one day after she went to work she felt an inexplicable fear.

It was a very hot day, the sun of late summer hung in the sky like a big oven, burning the leaves on the trees until they shrivelled, no wind stirred; usually ducks, chickens, pigs, or dogs would be heard in the street, now all the sounds of life had disappeared, the animals were resting in the shadows or on the water. The children were laying on the Kang having a nap, and Lian swinging a palm-leaf fan in her hand only spread a warm breeze on the boys sweating heads.

That afternoon, Lian looked at DaShan's face and thought as long as he has life I will remain tormented; she thought this was the best time to get rid of him, and placed a bed cover over his face that caused him to cry. Her hand got weaker as he struggled, and she removed it. The noise woke up the younger one and he started crying, she patted him lightly on his body, singing a baby lullaby, and soon had him in dreamland again. Soon after the baby went back to sleep, she resolved once again to cover DaShan's head and snuff out his life.

Lian was holding a pillow on DaShan's head, and she was saying. "Baby, I am letting you go, not because my heart is hard; it is because this family can't have you. Your leaving is for the best, go to be with your father; and in your next life I wish you have good luck, you must go..."

Chapter 89

MEANWHILE YINGLI HAD BEGUN to feel a strong anxiety, standing up and sitting down didn't help. In the beginning she thought it was caused by the hot weather. These days the sun was like a big oven hanging in the sky: the trees, grass, and crops leaves were all becoming dry, the river was covered with ducks; dogs were hiding in the shade of trees with their mouths open and tongues hanging out. Everyone was suffering from the heat with heat rash showing on their necks and chests. In her office she found a piece of newspaper to make a little fan that helped to make her feel cooler. The anxiety persisted; she thought blindly that DaShan might have a fever again, or that her mother in law might have fallen. She had noticed recently that her mother in law was always in poor spirits, she wondered dimly...if the baby had a problem.

Her thoughts were running wild, and with no patients to care for she started running back home. She could make the return trip running in 40 minutes. When she reached the house and saw the door was closed she thought her mother in law was really getting old that in such hot weather she didn't have the door open. When she entered the house, what she saw made her scream out. "What are you doing" she said.

YingLi rushed in and tore the pillow off DaShan's head. Saw his face had turned blue, and he was soaked in sweat, his breath was very weak and he was unconscious. YingLi used her fingers to pinch the mid point of his upper lip and said: "Baby! Wake up! You need to wake up now!" Then, she found a needle and did acupuncture on him.

Lian had fallen on the floor from the Kang, she had a blank look on her face and appeared to be neither feeling, nor thinking.

YingLi had woken up DaHai, and he was crying because he had been disturbed from a good dream, when he realised no one was coming to care for him he went back to sleep again.

DaShan opened his eyes, and his face was starting to regain its colour. YingLi finally began to unwind. She asked angrily: "What were you trying to do?"

Lian did not answer.

YingLi continued, her voice shaking asking. "What did you want to do? Why were you trying to kill him?"

When Lian heard the word "kill" her body started shaking, and she started weeping. YingLi took DaShan who was now wide awake and crying and held him cradled in her arm as he cried.

"Why?" YingLi continued: "You tell me why?! Speak! Did you have no reason? Or were you afraid of something? I know you did not expect I would back so soon. My son's soul called out to me, our hearts beat together. When I felt anxious, at first I was worried that something might have happened to you. You're not human! You are an animal!"

YingLi had tears on her face, as she said: "He is only six years old, why did you want to kill him? He is dumb, and you know why he is dumb? Because of you. Now I know for certain that you didn't give him medication, and you did not forget, you tried to kill him. You are very ruthless. Would you kill a six year old boy because he is has not your blood grandson? If you didn't like him you could have told me, and I could have taken him to my mother. Anyway, you know I planned to take him back to my mother. Don't you know how important he is to me? His father was my first love. He is the fruit of my love. You don't know, because you never experienced the emotion. You don't know about love, you never had love, you have never been loved by a man."

Lian started crying.

YingLi rocked her son cradled in her arm and he soon fell asleep again. She had seen his face. How dangerous it was, if she had been back a few minutes later, he would have been dead. She took a deep breath of fresh air and set out to find NianLin.

Chapter 90

S HE FOUND NianLin WORKING with his team in the manure pit.
: "Your mama tried to kill DaShan." She said loudly in front
of the team, through her tears.

The people who were working with NianLin were very surprised
and shook their heads in doubt. NianLin didn't believe YingLi. He
saw that YingLi had red eyes and tears on her face, and his leader
said: "Go home and find out what has happened"

When they got to the house, Lian was hanging a rope from
the house rafters to commit suicide. NianLin jumped up and tore
the rope down. Afterward he hugged his mama and asked very
nervously. "Ma, why did you do that? Don't do that, what has
happened? Tell me, I'm here, your son is here, tell me, what has
happened?"

Lian had red swollen eyes, she broke free from NianLin's arms,
sat down on the wet floor, patting her self on the chest and crying.
"Don't try to stop me; I don't want to live…"

YingLi asked. "If you don't want to live you could die by yourself,
why did you try to kill my son?"

"Shut up." NianLin said to YingLi.

The neighbours had heard a commotion, and they were
coming.

When Lian saw the people she started crying and said to YingLi. "You have wronged me! I have been caring for your child, treating you like my own daughter! Wow, everyone knows that is not easy. Looking after children my hands are in pee and shit, but I have not complained about it, and I like it. I have lived here for twenty years, whom have I hurt? Oh Wo...wo..."

Women tried to help Lian get up on her feet but she used all her strength to resist them.

NianLin whispered to YingLi: "Apologise and let her stand up, the floor is very wet."

"I will not apologise to her. She tried to kill my son. I'm the one that needs an apology."

"It can't be as serious as you say, you might have been mistaken in what you saw. "There is no mistake I saw very clearly." YingLi said resolutely.

"My mama is not the kind of person to do something like that." NianLin said loudly.

"You made your mother in law upset, to apologise is not too much to ask." a woman said to YingLi.

"NianLin" YingLi shouted back: "When I came back, your mama had his face covered with a cotton pillow. Are you saying, in this hot weather, that covering his head with a pillow she was not trying to kill him? My son's face was turning black and he was unconscious, is that not trying to kill? If I would have been a couple of minutes later getting back he would have been dead already." YingLi was sobbing too.

"How is it that is was so fortuitous that you came back when you did?"

"NianLin," YingLi said in very loud voice: "I suspected that today was not the first time she tried to kill him. When DaShan was sick, she didn't give him any medication, and that left him dumb."

"Don't talk shit!"

"I'm not talking shit! You go to the hospital and ask the doctors! They did a blood test. It was not me who said she didn't give him any medication it was the blood test and the doctors. I did not tell you, because I knew that you would talk to you mama and make her upset too. I still tried to think the best towards your mama.

I knew it was not easy for her to look after two small children, if she had forgot to give him medicine that was not her fault, she had always treated me well. Anyway it was too late to complain, and not necessary to make her unhappy. Now I know the truth!" Her words were interrupted by DaHai's crying, the shouting had awakened him from his dreams and he had wet himself, and was kicking his legs and crying to be changed.

YingLi held DaShan tightly.

DaShan did not understand what was going on, he looked blankly from one face to another in confusion.

NianLin said to YingLi: "DaHai is awake, go and take care of him."

YingLi did not move, she held DaShan very tightly as if she let go he would fly away and never return.

YingLi still looked very angry.

Lian was still crying and saying she would commit suicide.

In the people's view, the mama's heart was breaking and she was crying.

NianLin was upset with YingLi and hollered at her saying: "I don't believe it! Even if I die I would still not believe it! My mama is a good person she has always been kind to everyone." He pointed at YingLi and said: "I know you saw other girls go back to the city, and your mind has followed, you want to go back too. Because you're married you can't, and you are just making up an excuse so you can divorce me. You can go you don't need to make up any reasons. I'm not stopping you! If you want a divorce I will give you one. It is not necessary for you to pile shit on my mama's head! She is my mama, and I know her very well."

YingLi took DaShan and left the mountain village.

NianLin didn't try to stop her and the other people had no power to interfere.

Chapter 91

WHEN YINGLI RETURNED TO Long Shan City, Chairman Mao had died. This shocked the whole world, and made all China grieve. After Mao's death the political power structure changed; and the Cultural Revolution was ended.

During that time, YongHong realised that her political life could soon end too.

For ten years she had experienced ups and downs that required her to change fast, and did not have any big problems; but people who had joined the revolution before her had been arrested, and she had become very nervous. She was afraid of being kicked out by the new wave in society; and she had stayed home for three days and did not go to work.

Some one called ZhangYong because he was her legal husband. When ZhangYong learned that YongHong had not gone to work for three days he went to her apartment as soon as he hung up the phone.

ZhangYong understood YongHong's mood very well. He had been the same when he left the army and came home disabled. That year, he had risen to the high point of his life and then fallen to the lowest ever. It was LinLin who had helped him find his way. He very clearly remembered that year, in the spring; LinLin had used a tricycle to take him out. The first time out, they had gone to Songhua Lake, and rented a little fishing boat. The boat ploughed a path through the water, taking them past silent mountains, and only the sound of the motor could be heard. LinLin treated him like a big brother told him the names of the mountains, and what kinds of trees, and animals lived there; the history of the lake, and what kinds of fish were found in it.

ZhangYong had not only been there once, from primary school to high school, all the teachers brought the students here. This lake had been man made with Chinese slave labour during the Japanese occupation. A dam more than ninety metres high, and more than thousand metres wide, controlled the water of Songhua lake, to power electrical generators. Because it was built by the Japanese devils while occupying the Northeast, there was also a big hole where more than ten thousand people who died building it were buried. ZhangYong realised that this place had many memories and had been the scene of a national disgrace and the death and suffering of thousands of people. ZhangYong realised that LinLin had a goal on this trip also. The day he had been fighting with YongHong, LinLin and YingLi had seen them, and his strange actions had made people worry. LinLin must have been carrying out a request from those who had asked him to try to educate him. Many teachers had attempted to educate him and he had listened to many inspiring stories, but they had been like gentle breezes, passing but, never changing him. Yes, they wanted him to become like China's Pavel Korchagin? He can't write; become Chinese's Beethoven? He pondered these thoughts...until lunchtime when LinLin bought a live fish from a fisherman and took it to the fisherman's family who cooked it for them without charge. The fisherman's wife gutted the fish and threw it in boiling water for a few minutes with a little salt. It was simple cooking, but it tasted very original and delicious, it was better than any fish he had eaten before braised in soy sauce, or fried.

With chopsticks in hand Zhang dug into the fish and didn't stop until it was all gone, the big fish was devoured in no time at all. Afterwards, he felt guilty because LinLin had not eaten yet. LinLin looked like he didn't mind that. He was drinking wine he had brought from home, singing some thing that ZhangYong couldn't understand. All day, ZhangYong waited for LinLin to start trying to educate him, but, it never happened. In the evening, LinLin took ZhangYong home, and simply said: "Good bye!"

ZhangYong with his back to him said. "Bye!"

After a while, LinLin took ZhangYong out again. This time, they went to the park on the northern mountain. Lin took him under an arched bridge, and facing upward, asked: "This arched bridge has another name do you know what it is?"

"Break the soul's bridge?" Zhang guessed and said he was not sure.

"Usually humans lived with inspiration." LinLin said, as he took him in front of an ancient temple, which had three hundred years of history. Inside the temple was very much in disorder; Buddhist patriarch- Sakyamuni, Taoism founder Laozi, Confucianism sage Confucius, and Eight big Buddha's with 18 Arhats, were all laying on the floor, some with their arms or legs broken off.

LinLin pointed to them and said to ZhangYong.

"You see, even Buddhist patriarchs and immortal sages have suffered disaster, what about humans?"

ZhangYong smiled and his mood improved a lot.

LinLin asked casually: "What religion do you have?"

"Communism" This word took him back to when he was a teenager, full of vigour and daring, an energetic one. This recollection broke his good mood. He thought of ZhangYong at the prime of his life's full flowering had died; the self assured ZhangYong had died too.

"Well, what did you plan to do for Communism?"

ZhangYong looked at him, this man was older than him by more than twenty years, but his family position was that of a young brother in law.

LinLin took his time with him this trip around; it was not a question about Communism. The answer was so easy if he was not disabled. If he was a student, he would work hard to study; if he was a worker, he would do a good job, if he was a solder, he would take up a gun to protect the country...none of these were for him now. His face turned red suddenly, and he felt guilty.

LinLin looked at him and said. "Don't you think if you were Beethoven you would know what to do; If you were WuYunDuo you would know what to do...and don't think you since you are a Third class person who has rendered outstanding service too...that you are not just a common person. Like anyone on the street, without work you don't have money to eat, without study you can't find a job to live. Even though schools are closed and study is not advocated, we can't do any thing without studying. When you were a child, you had to learn how to walk, how to talk...and how to grow up, you learned to ride a bicycle, and play sports games...don't interrupt me, I know you want to say you are different now."

LinLin avoided using the word disability, and used different words that wouldn't hurt his self-confidence. "You can learn a skill to benefit society, which is better than what you have been doing lying on your back and sleeping."

ZhangYong was mad, he said: "I have not just been lying on my back sleeping."

"Explain what you have been doing then."

ZhangYong had no answer and realised that he had just been at home causing trouble just because he was disabled. "How can I escape from this way of life?" he asked. "What can I do?"

"Study, learn a skill, worker, technician, administration, or inventor...legs only help you walk, your brain can help you fly." From then on, he had accepted LinLin's teaching, and borrowed lots of his books to read and learn from. As a result he had become the leader in the factory for the disabled.

He had been downhearted, he knew how it felt, and he knew why YongHong had fallen into this condition too, and now she needed someone to help her out.

As he had guessed, Hong had been drinking, and he could hear her talking to herself from the hallway. In his memory, Hong was not much of for drinking, however she was feeling pretty good by the sound of things. She hadn't heard him coming, and she was busy drinking and talking to herself.

"Chairman Mao, what it is wrong with me? They said I need to be temporarily relieved of my post for self-examination, what have

I done wrong. Chairman Mao, you must speak the words of justice for me. You know, I'm very loyal to you; I want to follow you all my life. Oh, no, it is two lives, three lives...and the generations following. Since I was eighteen I have followed you and joined the revolution to rebel, I rebelled against my mama, and I did not hesitate at all. You said she was a Capitalist Roader, and of course I found it necessary to stand by your side. But, these people, do not listen to you, they have let her return to her position. I confiscated my own home, and other people's homes too. I also set fires to people's homes, and took people to the temples to destroy them...is that my fault? If I have a fault, why did you meet me in Beijing? You met me, and shook hands with me...Oh, Chairman Mao, that meeting, how exciting it was. How many people wished to meet you and shake your hand? They had no chance, and they are jealous, right? Hum, I don't have any faults, none..."

ZhangYong closed the door, and took off his shoes. YongHong saw him, nodded her head, laughed, and continued talking to Mao.

"YongHong, you really value your position; is power the most important thing in your life? We have to give it up now and forget about it, things are changing. You can see that your younger sister doesn't have power, and she still has a life. Don't you still want a life with WenJun? Ha ha; what do you want? Have another child? No. Marry? Maybe. Ha, Ming you are a ghost, we will see, what can you do? Oh, you were sick, haven't you died yet? I don't know, Shan didn't tell me. Oh, you didn't see Shan for a long time. Long time... long...WenJun; you are a son of bitch. You don't love me anymore. You left me, how can I continue my life? Why did you need to do that? It would be better to die. Go and die..."

When Zhang heard those words, he was worried and moved close by YongHong's side, wanting to talk to her: "No, don't go and die. You only are twenty something, too young to die, it is too early, stay alive, a live rascal is better than a dead hero. Hey. Who said that? Ha-ha. It is true. Alive...alive..."

Suddenly Zhang saw that bottle had been become a knife in Hong's hand, the knife flew to her neck and wrist, and she was bleeding. Had she lost her mind, what? Did she really want to commit suicide? No, he had to stop her, and reached out to grab her arm. Stop...in his life's last memory, it looked like he had grabbed her knife, then he wanted to find something to stop her bleeding and call emergency for help, then... he didn't know what happened, he hadn't done anything yet, and he was laying in a pool of his own blood.

Chapter 92

YINGLI NOW LEARNED THAT she would have to divorce NianLin. YingLi went back to Long Shan city, thinking about everything that had happened and she felt she hadn't done anything wrong. After a month NianLin had still not come to see her, and she kept asking herself: Could I have done something wrong; did I make a mistake? I really saw Lian using a pillow to cover my son's face, and he really was suffocating and she did not have an explanation but why did she do this? YingLi still did not have an answer, and felt very strange.

Unconsciously she wished for NianLin to come to her, and the feeling grew stronger day by day; she also missed DaHai very much. If Lian would give her an explanation, and NianLin would come to pick her up, she would go back with him. She planned to leave DaShan in Long Shan city to go to school. He was dumb, even though he still had his hearing he could not talk, and needed to be in a special school. YingLi thought perhaps Lian wanted to kill DaShan because he was dumb, and had not given him his medication; if this was true she never wanted to see her again

YingLi's mind swung in indecision, and time was quickly passing. One day, LuDongChun handed her a letter that made her decide she would have to divorce NianLin without hesitation. The letter was from LinLin, sent from the U.S.. It was the fourth letter he had sent to LuDongChun, but the first that she had received.

How it made YingLi feel it id difficult to say. Of course she couldn't believe it at first, she asked her mom: "Do you think it is true?"

"Yes, I think it is true."

"I can't believe it!"

LuDongChun replied: "It is hard to believe; but you must remember his body was never found."

"How can we find out for certain?"

"Well...you can reply to him, and ask for more information about our family and his history."

YingLi began writing right away. After getting a reply one day she told her mom: "Mom, I am going crazy! It is him! Wow, it is him!!"

YingLi hugged DaShan and told him in tears, and smiling: "Oh! My son, your father is coming back! He will come back soon!"

DaShan used sign language and said: "will we go back there again? I liked it there and I miss my little chicken and duck...and my young brother."

Now she had to divorce NianLin, but it was still not going to be easy; she recalled how kind and gentle NianLin had been with her; and recognising that she would lose her other son really bothered her.

LinLin said he would come back, but he was a "dead person" in China; how was he to report to the government, and get his HuKou. YingLi and LuDongChun both got busy trying to find out how a person who was officially dead could be reinstated.

Chapter 93

YINGLI DECIDED TO GO back to the mountain village to get her divorce.

NianLin and YingLi both left the divorce department, and continued walking together for awhile, when they came to the cross road, they stopped and looked at each other. YingLi had tears on her face; he was silently looking at the woman who had been his wife but was now going back to another man, he couldn't complain about her, he could only complain about his destiny.

She said: "You know, I'm not ungrateful."

"No body said you were." NianLin said as he looked far off at the sky where white clouds were passing by and below a few workers were panting a wall white over red words that said "Long live the proletariat dictatorship", the red was partly hidden with the white paint, but the red colour was struggling to show itself; the workers repeatedly panted over it until it became pure white.

"I will always remember you." said YingLi.

"Just remember DaHai that is enough." NianLin said.

When he mentioned DaHai, YingLi's eyes became red again, and said: "Will you listen to me and let DaHai's HuKou move to the city with me...?"

"I feel he will be fine where he is."

YingLi opened her mouth to speak, but no words came out. After awhile, she said: "Now that the national situation is changing, the mountain village will change too...find a good woman to marry."

His gaze was still fixed on the sky, the far off wall, and the workers. He said: "You don't need to worry about DaHai, mama and I will take care of him, and help him receive a good education."

"Can I come to see him?" YingLi asked.

"Of course, he is your son too, come any time." NianLin replied.

"Please don't complain to him about me." YingLi felt she had hard to say that but she really was talking about LinLin.

"I have no complaint, this is destiny." he said.

Having seen YingLi off, NianLin stopped a carriage from a neighbouring village to hitch a ride.

Mother in law problems with daughter in laws, had continued for a thousand years in China. Choosing between them was a tough choice for a man. A traditional son must choose his mother first, that would hurt his love with his wife. Since YingLi had left and gone back to Long Shan city, he had thought about it constantly. He believed what ever his mama did she had done by mistake; how could she hurt her own grand son? YingLi had been homeless and his mama had helped her; that was being hospitable, and it had made him a little jealous also. Maybe his mama did not balance her attention between two grandsons; that was normal, the little one was younger and needed more care. Why would she need to hurt DaShan? There was no reason. Since DaShan was born, his mama had cared very well for him. She had treated him like he was her own flesh and blood grandson. When she had no money she had sent him to sell eggs that even when she was sick she wouldn't eat herself. That show made YingLi weep and she had said: "NianLin don't you worry, even if all the other girls go back to the city I will not go. You and your mama are in my heart. If I left you I would not be human."

The main problem seemed to be that DaShan was dumb and she suspected that his mama had forgotten to give the medication to him. If she forgot that was normal; could her forgetting once or two twice make him dumb? But he thought YingLi had another problem too, she saw lots of students going back to the city again. He thought her heart had become anxious, she promised me before she would not go and now she needed to make an excuse. Yes, she had told him that Feng, had used her own body to get back to the city...was the city living really that great? If anyone asked him he would say, he liked the countryside better. Then YingLi had proposed a plan for him to move to the city, but if the deal was that his mama could not go with him, he had to refuse.

This choice was very hard, and he hadn't been able to choose. He didn't want to give up either his wife or his mama. His mama had given him life, and as long as he could remember, he was the only person in her life. For him, she had suffered most of her life, she didn't want to remarry, and saved her money so that he could have a family...she lived only for him. YingLi helped her to repay her for her kindness, and after she had the feeling to make love, they had a baby. During the past weeks he had been unable to make a choice but now it was too late.

He had lost his love, and been made a joke by the people, because another guy was taking his wife away from him.

He really hated the man named LinLin. Even though YingLi had told him many good things about LinLin he still hated him for causing him to lose face.

Chapter 94

WHEN LINLIN ARRIVED IN Long Shan city he went directly to city hall to find LuDongChun.

LinLin met LuDongChun in her office.

She was really very surprised, and said: "Hello! Why didn't you write or call to say you were coming?"

"I learned from people in the west and was trying to give you a pleasant surprise."

"I didn't think it surprising at all, we knew you would be back, we just didn't know when, it is nice to see you, sit down please."

"Mama, where is YingLi?"

"Oh, she went to the countryside to visit a child." LuDongChun didn't tell him she went there to see about a divorce matter.

In her view, he had not changed much.

However, she had changed a lot in LinLin's view, dense white hair could be seen growing out below the coloured layer on top very clearly, and her face was very wrinkled. Ten years ago she had still looked young and vigorous; the job of mayor had made an old woman of her.

She had returned again at the beginning of 1975 because Long Shan city's economy was on the edge of collapse. Long Shan city was the centre of national grain production, a very important area, abounding with maize and soybeans. The country's largest chemical industry base was located here also, three chimneys standing on the north side of the river, emitted blue and green smoke continuously 24 hours a day. The raging waves of red revolution had upset the traditional mode of production. The peasants learned "DaZhai"- a little mountain village, to show that human's were smarter than god: they could remake the landscape; hills were now terraced; the course of streams, creeks, and ditches had been changed...and workers did not work; they just studied theories that were very hard for them to comprehend. The residents of Long Shan city during this time were living on short rations, each person received once a month: 100 grams of Soya-bean oil, two pounds of flour, two or three pounds of rice, half a pound of pork (with bone), half a pound of salt; a quarter of a piece of soap, half a pound of sugar, five pieces of tofu; and once a year: tickets to buy seven yards of fabric...if they could find it.

The people were comparing their present mayor to LuDongChun; when she held the position peoples' lives had been much better than they were now. She had not recommended over fulfilling the national grain goal, believing that the peasants should be fed first, and that the support group should have a private grain depot so that when they were finished their assignment for the unified national goal; the workers could use the bonus to stimulate more pay for more work. She had received criticism from the leading body at a higher level at the time, but with Long Shan city steadily raising industrial output, and taking into account the "three years of special hard times", in which in all of Long Shan city no one had died of starvation while millions died in other parts of the country; LuDongChun had gained great respect.

The higher authorities now had to acknowledge her abilities and return her to her former position. The central leader now had a new slogan: "I don't care if the cat is white or black, if it can catch a mouse it is a good cat." The leader of the province personally made the decision to reinstate LuDongChun in her former position in Long Shan city hall.

"She just went yesterday, I don't know when she will be back, she might want to stay with the child a few days. She hasn't seen the little boy for a long time."

LinLin did not want to wait. "Can we call her?" He asked.

"This is not the US, our telephone system has not been developed yet." she said: "There is only one phone at the main group, and it is four or five miles from her ex-husbands' home."

When she mentioned YingLi's ex-husband, LinLin asked: "If I hadn't showed up, perhaps they wouldn't have gotten divorced?"

LuDongChun looked at LinLin and then changed the subject:: "You should think about your HuKou first, both YingLi and I have been running around trying to get you re-registered, they won't give the re-registration to anyone except you. How about letting me go to the police station with you?"

"There is no rush, I'm back to stay, not to travel." LinLin was not concerned about his HuKou; he just wanted to see YingLi as soon as possible.

LuDongChun was reading his thoughts, and said: "Ok, you're right, there is no need to rush to get your HuKou. How about I take you back my house? You can see your son's picture; he went with his mom. Did YingLi send you his photo? We have some at home, he is a big boy now even though he is only seven years old, and he is so tall his head reaches my shoulder already. He is like you, really the material of a great athlete. Wow, if he was not dumb."

"How did he get dumb?"

"YingLi didn't tell you? He was sick, and had a very high fever." LuDongChun's talk didn't involve Lian, because that had not been proven.

"Why didn't YingLi give him an acupuncture treatment?"

"She said she heard that acupuncture anaesthetized for surgical did not work well, some people had been yelling with pain."

"Acupuncture can work for the dumb. I know a few points, it is not a hundred percent, but we can try it."

"YingLi tried but it did not work. She said to do that with her hand shaking, was too dangerous, and could make him die. She said she felt bad enough that his condition was like it is, but if she made it worse she would not be able to face you!"

LinLin had no answer.

LuDongChun was watching the time, and said: "I am sorry that I am so busy, today I am scheduled to go to the countryside for meetings, and an inspection. I can't stay and visit with you and my driver will be waiting for me. How about, I send you to my home first? Here is the key. I think I will be back tomorrow or the day after tomorrow. You can rest by your self, and wait until I get back. I will pass near that village and can send word to tell YingLi to come back today or tomorrow."

"Mama, can I go with you?"

"You want to go?"

"I can pick up YingLi and see how the countryside have changed. It has been many years since I have been there." LinLin said.

LuDongChun thought about it, and said: "Ok, but I'm not going into the village, I can drop you off near the village, but you will have to walk three or four miles in, is that Ok? I'm very busy, and have to meet with a local leader that I have an appointment with. I will be a little bit late as it is but that will be ok, if I was too much later there would be no excuse."

"No problem. I can go by myself if you just tell me how to get there."

"I'm never been in there either, but you can ask someone."

"Don't worry about it, I'm not a three or four year old boy, it is no problem."

"You can bring her back right away but you will need to take the bus, I really won't have time to pick you up."

There had been a bad wind storm following many days of heavy rain and the street they started out on was blocked by a big tree lying in the road. The driver told LuDongChun: "We can go a different way that is a little further but we won't need to wait if you are in a hurry."

LuDongChun complained "We have been having terrible weather for days, heavy rain and wind. You can see the city is a big mess."

"Are you going to check on the disaster situation?" LinLin asked.

"Yes, the city and much of the province have experienced a disaster; my days are busy meeting with leaders to arrange supplies for the people. They reported that they had delivered the emergency supplies to the countryside, but I still need to see with my own eyes, before I can relax."

"You are being very conscientious, checking to see that the work has been done properly."

"Oh, that might not last long, I'm old, and I will soon be replaced by someone younger."

"You are right, you have worked hard all your life, you really need to relax. I see that your hair is turning white."

"Oh? Can you see that?"

"Hum."

"When I heard you were coming back soon I dyed it. If I had known it wouldn't cover everything; it would have been better not to do it."

LinLin was laughing, and said: "It looks like you did it yourself."

"Yes, how did you know that?"

"The front is coloured, but the top and back still have...white roots."

"Of course, I can't see there. I see that your hair is not white, you don't dye it, do you?"

"My hair is not white yet but my age is."

"Yes you're right, you said I am very conscientious about my job, I just want to do more in this life. What do you think? When a person doesn't have anything to do for years, and then suddenly is working again, and discovers that they are old, and many things have not been done, and you will have to give up your job and let someone else take over. I can not relax yet, the years have taken their toll but when I go to see Marx, how could I face him and talk to him, if I have accomplished nothing? I would lose face."

"I have accomplished nothing either. I became a ghost, and lived in exile a long time; the prime time of my life is over. Now all I can do is try to earn enough to buy food to feed my stomach."

"Don't talk like that. I don't want to hear that kind of talk. You just proceed step by step, register for your HuKou first, then look for a job, it is a good thing that your case has been redressed."

This made her think about YongHong, and what she had done for him. But, YongHong was in jail now. LuDongChun frowned and looked a little sad. LinLin noticed this and asked: "Does my case still have a problem?"

"No, there is no problem for you; all your documents are in YingLi's hands, you can take them to find job and you will have no problems. The county now needs professional people every where; you came back at a very good time, a job will be no problem."

"Job? What kind of job can I get?"

"What kind of job would you like?"

"Me? What I would like?"

In LinLin's experience, there had never been choices, one always had to obey the organization who allocated the jobs; there had been no respect for personal choices. He had expected that coming back he would have to accept a very menial job.

"You could go back to your old profession teaching if you want; would you like that?"

These words made LinLin very excited. But, after, he came down, he said: "I gave up my professional job many years ago, that would be hard to pick up again; I also must consider that I might lead the students to take the wrong road by mistake."

"LinLin I know you. You won't have a problem. How old are you, fifty-three or fifty-four? That is a very good age. What program did you graduate from?"

"Master's in Education."

"Now that you are back you can use your training, you still have more than ten years that you can teach. Lin, you need to open your mind, the government encourages every body to open their minds now. You need to forget thinking about whether you are a rightist or an anti-revolutionary. You are a Chinese citizen; you only need to think how this country became no stranger to hard work." LuDongChun was becoming very excited, she looked directly at Lin, and said: "The Cultural Revolution is finished. Our country is now on the economic track; it will be much stronger soon. Do you believe that? The country is like a person, she can fail, she can make mistakes; but after she finds the right way, she will become bigger, and stronger than ever."

"I believe what you say."

"Yang." She called out to the driver. "Turn on the radio, and let us listen to that music again." Then she turned to face LinLin, and said: "This music is called a Sonata of enthusiasm, it was written by Beethoven; this was once Lenin's favourite symphony. Ten years can pass in a moment, or can last a century also. This sonata really excites me, have you heard it before?"

LuDongChun had fallen under the spell of the music already, the notes that billowed and flowed through her lifted her heart. She appreciated it, and was excited, the muscles of her face followed the notes she felt surging through her.

"I don't understand much about music." he said.

"Oh" she said as if she was waking up from a dream and saw LinLin's face was showing his embarrassment. She laughed and said: "Let me explain it to you. This symphony has three movements altogether, Listen. In the first movement the rhythm is fast: da... da...the theme is solemn, and the melody is graceful. Listen, here, the author's mood has changed, the beat rises and falls, full of yearning for and expectation of life...The enthusiasm that can't be checked emerges here, the ideal has been broken.

"The struggle, the tempestuous wave is immense and equally magnificent, and the struggle, continues, after the struggle follows the second movement, in this state of variations, the whole movement permeates a kind of optimistic mood. Listen, the soul is not dead in agony and torment...the rhythm is becoming active, it is overcoming agony, unease and disappointment, it will stand up strongly again. The third movement, the Sonata of the state has two subjects that reflect the facts and offer pieces of mighty fighting scenes the one theme, there is indomitable imposing manner; the second theme has an equally staunch spirit of struggle.

"Who said Chinese don't understand Beethoven? Only Chinese can understand him because his music includes enormous agony, and also enormous struggle, and courage. Ok, tell me what you felt now that you have listened?"

LinLin said: "I know some of Beethoven's words very well, they are: "I want to clutch destiny by the throat, it must not make me surrender."

"I think you understood his music." LuDongChun said.

Chapter 95

LINLIN WAS STANDING UNDER shabby low eaves beside a sun dried mud brick wall that was so common in the countryside. There were three rooms, with the kitchen in the middle, and bedrooms on either side. The house appeared from the outside to be lower on the right side. A tall chimney stood beside the house, close to the wall, but there was no smoke coming out.

A handsome bare foot boy wearing ragged pants, with his feet covered in mud and animal dung was playing in the yard catching baby chickens; he already had one in his hand, and he was trying to catch another one. The little chickens were going in all directions, and he chased after them running; the mama chicken was cackling loudly in protest. He lost the baby chicken from his hand with out even noticing. His face was aglow and covered in sweat from the excitement, looking like a very ripe lovely apple. When finally with empty hands he came back, and found LinLin standing in front of the door, he called out: "Grandma, grandma."

From inside a voice answered very weakly: "You better come back in the house, don't make me hit you."

LinLin lowered his head to go in the kitchen and heard the voice coming from the room on the right and asked: "Can I come in?"

"Who is it? Oh, come on in."

Inside there were two Kangs, one on the south side and the other on the north side. A woman was sitting on the south Kang, supported by some bed covers; all the rooms smelled of dust and mould. LinLin sneezed several times and guessed that this was YingLi's mother in law.

"You can have a seat." she said as she struggled to open her bleary eyes to see who had come, at her first sight of him, she began to shake, and then she opened her eyes wide and stared.

LinLin sat on the Kang, less than two feet from her, and he immediately had a feeling that this face looked familiar from somewhere, but where? He couldn't remember and it seemed that it must be an illusion.

Lian felt that she was having an illusion too. She closed her eyes, and thought: could it be him? No, YingLi had said he was still in the US. However, this face had a black mole too, the size of a bean. This mole had been in her memory for how many years since he had left. Now, that he was almost face-to-face, she couldn't be mistaken; yes that black mole is his, those lips are his too. Only the face had become older, with the map of the lines of the years. When she opened her eyes again, tears covered her face.

"LinLin? You are LinLin? Oh you were my Lin..." she started to weep, and her voice was trembling too.

LinLin stared blankly, and suddenly realized what had happened.

"You, are you...are you Lian? Are you really Lian?"

LinLin asked standing up.

"Lian, why are you here?"

"This is my home; if I was not here where would I live?" Lian replied.

"Is, NianLin your son?"

"He is our son." she said the word "our" with heavy emphasis.

Lian had been sick for a long time; since YingLi had gone back to Long Shan city she had been trying to persuade NianLin to divorce her. She didn't want to see her son without a wife, but while YingLi's son-DaShan was still alive; he was like a ghost who would not die in any accident, and so long as he lived he was an obstacle to the family. When YingLi came back to divorce NianLin, she had given her information that Lin, was still alive, and that he would soon be back in China. This news had made her delighted and kept her awake all night. She kept asking her self he is YingLi's husband now not yours, why are you so happy? She didn't have an answer, but she was just happy anyway.

Now, he stood in front of her, and she could see him once again. How happy she was, she was contented now, even if she died now it would be without any regrets.

Lian forced herself to smile, and told him with a smiling face:

"How nice to see you again, now I can close my eyes and die in peace"

"Did you know that YingLi and I were married?"

"Yes, but when I found out it was already too late; they already had a child. Since she gave birth she has lived in my home, she never said anything about you or even if she had a husband. We were all guessing that the boy was a bastard and that she was just here to give birth and then leave. After she married NianLin we found out that she was a city student and when your case was redressed, I learned that she was your wife. She came to the countryside to hide when the child was born; when her mama went back to city hall, we knew she had a problem with her family birth too. She could not hide her child any other way. Does that make you angry..." She said sobbing, and couldn't continue talking.

LinLin moved beside her and touched her on the shoulder with his hand; he couldn't express what he felt in his heart.

He said: "The past is over, let's forgot about it."

"No" it is in my heart forever, clearly, forever. I have never forgotten. It seems like it happened yesterday. How can I forget? I can't."

"That is just abusing yourself; please don't do that."

"Abusing myself? I suffer from my own actions, I have no excuse."

"You never remarried?"

"When you left I knew my love life was over for this lifetime."

"I left so that it would be better for you and our child, to protect you, and not involve him."

"I knew that."

She sobbed again. The memories from many years ago returned: "She had grabbed a hold of his shirt and said: Don't go, please, don't leave me, don't leave this family. Let me be your horse or cow, and take care of you the rest of your life. Let me atone for my mistake in front of you ..." Outside it was pouring rain, he pulled her hands off his shirt, and had left in the drenching rain, never once looking back.

"Have you been all right all these years?"

She tried to stop sniffling, and said: "OK, how about you?"

"Me? Didn't YingLi tell you about me?"

"Yes, she said you had a job receiving waste, and that you had been a college teacher. It was my fault that caused you to have to collect waste to earn a living. I'm really the criminal. This life I owe you a lot..."

"These things in our lives are in the past; let's forget them and not mention them any more, is that is Ok?"

Lian nodded, and said: "Will you forgive me now so that if I die I will rest in peace."

LinLin looked at her pale face and said: "Let me check your pulse, and make a prescription for you."

Just then, DaHai came running in and said: "Grandma, I'm hungry."

"Go and wash your hands, you are a mess; Let's go and wash."

Lian got up off the Kang, put on her shoes, and took the little boy to the kitchen, pouring water in a basin, washed his hands, feet, and face. Then she carried him back to the Kang; laid him on a pillow, and gave him a bottle of milk. The nipple on the baby bottle had a very small hole that forced him to suck hard, making him tired, and he soon went to sleep.

LinLin said: "The nipple needs to be adjusted, so the milk will come easier."

Lian said: "That would encourage him to eat more, he is not hungry, he just wants to sleep."

Lian had barely finished speaking when he could be heard snoring already. She said very caringly and lovingly. "You see how old he is, he still can't go without milk. YingLi and NianLin both say I spoil him. However, without milk he is unhappy, he doesn't want any other food, if I see him not eating my heart gets uneasy, and I turn soft again. Let him drink, some children drink milk until they are eleven years of age, right?"

"What will he call me?" LinLin asked.

"Grandfather, of course."

"Oh, our family relationship is messed up now anyway," She recalled her actions, felt guilty for a moment, and said: "This is YingLi's fault, she didn't tell us she had a relationship with you."

LinLin interrupted. "You can't say that, her situation pushed her to lie, to protect herself and the child. I understand her very well, whatever she has done, and she is still a wonderful woman in my heart."

"She is different than me, isn't she?"

"Yes, she is different than you." LinLin answered without thinking.

Those words cut deeply and hurt Lian's feelings.

LinLin had not noticed that Lian's feelings had been hurt, he was thinking to himself; she dares to love and to hate, the life that she gave to me.

He said: "Whatever she has done with any man, I believe it was only because she had no other choice, I know that she loves me, and I love her, our life will be together."

LinLin's words struck like a rock slamming into her heart, his words were right, but for her they hurt because she loved him too. She was still crazily in love with him, she loved him, like a mama loves her own baby, always worrying, afraid he might fall, be hungry, catch cold or worse.

When she had reported his talk to the leader of the party, she expected that the party would help him on the road to the revolution, the road to a better life; she didn't know it would be a bad thing to do. However, no one had said her actions were good for him, even her friends, and coworkers...therefore she took their child and left the forest. She felt jealous because YingLi was of a higher class, she was low class...she knew she didn't have any right to be jealous, her rights had ended twenty years ago. When this man who had suffered so much and had been her whole life showed up again, she realised that her love for him had never ended. She was jealous, because she knew that a woman, who is understood by a man, has the best love, and the greatest happiness.

"Yes, she had to do any thing when there was no other way to go." Lian said in a low voice, saying one thing and meaning another. "Don't let them know about you and me before..." Her heart was suddenly getting big, a woman's emotions are very fragile, they cannot accept too much suffering, it had all began because of her, and it must be ended by her.

"I agree with you."

They had the same thoughts that later YingLi would bring LinLin to see the child. LinLin said: "Just tell them we never knew each other."

Lian didn't want the relationship to sound like that, and said: "We could just say we were coworkers in the forest."

"Ok, we were coworkers in the forest and..."

Lian continued: "Our parents were good friends."

"Ok. and...?"

Lian smiled, quite contented. Finally she had an understanding with him; this was the first one and was to be the last one also. She said with tears on her face: "We grew up together, after you went to study in collage, and became a teacher, I'm...I'...what?"

"You decide, and tell me."

"I got married, you got married too."

"Ok."

"It has been twenty years since we saw each other."

"That is true." LinLin said emotionally.

"It is all true, we were coworkers, it has been twenty years since we have seen each other, we are..." Hot tears poured from her eyes, she wanted to pour her heart out to him and have him understand the guilt she had lived with and the fact that she had never stopped loving him over all these years.

Suddenly she saw NianLin coming with a stick as thick as a fist raised high, and it was aimed at LinLin's head.

LinLin had his back to the door and didn't see or hear NianLin coming up behind him.

Lian saw this, her throat was suddenly full of phlegm, and she didn't have time to speak so she opened her arms and used her body to shield Min's head. The blow intended for Lin landed on her head, knocking her backwards onto the Kang with blood flowing from her head.

Summoning all of her strength she screamed: "Don't hit him! Don't hurt him! He is your father..."

Chapter 96

WHEN HE RETURNED FROM town after getting his divorce the village people told him a stranger had entered his house. Some said: NianLin, that man came to take your wife, why are you so stupid? When she wanted to divorce you why did you not beat her? Beating her not only gives vent to your anger, it can also take away your bad luck. You don't want to be unlucky the rest of your life do you? Is a farmer a lower class than this man who came to take your wife? Why is he taking your wife, is it because you are so weak, is that your personality, it is not the way of mountain village men. We men of the mountain villages don't care if a woman stays or leaves, because we are poor, if we can't offer her enough food or clothing, and she wants to leave, we let her go.

Your wife is a different story: she had another man so she left you. This is reason enough even in other countries for a fight between two men. They call it a duel, if white people dare to duel, why don't you? If you don't dare to hit him yourself, we will go with you. Go and fight with him yourself; hit him, don't show yourself as a coward. NianLin asked himself if Lin had not come back, would YingLi still of divorced him. The answer could be yes or no. YingLi's divorce had really thrown him from the peak of his life to the lower end in one night. He also knew that fighting was not only to keep a woman, it was also for a man's self-confidence, and to preserve face. But he was roused to anger by the people's talk, and he took the stick from the other guy's hand, and ran home to give LinLin a beating.

When he saw that the blow had landed on Lian's head, NianLin threw it aside. NianLin saw that his mama's eyes looked stunned, and heard her speak imploring him. He clearly heard her say: "NianLin, my son, my good son, you can't hit him; don't hit him, he is your father."

NianLin shook his mothers' shoulders asking: "What did you say? Who is he?"

Lian was startled by NianLin's question, and still wanting to keep it from him she said: "what did I say? I said he is …is"

NianLin said it for her: "You said he is my father." NianLin said pointing at LinLin.

LinLin was busy looking for something to bandage Lian's head, it was bleeding a little and had made her hair wet. LinLin used a cigar to stop the bleeding, and then he tore off part of his shirt to wrap it.

Lian avoided NianLin eyes, and said: "I said he is DaShan's father."

"Ma, you lie, you said he is my father. Tell me, what happened? Who is he?"

"Oh, my son, your father is …is…" she wanted to say "dead" the story she been telling him for twenty years, but now she could no longer say that.

"Mama, tell me the truth. Please, tell me the truth"

Sudden compassion for his son made LinLin forget what he and Lian had agreed to conceal. He said: "Don't hide it from him. Yes, NianLin, I'm your father."

"Mama, tell me everything; he says he is my father; you said my father died a long time ago. Tell me what has really happened?"

The room fell as silent as a cemetery at midnight.

Lian thought to herself: My god, he told him already, what can I do?

LinLin saw that NianLin had very strong feelings from deep in his heart; he looked closely at NianLin and saw clearly that he was his son, the wide forehead, the little thick lips, the high bridge of his nose, and the bright eyes.

Lian spoke first facing her son who was wide eyed, waiting for her to explain to him and said: "NianLin, it is true, he is your father. I lied to you because it was entirely my fault; I got your father involved in…" her words were interrupted by LinLin:

"NianLin, we both had faults in the past, I can't say who was right and who was wrong, and you young people don't understand either. Any way, I feel very sorry that I didn't have the chance to help you grow up." He wanted to tell him that he went back and tried to find them but they had left; however those words remained unsaid.

"Mama, please tell me clearly what happened. Tell me."

"NianLin…" Lian said crying.

"NianLin, you need to calm down." LinLin said trying to calm him down.

"Calm down? You want me to calm down? How can I? Since I was little up until now I believed my father was dead. My father died, and my mama raised me, it was not easy; I always treated my mama very special. One day, my father suddenly appears from the sky, and I discover that my father has the same woman for a wife as me. If this news gets out, how can I live in this world? I will have no face."

"NianLin, when you were with YingLi you didn't know, and I understand; I believe other people will understand too" NianLin interrupted him saying: "Will understanding help everyone? You tell me, tell me how we can distinguish between DaShan and me; are we brothers or father and son? Are DaShan and DaHai brothers or uncle and nephew? Do you understand? If this gets out, people will laugh until their teeth fall out. This story can spread for a hundred years, a thousand years, ten thousand years or more. Since I was little I have been a joke to other people; they said I was a bastard, now I will be laughed at by people saying I have committed incest." then he started sobbing. He had grown up in the traditional way, and really couldn't accept this.

LinLin had thought only he would have a hard time accepting what had happened; now he knew he had been wrong. NianLin was suffering even greater anguish than he was. In the future this may not be a big thing, but for the present they both must suffer.

When LinLin left the mountain village, he carried a heavy load on his shoulders thinking that his telling the truth to NianLin maybe was a mistake; he was leaving NianLin to carry such heavy psychological pressure. According to Chinese tradition, they should really be cast aside and shunned by the people. Fate had surely given the family a place in history that even Darwin would find a difficult problem to sort out. It seemed that to obtain a solution they would all need enough time and courage.

Chapter 97

AFTER LINLIN LEFT NIANLIN pressured Lian to tell him everything that had happened. Lian really had no choice, she just hoped that her son would understand her, and she told him everything; but it made him very mad and he said:

"I hate you. Why did I have to have a mama like you? Your have been mean and shameless. You set up a trap for your own family..."

"No." Lian screamed: "I did not set a trap for your father, I did not. For sure, I did not. I loved him so much. I did that because I wanted to help him have a better life and to protect him..."

"You tell me why DaShan is dumb, you caused that didn't you? Don't tell me you didn't. I know you did. Even when I had to face YingLi I said firmly my mama is not that kind of person; but in my heart I suspected you already, I just didn't want to talk about it, or believe it. You are my mama, in my heart you were always a wonderful person, I loved you so much, so much. But it is you who is to blame, am I right? Admit it and tell me Yes."

"Yes." Lian answered honestly. She said: "I thought that would be the best for our family, the best for you and YingLi."

"Saying that tells me you knew who YingLi was. Why did you want me to marry her? I'm so low? Without a woman I could have

359

lived single? Even if I lived single all my life I wouldn't want to be married to the same woman as my father. Do you understand that? What kind of man am I now? Anywhere I go people will point their fingers at me. Do you know that? Are you happy? You ruined your husband's life, and later you ruined your son..."

Lian interrupted him: "NianLin, my good son, it is not like you think. When I discovered who YingLi was it was already too late, you had a child with her already..."

NianLin interrupted her: "If you knew early or late who can believe you? Since today, you are not my mama any more. I don't want a mama like you. You made me lose my father many years ago, and now you make me like no human. I am like a ghost also."

"My son."

"I tell you again, I'm not your son anymore." he said, as he left the house in a rage, full of anger.

He left Lian with a broken heart, her only reason for living the only dream that she had left, the source of her existence, courage and strength...in a moment had left her. She silently put on the clothes that she had worn to her wedding so many years ago, then she powdered her face, she picked up a little mirror to check her work, and felt good, then she combed her hair, and braided it in two pig tails. When she finished her preparations, she put a rope over the ceiling beam climbed up on a chair, and ended her life.

Later when NianLin returned and found her, he screamed and cried at her: "Ma, open your eyes please, wake up please; you are not dead, you are scaring me. Are you listening: you are my mama, my good mama. I'm your son; mama wake up, please, please. Don't scare me like this; listen, I have already forgiven you. Your son has forgiven you. I know that it was not fair to say it was only your fault. Don't go; don't leave me. Please..."

Lian's eyes were closed, and in the dim light and silence her face wore s smile. She was gone, and didn't need to consider the vexations of this world any longer. She knew, she had lived an unsuccessful life. If life was a game as many people said; she had lost, and lost very miserably, she had lost both her husband and son by her own actions.

If you believe the world is a stage and people just actors she was an unsuccessful clown, and she didn't like the ugly face she wore. As the rope tightened she prayed that in her next life she would change her life style, and learn how to love and respect family members and her self.

Chapter 98

WHEN YINGLI GOT BACK from the mountain village her mother LuDongChun was not home. She also unexpectedly found a letter from her older sister waiting for her.

"My dear sister YingLi:
I have more feelings in my heart than I can express. I remember that 29 years ago we came into this world together; when I learned that you were my twin sister I was three years old. We were twin girls from the same womb on the same day and hour. Even though I arrived just half an hour earlier, that was enough to satisfy my vanity and self-respect. Memories of my childhood are like being a little adult, always raising my arm to protect you. In the kindergarten, if someone insulted you, I would defend you and scratch their face...we were like actors on a stage, following each other. We made dad and mom proud...dad liked to carry us one in each arm, you liked him to kiss you first, I liked him to kiss me first...we were always quarrelling about little things, then in a few minutes all was forgotten and we were like one person again. The memory of dad's passing away hurt both of us very much. He was the centre of our lives before he got sick, and then he turned into a bag of bones that made me scared to look at him. You were better with him than me; you would feed him, putting the food in his mouth, and

also help him light a cigarette. You said you were not scared, but your fingers shook, and once or twice you burned his moustache. I don't know why he left us, and why when he left we did not cry or weep. You did not cry, I didn't cry and mama didn't cry either. Why? We were so young at that time, I really can't remember.

When we got older we were not always together, and our minds have always been different too. I remember when we were in high school and you said you wanted go to college, and become a teacher; I wanted to go to the military project institute, and become a military engineer. You said a girl was no good for that job, and made me very unhappy; for three days we did not talk to each other, until mama came back from another city, and we had to show smiling faces again. I thought that was the biggest disagreement our relationship would ever have; who could know that later in the Cultural Revolution our relationship would be broken. I knew you hated me for my actions. I'm a very self-confidant person, on the surface it may look like I didn't care, but in my heart I was really sad. I know why you don't like me and hate me, I hurt your feelings very badly, later I wanted to make up with you, but you refused me.

My sister YingLi, will you believe me this one time? When I wrote the big character poster for mama the idea was immature and selfish. I didn't understand why others should be able to join the revolution and I couldn't because mama's family were Capitalist Roaders. It was not my fault what my family did before the revolution; they said a family were all the same and no one could choose their own road. I just wanted them to see me, YingHua; in time I changed my name to YongHong, the real me. The name YongHong made them treat me like somebody important with increased respect.

If mama was a traitor or not I really didn't know; but I saw lots of high position cadre in Beijing who during the revolution got this label. I thought if mama was captured and raped by the Japanese devils; that was a strong reason she could have become a traitor. I was the first to say that mama was a traitor and that gave me power because I was her daughter. When the big-character poster was stuck on the wall, they really treated me very well, they said: "You are the greatest". I asked myself how could I have done it any other way? I knew that if I did not write it someone else would. I knew I better do it first...later when they ordered me to marry a disabled guy you said I could say yes or no. If I said "yes" my love life was over before it began; if I said "no", my political life would have been ended right away.

Later they wrote material for me to talk about, saying how many times I had struggled with my mind; then learning what Chairman Mao had said. Then I woke up and began to realise my mistake. For the things I had done I cried many times with no body knowing; at that time I really didn't want to kill Zhang. When I think about that material for the talk show I still have a red face. I was just an actor, a political actor, wanting to be accepted; I had no control over my own life.

Please tell mama. I know she hates me and I know I hurt her very much; I am very sorry, and if I have a next life, I will be her daughter again and make amends for my faults with good deeds, and give presents to my elders and superiors.

About support for my daughter GuoGing, I need your help, when I get out of jail, I will work to repay you.

...

YingLi had tears on her face as she read. Her sister had cooperated with the police after mama LuDongChun had strongly pressured her. The police charged her with accidental death, and she was sentenced to serve eleven years in prison.

YingLi's son used sign language to ask her: "Mom, when will my other father be back?"

YingLi held him tight, and said: "My son, you only have one real father. He is your real father, and he told me, he would give us a surprise. When? I'm not sure. Just soon, very soon..."

End.